Son and Servant of Shropshire

For my children
Alastair, Richard and Charlotte
and my grandchildren
Jack, Hannah and Samuel, William and Edward

Son and Servant of Shropshire

The Life of Archdeacon Joseph (Plymley) Corbett
1759-1838

by

Douglas Grounds

Logaston Press

LOGASTON PRESS
Little Logaston Woonton Almeley
Herefordshire HR3 6QH
logastonpress.co.uk

First published by Logaston Press 2009
Copyright © Douglas Grounds 2009

ISBN 978 1 906663 13 1 (paperback)
ISBN 978 1 906663 14 8 (hardback)

Typeset by Logaston Press
and printed in Great Britain by
Bell & Bain Ltd., Glasgow

Contents

Illustrations
(with acknowledgments)

Front Cover
The Lawley from the Longmynd (by kind permission of Richard Warren) and William Joseph Plymley snr. (by kind permission of Mr. and Mrs. T.W.E. Corbett)

Rear Cover
The plaque of Joseph Corbett's coat-of-arms hangs in a corridor of the Royal Shrewsbury Hospital

Colour Section *(between pages 18 and 19)*
William and Joseph Plymley snr. (by kind permission of Mr. and Mrs. T.W.E. Corbett)
The Refectory, Chester Cathedral — the schoolroom of King's School, Chester in Joseph Plymley's schooldays (by kind permission of King's School, Chester)
Pembroke College, Oxford
'The Bank' or 'Bank House', now 'The Dower House' (by kind permission of Mr. and Mrs. T.W.E. Corbett)
'Plas Gwyn', Pentraeth, Anglesey
Pentraeth church, Anglesey
The altar picture presented by Joseph Plymley at Pembroke College, Oxford (by kind permission of the College)
St. Mary's church, Longnor
St. Mary's church, Longnor: the pulpit
St. Michael's church, Madeley

Black and White Section *(between pages 50 and 51)*
Portraits of Sir Richard and Sir Uvedale Corbett (by kind permission of Mr. and Mrs. T.W.E. Corbett)
Longnor Hall in 1792 (by kind permission of *Country Life)*
The entry of the Rev. Joseph Plymley's first marriage in the register of Pentraeth church (by kind permission of Anglesey County Record Office)
Thomas Clarkson at the age of about 26
Extracts from Katherine Plymley's journal (by kind permission of Shropshire Archives)
A page from the Rev. Joseph Corbett's diary (Shropshire Archives)
A page from the Archdeacon's report on Woolstaston parish (Shropshire Archives)
A page from the Archdeacon's report on Acton Scott parish (Shropshire Archives)
The statue to commemorate the end of slavery in Barbados (by kind permission of Tony Peck)

Second Colour Section *(between pages 178 and 179)*
St.Mary Magdalene's church, Little Hereford
The Archdeacon's illustrations of St. James' church, Cardington (by kind permission of Mr. and Mrs. T.W.E. Corbett)
The Archdeacon's illustrations of Holy trinity church, Hol(d)gate (Mr. and Mrs. T.W.E. Corbett)
Title page of the Survey of Shropshire Agriculture (by kind permission of Shropshire Archives)
The Corbett coat-of-arms in the east window of St. Laurence's church, Church Stretton
St. Mary's church, Leebotwood
Shrewsbury Prison: the gatehouse built in 1793
Holy Trinity church, Hol(d)gate
Portrait of Archdeacon Corbett (by kind permission of Mr. Panton Corbett)
The interior of Longnor Hall (by kind permission of *Country Life)*
Longnor Hall today (by kind permission of Mr. A.V. Nicholson)

Foreword

Douglas Grounds gives us a fascinating snapshot of life at the end of the eighteenth and beginning of the nineteenth centuries in Shropshire. So different in so many ways and yet involved with issues which are still live today.

Rural poverty concerned Joseph Plymley greatly and he was involved with charities and provision for the poor. The situation in the country resonates with the credit crunch today. There was concern over the viability of the banks and the economic plight of the nation. There is still rural poverty which may be more hidden but certainly exists. The Archdeacon was asked to do a survey on agriculture which would feed into national thinking.

He also used much of his energy in working with William Wilberforce and Thomas Clarkson to bring an end to the slave trade in the British Empire. It was a long process with many disappointments but also much rejoicing when finally the Act was passed. As Bishop and Archdeacon of Ludlow I spoke at the launch of an exhibition in St Laurence's Church Ludlow, which was a celebration of the 200th Anniversary of the successful passing of this Act.

The Archdeacon lived all his life in Longnor and surrounding area, except for the time he was at Oxford University. He was a local man who was ordained and became Archdeacon of Salop. The Diocese of Hereford today has had a strategy, which we call Local Ministry, for 15 years, which encourages people in a vocation to ordination and then to continue in the local area to which they are committed.

It is one of the Archdeacon's duties to carry out Visitations each year. I am amazed at the energy of Archdeacon Plymley in visiting every church and parish with a questionnaire, writing up a report, and sketching each church building in less than two years of becoming Archdeacon. He managed this in days when transport was not easy and showed great concern for the people and clergy of the parishes of the Ludlow Archdeaconry.

The Archdeacon was faithful in the conduct of worship and prayer, but also saw that the whole world belongs to God and exercised a right involvement in politics and public life. He rose above the issues of party politics because of his care for everyone, but realised he needed to be involved, because that is where decisions are taken that affect the lives of the poor and the wealthy.

Joseph Plymley, who changed his name to Corbett in order to inherit estates, was also a magistrate almost to the end of his life. He took this work very seriously and was greatly respected.

It has been a privilege to write this foreword for a book about one of my predecessors. Since Joseph Plymley/Corbett's time the title of 'Archdeacon of Salop' has been changed to 'Archdeacon of Ludlow' so that the Archdeacon in the Hereford Diocese is not confused with the one in the Lichfield Diocese in North Shropshire. So many of the issues with which the Archdeacon wrestled — local ministry, banks, financial situation, agriculture — are all issues with which I have dealt in my time as Archdeacon of Ludlow over the last seven years. The historical text of this book comes alive as you read it with the eyes of today.

+ Michael Ludlow

Right Reverend Michael Hooper
Bishop & Archdeacon of Ludlow   Ash Wednesday 25 February 2009

Preface

The 250th anniversary of the birth of Joseph Plymley falls in May of this year 2009. It happens that this same year also marks the 200th anniversary of the birth of Charles Darwin, Joseph's more illustrious fellow Salopian. Darwin is rightly hailed as a man of international stature for his revolutionary research into the origin of species. Yet young Charles was reared in an environment of scientific inquiry that had been nurtured and promoted by Joseph Plymley and his friends and associates (including Dr. Robert Darwin, Charles' father) in what has been called 'The Shropshire Enlightenment'. Joseph's sister wrote of his 'love for natural history in all its branches', and she, like her father, excelled in paintings of plants, insects and butterflies.

I first became interested in Archdeacon Plymley (later Corbett) when researching the history of St. Laurence's Church in Church Stretton. It was his monumental survey of the archdeaconry that provided an invaluable description of the church at the end of the eighteenth century. And it was to him, as a figure of integrity and authority, that young rector Pemberton turned for support when he encountered opposition in his congregation to his planned re-ordering of the interior of the church. The more I read about the Shropshire of those days the more I discovered that the Archdeacon was involved in almost every sphere of activity, above all as the leader of the anti-slave trade movement in the region. Indeed, for nearly half a century he was at the forefront of life in the county.

What, for me, transformed a passing interest into a lengthy piece of research was the discovery that Joseph's sister, Katherine, kept a journal for thirty-five years, and that this journal, running to nearly one hundred and fifty notebooks, was held at Shropshire Archives. Katherine's journal, which she maintained from 1791 to 1827, is a literary work in its own right, an illuminating account of her life and, since her brother was much more fully engaged in the Church and society than she was, of Joseph's life, activities and family. Much of this biography is inevitably drawn from Katherine's pages, so much so that I have only occasionally given specific references but have included many other passages marked only by quotation marks. From 1814 to 1827 Katherine's journal is supplemented by Joseph's own diaries, while from 1827 to 1829 and from 1832 to 1835 these alone provide details of what he was engaged in. Whereas Katherine's journal is written in continuous prose, giving often vivid accounts of what was going on in the family, Joseph's diaries are more the *aides-mémoire* of a busy man, noting meetings and correspondence, but occasionally giving insights into what he was reading, what his children were doing, his health, and his spiritual life.

The massive survey of the archdeaconry, written up in his own hand, and his published *A General View of the Agriculture of Shropshire* furnish valuable evidence of his interests, activities and opinions. Further details of his life have been gleaned from family records, local newspapers, diocesan records at Hereford, the Record Office in Anglesey (where he met and married his first wife), the archives of Pembroke College, Oxford, the copies of some of his correspondence with William Wilberforce and Thomas Clarkson that Katherine preserved, and some records of the campaign for the abolition of the slave trade.

The documentary evidence is happily supplemented by the preservation in the village of Longnor, near Shrewsbury, of the two houses in which he spent virtually the whole of his life — The Bank (now the Dower House) and Longnor Hall — as well as many of the dwellings of his day and the church in which he ministered for over fifty years. So little is altered, especially in the church, that it is still possible to stroll around the village and sense a little of the atmosphere of his life there.

I have tried to depict that life in largely chronological order, but with special treatment of the anti-slave trade campaign and his roles as magistrate and Shropshire Bible Society president. References to local events and elections, and to important national and even international developments, are intended to help the reader to place Joseph's life in a wider perspective.

If my greatest debt is to Katherine, I am pleased to place on record my gratitude to the living who have assisted me in researching Joseph's life story. To Mary McKenzie and the staff, particularly Kerry Dickins and Derek Moore, at Shropshire Archives I owe especial thanks. I wish to express my gratitude, too, to the staffs at the County Record Offices in Hereford and Anglesey, and at the Bodleian Library in Oxford, and to the archivists at King's School, Chester, and Pembroke College, Oxford.

My personal thanks go to Bishop Michael Hooper of Ludlow, Joseph's distant successor in the role of Archdeacon of Salop, who most kindly agreed to write the Foreword. Tim Corbett, Joseph's direct descendant, and his wife Cilla have been extraordinarily kind in showing me round their house where Joseph was born and spent the greater part of his life. They have shared with me their extensive knowledge of Katherine, and allowed me access to the portraits that line their walls and to the volumes of miniature paintings of the churches that complemented the written details of the parishes of his archdeaconry. Panton Corbett, though rarely in Longnor, was good enough to let me photograph the portrait of Joseph painted in 1819. Richard Warren promptly and most helpfully found in his collection just the photograph of the Lawley that I wanted for the book cover, Tony Peck kindly brought me back from Barbados his photograph of the statue commemorating the end of slavery, and Tony Crowe gave me the benefit of his knowledge of heraldry.

It has again been a pleasure to work with Andy Johnson of Logaston Press as my knowledgeable, wise and discriminating editor.

My greatest debt of gratitude is to my wife, Adele, photographer, proof reader, Index assistant, and encourager-in-chief. Her reading and re-reading of the text and her readiness to discuss and debate chapter by chapter have been enormously helpful.

I must bear, however, the responsibility for any errors or imperfections that remain. And I have the pleasure of dedicating this volume to my children and grandchildren, who have already caught, or are catching, my love of history.

Douglas Grounds,
March 2009.

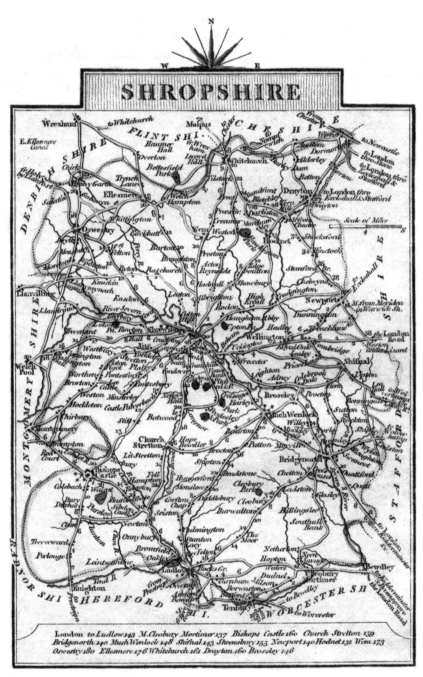

Map of Shropshire engraved by J. Cary in 1814

1 *ANNUS MIRABILIS*

If you were British, 1759 was a most auspicious year in which to be born. It was hailed as the *Annus Mirabilis,* the year of a succession of victories over the French on land and sea in the global Seven Years' War. Each one was celebrated throughout the country by the ringing of bells and the lighting of bonfires.

Joseph, the subject of this biography, was born on 17 May in that memorable year. Already, in its first four months, the French had abandoned the siege of Madras and were losing their hold in southern India, while in the West Indies British ships and soldiers had completed the conquest of the French island of Guadeloupe. News of these victories boosted the prestige of Britain's great war minister, William Pitt, whose second son, named after his father, was born on 28 May. As the future Prime Minister for over twenty years — in the most active period of Joseph's own life — the younger Pitt was destined to lead Britain in an even greater war against France.

Yet in the first weeks of Joseph's life final victory in the war was still in the balance. The greatest threat came from the huge French invasion fleet of flat-bottomed boats that was being assembled in Le Havre and the Breton ports. Further east there was stalemate in the Rhineland where an Anglo-Hanoverian army faced the French, and Britain's ally, Frederick the Great of Prussia, had his hands full against the Austrians and Russians, allies of France. And across the Atlantic the British forces in Canada were making only slow progress towards Quebec, where the French commander, Montcalm, had time to strengthen the fortifications.

August, however, brought two exciting victories. On the continent the first day of the month saw British soldiers — notably the Royal Welch Fusiliers — distinguish themselves in the battle of Minden, which enabled the Anglo-Hanoverian army of Prince Ferdinand of Brunswick to drive the French from Westphalia and end the threat to George II's homeland of Hanover. Less than three weeks later, on 19 August, French hopes of a successful cross-Channel invasion were gravely damaged by the stunning victory of Admiral Boscawen and the Mediterranean fleet over the French Toulon fleet (itself endeavouring to link up with the northern French fleet at Brest) in Lagos Bay off the coast of Portugal; the French fleet lost five ships of the line and 500 men.[1] Totally unnoticed — of course — between these two stirring battles was the birth on 4 August of William Wilberforce, who would in the future become the close friend of the younger Pitt and the Parliamentary leader of the anti-slave trade movement — in which he would welcome his contemporary, Joseph, as a valued fellow-labourer.

The news of Boscawen's triumph did not reach London until 6 September; the delay is a reminder of how slow communications were two and a half centuries ago. It meant also that government and people rejoicing in Britain were unaware that the critical moment in the campaign to capture Quebec was fast approaching. It was on 13 September, two hours before sunrise, that Wolfe's forces landed at the foot of the cliffs leading to the Heights of Abraham. Yet by 8.00 a.m. nearly 5,000 soldiers were drawn up in line of battle less than a mile from the western walls of Quebec. Within hours the French had been driven from the field, although General James Wolfe died of gunshot wounds at the moment of his greatest triumph. Quebec surrendered five days later. When the news did reach London in late October the capital and the country went wild with excitement. Professor Black records that 'The ringers at York Minster were paid four times between 21 August and 22 October for celebrating victories, beginning with the triumph at Minden and ending with the capture of Quebec'.[2] That capture was probably the most spectacular success in a year of victories and made legendary, as Pitt said in his triumphal speech to the House of Commons, by Wolfe's death 'in the hour of victory'.

How much Joseph's infant slumbers (or those of his to-be-more famous contemporaries) were disturbed by the local victory revelries we cannot know, but the celebrations would have been some time later than those in London because the fastest coaches from the capital to Shrewsbury then took several days and the *Shrewsbury Chronicle,* which became the main source of news, both national and local, for the people of Shropshire, did not begin publication until 1772.

By November the French position in India had become critical if not yet desperate. Yet for Britain the threat of invasion remained. One more great victory was to come. Admiral Sir Edward Hawke had been given the responsibility of blockading Brest and the French warships there that were intended to protect the invasion flotilla. Severe storms in early November so damaged

Hawke's ships that he had to return to England, giving the French fleet the opportunity to escape and head for Morbihan on the south Brittany coast to collect invasion transports. Then, however, renewed gales blew the French ships right off course, and on 20 November Hawke caught up with them in Quiberon Bay. In the ensuing engagement the superior British seamanship in vicious squalls and heavy ocean swell gave Hawke a famous victory. He lost two ships and 400 men; the French five ships, including two flagships, and 2,500 men. For France Quiberon Bay was an utter catastrophe; for Britain, with the threat of invasion lifted, it set the seal on a year of victories. '1759 effectively made Britain the global superpower of the eighteenth century; it was the first time a genuine British Empire could be discerned, and it laid the foundations for the dominance of the English language in the modern world.'[3]

As the year ended young Joseph and his sister Katherine would have been blissfully unaware of the high drama on the international stage. They were at peace in the bosom of their family in the heart of Shropshire.

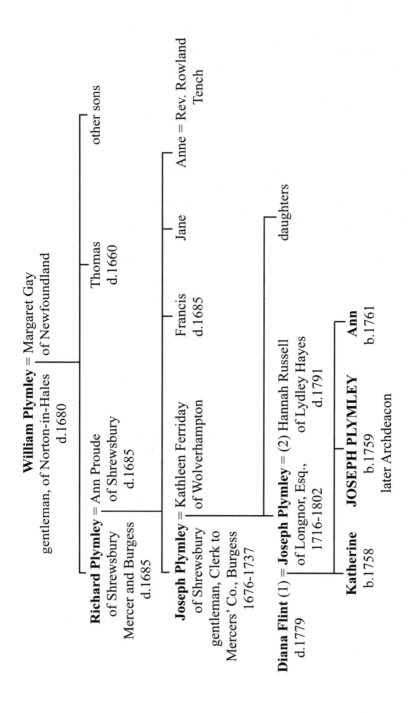

A simplified Plymley Family Tree

William Plymley = Margaret Gay
gentleman, of Norton-in-Hales | of Newfoundland
d.1680

other sons

Thomas
d.1660

Anne = Rev. Rowland
Tench

Jane

Francis
d.1685

Richard Plymley = Ann Proude
of Shrewsbury of Shrewsbury
Mercer and Burgess d.1685
d.1685

Joseph Plymley = Kathleen Ferriday
of Shrewsbury of Wolverhampton
gentleman, Clerk to
Mercers' Co., Burgess
1676-1737

daughters

Diana Flint (1) = **Joseph Plymley** = (2) Hannah Russell
d.1779 of Longnor, Esq., of Lydley Hayes
1716-1802 d.1791

JOSEPH PLYMLEY
b.1759
later Archdeacon

Ann
b.1761

Katherine
b.1758

2   THE PLYMLEYS & THE CORBETTS

Young Joseph and his sister were the children of Joseph Plymley and his wife Diana. Their first child, Katherine, born the year before Joseph, later traced her family back to her great-great-grandfather, William Plymley, of Norton-in-Hales near Market Drayton. William had married Margaret Gay, a native of Newfoundland and believed to be the first British subject born there. They had several sons, one of whom, Richard, became a successful mercer in Shrewsbury, being admitted to the powerful Mercers' Company in 1660 and made a member of the Corporation. He married Ann Proude of a good family, and became wealthy enough to buy property in Milk Street — most likely Proude's Mansion — as well as in Butcher Row and St. John's Hill from her improvident brothers.[1] But both he and his wife died early leaving two young daughters and a nine-year-old son Joseph. Their affairs were misman- aged and Joseph later had to sell the original family property at Norton to give his sisters their share of their father's estate. After a period as a clerk at Clement's Inn, he settled as an attorney in Shrewsbury, serving as Clerk to the Mercers' Company and, like his father, becoming a burgess. His wife, Kathleen Ferriday of Wolverhampton, gave birth to several daughters and a son, also Joseph, born in 1716.

This second Joseph Plymley was sent at the age of six to the Free Schools of Shrewsbury, where the Second Master, the Rev. Rowland Tench, had married Joseph's aunt Anne. This relationship and his clerical profession notwith- standing, Tench was very severe with Joseph and the other boys, with the result that when he reached the age of twelve Joseph was very glad to be transferred to Dr. Phillips in the Upper School, where he was much happier and where he developed his earlier love of painting and natural history. After two years in the top form he transferred to a writing school in Shrewsbury, considered necessary training in deciphering different hands for a prospective lawyer. His intended legal career fell through, however, and at sixteen he was apprenticed to Mr. John Thornton, a Shrewsbury apothecary and a distant relation by his

5

marriage to Elizabeth Lacon. Unfortunately Joseph's parents did not prosper and had to let part of their home in Milk Street to lodgers. They both died when Joseph was approaching twenty, leaving nothing but their house to their children. Joseph left Mr.Thornton after eight years when Thornton's young son was apprenticed to his father and seemed destined to take over the business. At the age of twenty-four Joseph determined to seek his fortune in London.

Arriving in the capital in 1740 he served first as a journeyman with Mr. Bowden, an apothecary in Palace Yard, Westminster, and then with Mr. Longbottom of Lombard Street. When the lure of the capital began to fade, he responded to an invitation from his old teacher Rowland Tench, now rector of St. Laurence's, Church Stretton, to take over an apothecary's business there. On consideration he felt the place, after Shrewsbury and London, to be too small — and likely to involve a lot of riding to outlying villages and farms. So instead he returned to Shrewsbury to become the partner of his old boss, John Thornton, whose son had recently died. It proved a wise decision, for when Thornton died in 1751 he left most of his fortune to his partner. At the age of thirty-five Joseph found himself the owner of a house at Lyth, then occupied by Thomas Gould, yeoman, a house at Exford Green, and Thornton's own house in Shrewsbury (possibly in Shoemaker Row) with its outbuildings and gardens, as well as a leasehold estate in Rowsell (Rous Hill), Shrewsbury, for the remainder of the ninety-nine year lease granted by the Mayor and Corporation in 1718. He was also left all his household goods and plate.[2]

Joseph was now in a position to indulge in his hobbies of natural history and painting, particularly of insects, butterflies and birds. In these interests he had already been encouraged by Sir Richard Corbett, one of Shrewsbury's M.P.s until 1754, a man of very considerable taste, much improved by travelling, and his brother Edward Corbett, who had presented Joseph with a three-guinea box of watercolours. Early in 1756 Joseph decided to sell the business and leave Shrewsbury. In July, at the age of forty, he married Diana Flint, nine years his junior, 'to whom he had been for some time attached'.[3]

The first offspring of this union was Katherine, born in January 1758. There followed Joseph, the subject of this book, born on 17 May 1759, and Ann born in July 1761. It was through their mother, Diana Flint, that the children were related to the Corbetts of Longnor, a relationship that was profoundly to influence their lives.

⚜

This branch of the Corbett family could trace their roots back to the 14th century, but they were almost certainly descended from the Corbet who had probably accompanied William the Conqueror in 1066, as by the time of Domesday Book (1086) Roger and Robert, sons of Corbet, held extensive lands in Shropshire. Corbetts (who had now gained the second 't') were established at Longnor, eight miles south of Shrewsbury, by the 15th century, and on 20 June 1642, on the eve of the Civil War, Edward Corbett was created a baronet by the king. In 1651 he served as Sheriff of the county under the Commonwealth, but died two years later; he was buried at Condover. He had married Margaret, daughter of Edward Waties, a member of the Council in the Marches, through whom he inherited the Leighton estate in Montgomeryshire.

Sir Edward's son, also Edward, married a daughter of Lord Newport, but predeceased his father. His son Richard succeeded to the title, and served from 1678-81 as a member for Shrewsbury in the fractious Parliaments at the end of the reign of Charles II. These were the exciting years of the Popish Plot and the Exclusion Crisis, the attempt to prevent the accession of Charles II's Roman Catholic brother, James, when the king should die. As Chairman of the House of Commons Committee of Elections, Sir Richard was deeply involved in the emergence of the first political parties: Whigs, who supported Exclusion, and Tories who wanted to maintain the legitimate succession. There is no doubt where Sir Richard stood, for he was a close friend of Lord William Russell who was executed for complicity in the Rye House Plot to seize the king. He appears to have been a man of intellect and vigour for he was a Fellow of the newly-founded (1662) Royal Society, and had begun the building of Longnor Hall in 1670. He died in 1683, when only forty-three years old, and was buried in St. Margaret's, Westminster. His marriage to Victoria, daughter and co-heir of Sir William Uvedale of Wickham, Hampshire, however, proved very fruitful, and their eldest son, named Uvedale after his mother's family, succeeded as the third baronet. In politics he followed his father, founding the Uvedale Club in Shrewsbury 'for the maintenance of Whig principles in the country'; it held quarterly dinners for the next hundred years.[4]

It fell to Uvedale, in about 1694, to complete the building of Longnor Hall, begun by his father. It is a large rectangular house with two main stories plus basement and attics. The principal facades, each of seven bays, face north and south. 'The disproportionately large hall and unimpressive staircases are legacies from the earlier 17th century, but in its compactness and symmetry the plan is typical of the fully developed Renaissance house'.[5] An elaborate and ornate third staircase is thought to have been the work of Uvedale Corbett shortly before his death in 1701. Although Uvedale died young, at only thirty-three years of age, his wife Mildred, a daughter of James

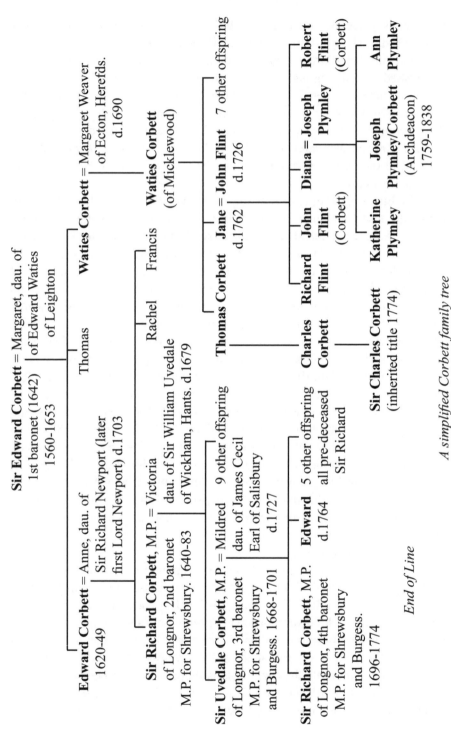

A simplified Corbett family tree

8

Cecil, Earl of Salisbury, had given birth to seven children. It was the eldest son, Richard, who became the fourth baronet, succeeding to the title when only five years old, but living for another seventy-three years.

Sir Richard, as he grew up, adopted the political principles of his grandfather and father and served as an M.P. for Shrewsbury for twenty-five years, half of them when Sir Robert Walpole was Prime Minister and the dominant figure in political life. He first gained his seat in the Commons in 1722 along with Orlando Bridgman, when their opponents were unseated after a Parliamentary inquiry into voting irregularities. He did not stand at the 1727 election but returned in 1734 when he gained the sobriquet 'Tawney Dick' (on account of 'the colour of his hide'!) and was elected with his fellow Whig William Kynaston, nicknamed 'Heavy Billy'. It was at that election that 'there must have been great local feeling and excitement as it is stated that six Companies of Foot were encamped in Kingsland and two Companies quartered in Abbey Foregate during the polling'[6] — one diarist claims so as 'to support the Corporation and overawe the other party'.[7] Sir Richard and Kynaston were elected unopposed in 1741 and again, after a poll, six years later. The 1747 result was challenged by a petition alleging corrupt practices by the Members and illegal conduct on the part of the Mayor. The petition, however, was subsequently withdrawn by leave of the House. Sir Richard retired from Parliament at the election of 1754. His electioneering had cost him dear, for he had had to sell some very fine estates, including the Hampshire ones brought into the family by Victoria Uvedale in the previous century. He also left a mortgage on the Longnor estates, which would be discharged by his successor at Longnor, Robert (Flint) Corbett.

Years earlier, and shortly before the end of his first term as an M.P., when he was only thirty years of age, Sir Richard responded generously to the needs of a young kinswoman, Jane Flint, the daughter of Waties Corbett and, like Sir Richard, descended from the first baronet, Sir Edward Corbett. Jane had married a local man, John Flint, in 1720, but they struggled to make ends meet as their family expanded. At length John left for London to seek employment, never to return home. All that is known is that he became a journeyman with a stationer, fell ill and died in St. Thomas's Hospital.[8] His wife was left in distressed circumstances, with a young family of two sons and a daughter and expecting another child shortly. Sir Richard placed her in the house of his steward at Ryton until the baby was born, and then took the whole family to live with him at Longnor Hall. This change in his personal circumstances may be the reason why he was not a candidate in the 1727 election. Jane became his housekeeper and served him in this capacity until her death thirty-six years later in 1762.

9

Jane was only a few years older than her benevolent and unmarried kinsman, and her children — Richard, John, Diana and Robert — must have been brought up to look on Sir Richard as their guardian and he to regard them almost as if they were his own children. The boys went to school locally, but Robert, the baby of the family, had more pains taken with his education than the others and Sir Richard himself, when not away during Parliamentary sessions or on his travels, instructed him in Latin. Diana was the most favoured for she 'was educated at the best boarding school for young ladies in Shrewsbury', and afterwards introduced to the most respectable families in the neighbour-hood. She was particularly intimate with Mrs. and Miss Edwards and used to pass weeks together with them at Frodesley Lodge.

John was the first to leave home, being apprenticed to a stationer in London, and the first to marry — to Elizabeth, daughter of Edward Tipton of Frankwell, a grocer and tallow chandler, in 1751. He settled in Shrewsbury. Richard, the eldest, 'was much about Sir Richard's person', and when he married Eleanor Atkis of Longnor in 1759 made his home in the village. Meanwhile, Robert had married Anne Russell of Lydley Hayes in February 1756, taken up residence at Micklewood, 'a pretty house built by his grand-father on Sir Richard's estate very near Longnor', and become Sir Richard's steward. Their mother and Sir Richard — who had retired from the Commons at the 1754 election and was spending more time at home — were probably concerned that their sister, Diana, had reached thirty and, in spite of being named after the goddess of hunting, had made no capture. There was great joy, then, when Joseph Plymley, the Shrewsbury apothecary whose artistic talents Sir Richard and his brother had encouraged, 'began to show an attach-ment to Diana'.[9] On their marriage at Longnor on 16 July 1756, when Joseph was forty and Diana thirty-one, Sir Richard was so pleased that he had a house built for them in the village and they moved there the following winter. This became known as 'The Bank' or 'Bank House', only a stone's throw from Longnor Hall on the other side of the Cound brook, which runs through the centre of the village. Thus, in his later years, Sir Richard, who never married, had his nearest relations all about him, 'and it may most truly be said that they contributed as much to his happiness and comfort as he did to theirs'.[10] This close relationship was to have very important consequences in the future.

Joseph and Diana's marriage united the commercial and professional Plymley family with the landed Corbetts who, by shrewd marriage alliances, had built up large estates over the centuries. The marriage proved to be a very happy one and produced the two daughters and the son Joseph, to whose early life we can now turn.

3 THE FORMATIVE YEARS

Joseph was just over two years old, and his sister Katherine three and a half, when their sister, Ann, was born in July 1761; two further sisters born later did not survive infancy. So Joseph grew up with his two sisters at The Bank, the substantial house that Sir Richard Corbett had provided for their parents, and which was enhanced in time by a cottage built in an infant coniferous plantation in the extensive garden. It was a loving family but a restricted environment, for Longnor was little more than a hamlet. When Joseph was a child the population was probably about 150 — it was to reach 177 by the first national census in 1801. The village stood principally on the road that leaves the ancient Watling Street at Longnor Green and runs north towards Ryton and Condover. Most of the houses were timber-framed and had been erected in the 17th century. Some were situated on a road running half-circle to the north of the village. The largest and oldest of these was Moat House, by this time a farmhouse. The mill stood across the road from The Bank, and at the northern edge of the village were a few houses near the Forge and iron furnace that had been opened in 1605. There was a smithy and, it seems, an inn — 'The Bowling Green' — on the main Shrewsbury to Ludlow road, where it was joined by the road that ran from the village past Longnor Hall.[1] A number of the cottages were, or came to be, occupied by miners from the Leebotwood colliery just across the parish boundary; some of the larger properties were the homes of the more prosperous tenant farmers.

Writing half a century later, and prompted by a visit to the Smythes at Frodesley, Katherine recalled that she used to visit the family twice a year in her childhood when 'our life was very uniform and retired'. It is doubtful, then, if Joseph and his sisters were allowed to play with the local youngsters from the homes of the neighbouring farmers and labourers.

They will, of course, have accompanied their parents on family and social visits. Their grandmother, Jane Flint, lived only just down the road at Longnor Hall, where she served as Sir Richard's housekeeper until her death in June 1762. Joseph was then only three and in later years probably could not remember her. Sir Richard, however, with no children or grandchildren of his own, and especially with his long Parliamentary career a past memory and more lonely after the death of his brother Edward in 1764, will always have been glad to see Diana and her husband and the children. Aunt Hannah, their father's sister, an inoffensive woman, nervous and of a weak mind, lived with them for twenty years, and their maternal Flint uncles lived nearby — Richard in Longnor, Robert at Micklewood, and John, after his return from London, in Shrewsbury. There would also have been social calls on local families, particularly Sir Edward Smythe and his wife at Acton Burnell. No doubt the family will have been regular in attendance at church on Sundays for Joseph's mother would be remembered for her piety.

The children's initial — and, for the girls, continuing — education will have been at home. Years before, Sir Richard had instructed their uncle Robert in Latin and, if he was now too elderly to repeat this, his conversation about his experiences in the House of Commons, in the hurly-burly of contested elections in Shrewsbury, and on his extensive travels — not to mention his fascination with inventions — will have broadened and enriched their minds. Their father, Joseph, passed on to them his passion for natural history, his love for and something of his skill in painting, and some of the medical knowledge he had acquired in his years as an apothecary. Katherine, in particular, inherited her father's gift for portraying butterflies and insects. Her journals reveal her love of nature as well as the breadth of her reading and her deep interest in current affairs, while her sister Ann from an early age assisted her father in dispensing medicines to local people — which practice, in spite of being plagued by ill-health herself, she continued after his death. The children's mother, Diana, will have paid particular attention to their spiritual development, their social skills, and probably their musical appreciation and performance.

Joseph and Diana's children, then, enjoyed all the benefits of growing up in a cultured as well as a loving home. Young Joseph, however, as the son and heir, had to have a formal education too. His father's memories of his unhappiness in the lower forms at Shrewsbury School, and his general disapproval of 'schools on a public foundation' (shared by his contemporary William Pitt the Elder),[2] led him to place his son, at about nine years old, at a school in the Warwickshire countryside with nearly a hundred boarders. Joseph's experience there showed that his father had been deceived as to its merits, and he was withdrawn after three years. Perhaps his father had been attracted by an advertisement similar to this one published three years earlier in the Chester *Courant*:

Free School in the City of Chester. The Reverend Dean and Chapter
of the Cathedral Church of Chester, having been pleased to appoint
me the Headmaster of the Free Grammar School of King Henry VIII,
founded in that Cathedral, a very generous subscription having been
entered into for my encouragement by the Nobility, the Dean and
Chapter, and the Gentry of the Town and Neighbourhood. ... I enter
upon the School, with the sincerest Resolution of exerting every Effort
of my Abilities, to render my Service acceptable to my present and
future Benefactors ...

I have taken a very commodious airy house for the Reception
of young Gentlemen and shall be ready to receive them at Candlemas
next [1768].

Truly sensible that the Manners of the Pupils I may be favoured
with are, especially with their Literature, the object of my Attention, I
shall be impartially careful of both, and in this Branch therefore of my
Duty, as well as in every other, the Pupils may depend upon the most
sollicitous [sic] Attention of

Their Obedient Servant,
Robert Vanbrugh.

The cost of 'Diet and Lodging' was set at fifteen guineas yearly and
'Schooling Two Pounds or Three Guineas, and Entrance Five Shillings or
Half a Guinea' according to the pupils' age at entry. Boarders were to be
accommodated in Mainwaring House in Watergate Street. For their tuition
they would have joined the twenty-four Foundation Scholars in the Cathedral
Refectory.[3]

Mr. Plymley decided in 1772 that this was the school to which he
would send the now thirteen-year-old Joseph, relying presumably on good
reports from others as well as the fulsome advertisement. The Revd. Robert
Vanbrugh, educated at Sedbergh, Eton and St. John's College, Cambridge,
was forty-three years of age and well settled into his appointment at King's
School, Chester. Katherine Plymley later recorded that Mr. Vanbrugh was 'a
man of merit, and much beloved by his scholars; my Father and Brother were
equally pleased with the exchange'.[4] Another master there who had an important influence on Joseph was Mr. Thomas Falconer, a graduate of Brasenose
College, Oxford,[5] a High Churchman and 'a man of great learning'. He had
prepared for the bar at Lincoln's Inn but had suffered a nervous disorder and
decided to take up teaching. He was to become a family friend who once or
twice a year would spend a few days in the Plymley home.

It was during Joseph's years at Chester that Sir Richard Corbett died in
September 1774 at the age of seventy-eight and having held the baronetcy

since 1701. His memorial in Leebotwood Church pays tribute to his public life and character:

> A friend to the constitution, to liberty and toleration
> he served his country as a true Patriot in many Parliaments,
> in his retreat as a useful Magistrate
> and a zealous Patron of all such Design
> as promised Ornament or Utility to the Public.
> In his manners he was gentle, kind and
> Condescending, Engaging the love as well as
> the Esteem of all who knew him.
> He died 25 September1774
> In the 79th year of his Age
> Having survived his younger Brother Edward 10 years,
> With whom through life he had been intimately united
> In all the offices of the most tender and unreserved Friendship,
> And with whom he desired to be joined
> In this last Memorial to his Fraternal
> Regard and Affection.

Even allowing for the customary hyperbole of epitaphs, such a man would have been greatly missed by many, not least fifteen-year-old Joseph, who must have learned much from his company and whose long-term debt would be even greater. For Sir Richard had altered his will in his last years in a series of codicils. His title descended to Charles Corbett, his nearest heir in the male line, but the estate, which had long been bequeathed by will to Charles Corbett also, was now to go to the children of Jane Flint (*née* Corbett), his relative and housekeeper for many years. For reasons to be examined later, the immediate beneficiary was her youngest son (and Sir Richard's steward), Robert. If he left no male issue the estate was to be entailed on Richard and his male heirs, then John and his male heirs and, finally, on Diana's male heirs. On Sir Richard's death, therefore, Robert Flint adopted the surname Corbett, as required under the will, and moved into Longnor Hall.

When Sir Richard died Joseph still had another two years to spend at King's School, Chester, where he was happy, had profited from his studies and had made good friends. Chief among these was Paul Panton, son of a lawyer and landed gentleman from Anglesey, to whose house he seems to have been invited on several occasions. Fifty years later, on Paul's death, Joseph would recall their first meeting in September 1772 and how they became close friends. It was on 28 March 1776, when he was two months short of his seventeenth birthday, that Joseph Plymley's name was entered in the Matriculation Register at Pembroke College, Oxford. The reasons for the choice of university and college are nowhere recorded, but Pembroke may have been commended to Joseph and his father by their friend Robert More, M.P., and by a young clergyman whom More had presented to two livings in his gift and who had graduated from the college in 1771. The new Master of Pembroke, Dr. Adams, came from Shropshire, and Kynaston Powell (later Sir John), who would begin a thirty-eight year stretch as Knight of the Shire (M.P.) for Shropshire in 1784, had also only recently graduated from the college. It may have been generally known, too, that in Doctor Samuel Johnson (who visited the college in the very year that Joseph went up), the great jurist Sir William Blackstone, the poet William Shenstone, and George Whitefield, the famed evangelical preacher and friend of John Wesley, Pembroke could boast four figures of national stature among their 18th century *alumni*.

The university of Oxford was generally at a low ebb in these years, with the lowest recorded number of freshmen, 182, being admitted in 1759.[6] Pembroke was therefore probably a community of between only 40 and 50 when Joseph went up in 1776, all male, of course, as Fellows had to resign if they married. Among his fellow undergraduates were James Watson, who would become a judge, Henry Ford, who only four years later would become Professor of Arabic, Edward, the brother of Samuel Taylor Coleridge, and, most famous of all, Thomas Beddoes, born in Shifnal, the son of a Shropshire

An engraving of Pembroke College, Oxford made in 1675

15

farmer.[7] Beddoes became a physician in Bristol and a renowned writer. He is best remembered as a pioneer in the study of chemistry. He had links with the Lunar Society in Birmingham, encouraged Humphrey Davy, and his work was later greatly valued by Darwin. On his death, the poet Southey was to write: 'From Beddoes I hoped for more good to the human race than any other individual', and Coleridge lamented that 'more had been taken out of my life by this than by any former event'. Joseph must have been intellectually stimulated by living alongside such figures in the small community of the college. There were naturally other students who comported themselves very differently. William Shenstone, who had studied at Pembroke in the 1730s, had identified four different groups to which he had been briefly attached:

1. 'A very sober little party, who amused themselves in the evening with reading Greek and drinking water.'
2. 'A set of sprightly young fellows' who drank ale, smoked and sang their 'pious orgies'.
3. Some gentlemen-commoners, 'bucks of the first head', who drank port and claret.
4. A literary circle who 'read plays and poetry, *Tatlers* and *Spectators* and other works of easy digestion, and sipped Florence wines'.[8]

Joseph had entered the college as a commoner, socially below any nobles and gentlemen-commoners, but above the servitors, poorer students who helped to meet the costs of their university education by waiting on their fellows. We do not know which of his fellow-students Joseph became closest to, but, like other freshmen, he would have been struck by the heavy drinking that was the norm.

He was inevitably influenced by the Master of Pembroke, Dr. William Adams, a native of Shrewsbury and former rector of St. Chad's, who was appointed, at the age of sixty-nine, only the year before Joseph's arrival. 'Over the college he presided with universal approbation and engaged the affections of the students by his courteous demeanour and affability, mixed with the firmness necessary for the preservation of discipline'.[9] His epitaph in Gloucester Cathedral recalls that 'ingenious, learned, eloquent, he ably defended the truth of Christianity'. He was said by one student to be 'considerably deep' into chemistry, and the college was the focus of much of the growing excitement for chemistry at Oxford, producing not only Thomas Beddoes but, shortly after Joseph's day, James Smithson, founder of the Smithsonian Institution in Washington, D.C.

Although no details of Joseph's life in college have survived, his sister's journals contain some crucially important comments. It seems that, young as he was, Joseph was 'designed for the Church', perhaps on account of the influence of his mentor from Chester days, Thomas Falconer, but more probably as a result of his mother's encouragement, for she had 'got Mr. Corbett [uncle Robert, Sir Richard's heir] to agree to give Leebotwood and Longnor — the only livings in his gift — to Joseph on Mr. Rice's death'.[10] But after a year or two at college Joseph, still of course in his teenage years, and in spite of the Christian influence of the Master, 'felt a disinclination to take orders and often said he did not intend it'. Neither the reasons for his change of heart nor its immediate impact on his life are clear, but there are two strong pieces of evidence that he actually left Oxford after two years: first, his last entry in the college's battel books (accounts of student expenditure on rent, food, tuition etc.) was in May 1778, and second, he was not awarded his B.A until 1786. His parents and family must have been taken aback by his decision to leave Oxford without proceeding to his degree, but they wisely accepted this assertion of independence. It seems likely that they realised that he needed time and space to sort out what he wanted to do with his life.

What her brother did after coming down from Oxford, Katherine does not record, but young men of his age can usually find ways of filling their time. One thing he surely did was to ride over — or take the family — to see the wonder of the Iron Bridge, completed in 1779, which spanned the River Severn then carrying increasingly heavy commercial traffic as the mines and ironworks of East Shropshire developed. The bridge, designed by Thomas Pritchard, a Shrewsbury architect, and built by Abraham Darby and John Wilkinson, two great captains of industry, was striking local evidence of the progress of the Industrial Revolution. It boosted the spread of a network of turnpike roads in whose development Joseph was soon to play a part.

Later that same year an event occurred that had a profound effect on him. His mother, whose health had been in decline for some years, 'was seized in September 1779 with a painful illness, occasioned by some internal obstruction, which terminated in her death on 2 November'. Diana Plymley receives far less attention than her husband in Katherine's diaries because she did not begin these until 1791, but looking back in her memoirs written in 1795 she describes her mother as 'tall and fair, with blue eyes and light brown hair'. Her elder daughter's recollection of her was of a woman of 'an excellent understanding, admirable discretion, great activity, prudence in her domestic concerns, generous, charitable and eminently pious'. She generously added that she 'retained to the last a great share of that beauty which distinguished her early years'. As already remarked, Joseph's initial intention to seek ordination was probably with his mother's encouragement. Did she in her final illness, even on her deathbed, prevail on her son to set aside his recent doubts and commit himself to the service of God as a clergyman of the Church of England? What happened next suggests that such a promise was made, or that the shock of the death of the mother he loved led him to re-think his intended course in life.

William Plymley

*Joseph Plymley,
1716-1802,
the Archdeacon's
father*

The Refectory, Chester Cathedral — used as the school-room for the scholars of King's School, Chester, in Joseph's day

Pembroke College, Oxford. The large quadrangle, looking south.
On the right is the chapel which contains Joseph's gift of an altar picture

Pembroke College. The hall at the north end of the large quadrangle

*'The Bank' or 'Bank House' (now the Dower House), Longnor,
where Joseph was born and lived until 1804.*

*'Plas Gwyn' (the White House), Pentraeth, Anglesey,
where Joseph met his first wife, Jane Josepha Panton*

*Pentraeth church, Anglesey, where Joseph married Jane Josepha Panton,
13 March 1783*

The altar picture in the chapel of Pembroke College, Oxford.
'A graceful copy by Cranke of our Lord's figure in the picture executed by
Rubens for the Petit Carmes ... it was given about 1786 by a
Fellow Commoner, Mr. Joseph Plymley' (from Douglas Macleane's History of
Pembroke College, Oxford, *1897)*

The interior of Longnor church

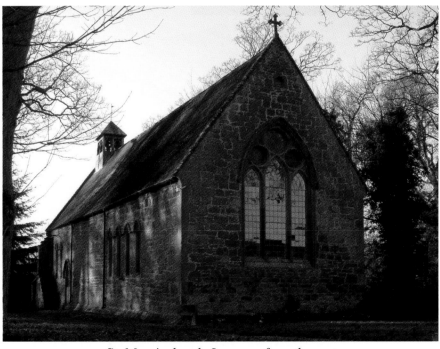

St. Mary's church, Longnor, from the east

The pulpit in St. Mary's, Longnor, from which Joseph preached over a period of half a century

Below: St. Michael's church, Madeley, built by Thomas Telford in 1796, early in Joseph's time as Archdeacon

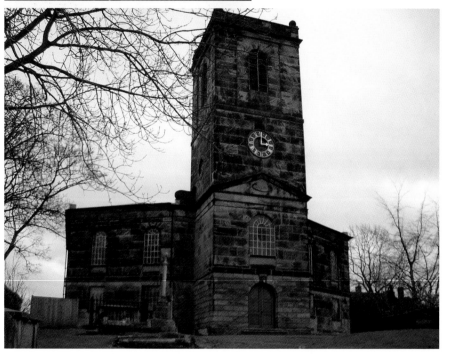

4 ORDINATION AND MARRIAGE

'My Brother afterwards resumed his first inclination and was ordained at as an early an age as the Church allows', was Katherine's rather bald comment confided in her memoirs years later.[1] This makes Joseph's decision sound almost casual, but it was surely the result of much heart-searching. It was, after all, to determine the course of his life.

Joseph must have discussed the question of ordination with his father and sisters, the local clergy, his former teacher Thomas Falconer, and other friends. Prominent among these was Robert More, Esq., of Linley, a distinguished and much travelled botanist, who had been M.P. for Bishops Castle and later succeeded Sir Richard Corbett as M.P. for Shrewsbury. More was the friend of Joseph's father who had regularly invited Joseph to spend part of his school holidays, and then university vacations, at Linley Hall, to the west of the Longmynd. Mr. More even consulted his young friend about appropriate decorations and furniture for the hall as it was extended. What made the lord of Linley such a valuable confidant at this particular time was his patronage of two livings in the west of the county, More and Shelve, to both of which he had recently presented the Rev. Robert Taylor. Since he had graduated from Pembroke College, Oxford, only five years before Joseph's admission, he and Joseph will have had much in common. The young rector's experience of life as a parish priest will also have been most helpful to Joseph in making up his own mind about his future.

It comes as no surprise, then, to find Robert Taylor's signature first on the testimonial that Joseph sent to the bishop with his application for ordination as deacon in September 1781. The other signatories were the Rev. Lewis Williams, rector of Woolstaston, and the Rev. Francis Kinchant, vicar of Stokesay. They testified that they had known Joseph for the last three years during which time he had lived 'piously, soberly and honestly'. His application papers[2] also included a certificate of age and confirmation that the notice of his intention to offer himself for deacon's orders had been read in Condover

Church (of which Longnor had been a chapelry) on 9 September and met with no objection. Most important was the letter signed by Robert Taylor, in his capacity of rector of Shelve, to nominate and appoint Joseph as his curate in that parish, allowing him £25 per annum for his maintenance until he gained some other ecclesiastical preferment. His application was approved, he made the necessary subscription to the 39 Articles of doctrine and to Church discipline, and on 30 September 1781 he was ordained in Hereford Cathedral. Whereas most of the other ordinands on this occasion stated in writing their college and university, Joseph merely appended 'Longnor, Shropshire' to his signature.[3]

It was an exciting moment when, in early October, the young curate set off on his horse from his home in Longnor across the hills to Shelve to take his first service. He may have had different feelings as winter set in, for Shelve stands 1,150 feet above sea level and could be cut off in severe weather. This is surely the explanation for his move in August 1782 to the much nearer parish of Woolstaston where the Rev. Lewis Williams was another friend; here he was to receive 25 guineas annually. Since Mr. Williams was also the incumbent at Longden and had served as curate at Stapleton since 1763, as well as sometimes helping out the very old priest at Leebotwood and Longnor, David Rice, he would have welcomed another pair of hands. But there was a further reason for the appointment. His mother's original intention had been that Joseph should be granted the Corbett benefices of Leebotwood and Longnor, to which she persuaded her brother Robert, now Mr. Corbett of Longnor Hall and recently honoured as Sheriff of the County in 1778, to agree to present him. But when Joseph lost his sense of vocation and left Oxford, Mr. Corbett had promised his friend Lewis Williams that he should have Leebotwood when it became vacant. On his ordination Joseph quite properly refused the prospect of Leebotwood offered by Mr. Williams and instead, as we have seen, became his curate the next year. All in all it was a very subdued start to his ecclesiastical career.

Joseph, however, had other things on his mind. On his visits to his school friend Paul Panton at Plas Gwyn on Anglesey, he had met and been attracted by Paul's cousin, Jane Josepha, who was living with them. She was a daughter of Thomas Panton, the younger brother of Paul Panton snr., barrister and Recorder of Beaumaris, who had married Jane Jones the heiress of the Plas Gwyn estate.[4] Thomas had been educated at Westminster School before — as a younger son — going into commerce and accepting a place with a merchant at Leghorn (Livorno) in Italy. He settled as a merchant there and married the Consul's daughter, Miss Douglas. Years later, when their family had grown large, illness suddenly struck — was it congenital problems, the exacting climate or an epidemic? — and Thomas lost his wife and four children. There remained only one son, who was to inherit the business, and a daughter who was herself in a delicate state of health. In order that she should benefit from a gentler climate, he sent her in 1774 at the age of eleven to live with his brother, himself the father of Paul and two girls.

As at that time Joseph was still at Chester School as a boy of fifteen; it was probably a little later when he first met Jane Josepha. Plas Gwyn was a splendid house to visit, a fine Georgian country mansion built about 1740 and unexpectedly with a red-brick frontage as Plas Gwyn means the White House. As time passed, however, it was not the house, nor even Paul, but Jane Josepha that drew him there. These were the years of the War of American Independence, heralded by the clashes of the colonists with the Redcoats of the British Army at Lexington and Concord in April 1775. The bid for independence, enshrined in the Declaration of 4 July 1776, developed into a protracted war in which the French joined, glad of an opportunity to gain revenge for their losses in the Seven Years' War after the disasters of 1759. The war clearly provoked much discussion in the Plymley household, for Katherine later recalled that her father had sided with the colonists whereas her sympathies were with the loyalists. For Joseph the War of Independence, whichever side he took, had a silver lining, because it was decided by her family that the dangers of an attack at sea were too great to risk Jane Josepha's return to Italy. But after news of the British surrender at Yorktown in October 1781 reached London, nearly six weeks later, and was seen to foreshadow the end of the war, Jane Josepha's father made arrangements to send a friend to accompany her home in the summer of 1782. Clearly Joseph got wind of this because before the friend arrived he had asked her to marry him — and she had agreed.

There seems to have been no opposition to the match from her father, for the families entered into negotiations over a marriage settlement. As both Joseph's friend Paul and his father were barristers, Jane Josepha's interests were carefully safeguarded, for all knew how unexpectedly death could strike.

The settlement,[5] signed on 23 January 1783, was between Joseph Plymley snr. and his son Joseph, Thomas Panton and his daughter Jane Josepha, and her uncle Paul and cousin Paul. The settlement set up a trust, with the Pantons, father and son, as trustees for the properties demised by Joseph Plymley the elder for the future benefit of his son and Jane Josepha. The properties were, first, a 'messuage', or house, on Pride Hill in Shrewsbury, owned by Mr.

Plymley and currently leased by William Lawrence, a glover. In addition he passed to the trust the house he lived in, The Bank, which had fifty-one years left on the lease granted by Sir Richard in 1765, the land in Longnor leased to him, also in 1765, by Robert Corbett (then Flint) for sixty-six years, and the land and buildings on Roushill in Shrewsbury originally leased to John Thornton, Mr. Plymley's former partner, by the Corporation. The income from these properties was to go to Mr. Plymley for the remainder of his life, and then, in order, to Joseph, Jane Josepha and their heirs. If, at a future date Joseph were to inherit Sir Richard's estates he would be required to improve his wife's settlement. Finally, when the marriage was solemnised, Thomas Panton agreed to pay his son-in-law £100 at once and £50 a year for life until the properties assigned to the trustees produced an equivalent regular income.

The wedding took place in the little church at Pentraeth, only a few hundred yards from Plas Gwyn, on 13 March 1783.[6] Jane Josepha was nineteen and Joseph twenty-three. Paul Panton must have been best man — he signed first as a witness — and his sisters bridesmaids for they also signed. Joseph's family was not present (not unusual at that time), for Katherine recorded that the bride 'was not personally known to any of us till my Brother brought her to Longnor as his wife'. She apparently agreed without hesitation to come to live in Mr. Plymley's house. Katherine's first impression of the young bride was very favourable: 'Rather under middle size, delicately and elegantly formed, fair, blue eyes, brown hair and aquiline nose ... If she was not strictly speaking beautiful, she was certainly charming'. Katherine was even more generous in her appraisal of her new sister-in-law's nature: 'In my mind every man may have wished to marry her, for she possest [sic] every virtue, and was adorned with every native grace that could make a woman amiable'. Jane Josepha was also very fortunate, for she had not only married a good man but had come to live in a truly loving family whose members held one another in the highest esteem.

Unfortunately, though understandably, Katherine gave no description of her brother. Though we know that she had the highest regard for him and when she commenced her journals in 1791 made constant reference to his activities and virtues, she gave no hints as to his physical appearance, and his portrait was not painted until many years later. As regards his character as a young man, we can only surmise, through interpretation of what is known of his early life, that he shared his family's deep concern for human freedom, that he enjoyed learning — even though he left Oxford without taking his degree — that he had had serious misgivings over his intended career in the

Church and had only committed himself after much soul-searching, that he had the capacity to forge strong and enduring friendships, and that he had been swept off his feet by the charms of Miss Panton.

The young couple settled happily at The Bank, for Jane Josepha was a home-loving girl who, 'though only nineteen, much admired and extremely cheerful in domestic society', was always content to be in her new home — which greatly pleased her father-in-law.

Less than three months after the marriage, Joseph took priest's orders at Hereford on Trinity Sunday 1783. This time his testimonial had been signed by Mr. Taylor, Mr. Williams and the Rev. Richard Wilding, rector of Easthope. In addition to the customary approval of the applicant's way of life, they added that he had 'diligently applied himself to his studies', which suggests that he now intended to proceed to his degree.[7] Early the next year his financial position improved a little, too, for on the death of David Rice on 7 March 1784, he was presented to the family living of Longnor while, as promised, Leebotwood went to Lewis Williams. Nonetheless, as his curate, Joseph continued to serve there also, taking the morning service in one and Evening Prayer in the other every week. Longnor parish had once been a chapelry of Condover parish, but Joseph now served as 'perpetual curate'. St. Mary's, which dates back to the late 13th century, 'is that rarity among English parish churches — a building entirely of one medieval style, in this case Early English'.[8] Joseph, who was to minister here for over fifty years, preached from the same pulpit to his congregation sitting in the same box pews as today. As the congregation grew, the western gallery, approached by external steps, was extended in Joseph's time (and again in 1840 when, after his death, the west door was inserted as the larger gallery blocked the south and north doors).[9] As Mr. Rice had been 'perpetual curate' at Church Preen, the patron, Mrs. Sarah Windsor, presented Joseph there too. Although they had been somewhat augmented by grants from Queen Anne's Bounty (a resource established to assist under-funded parishes), the stipends of all these benefices were very small, which is why so many of the clergy were pluralists, paying often temporary curates even less to serve in their place. Joseph himself, fully occupied on Sundays, employed Mr. Prosser to take the Preen services which were now fortnightly — previously they had been monthly. Katherine also noted that he 'constantly puts the children there to school', as he did also in Longnor where a charity school, endowed under Sir Richard Corbett's will, had just been opened. It is apparent, nevertheless, that the late 18th century Church was at a low ebb. For a conscientious clergyman, as Joseph was to prove himself, there was a very demanding task ahead.

But when David Rice died, Joseph's thoughts were not primarily on his clerical prospects, as five days earlier, on 2 March, Jane Josepha had given birth to their first baby, a son who at his baptism was given the name Panton. He was, Katherine remembered, 'a beautiful infant whom we all loved with a true fondness'. The joy of the young parents seemed complete. Joseph Plymley snr., with his two daughters unmarried, must have been delighted by the birth of his first grandchild but, unlike the new parents perhaps, would not have been so pre-occupied with the new arrival that he was unaware of the extraordinary political fever in the country. This stemmed from defeat in the American War, a struggle in which the Plymleys had taken a keen interest, and the consequent fall of Lord North's ministry after twelve years in power. The king was forced to accept two short-lived ministries composed of Whig groups that he hated, while the peace negotiations dragged on until the Peace of Paris was signed in 1783 and the independence of the United States was recognised. But what George III found intolerable was the unholy alliance of the ebullient Whig Charles James Fox and the conservative Lord North, a ministry that the king had to accept — just at the time of Joseph's marriage — as no other political figure could command a majority in Parliament. Yet a few months later the Fox-North coalition was defeated on the East India Bill and, at the king's invitation, William Pitt, only twenty-four years old, the same age as Joseph, became Prime Minister in December. In spite of its being lampooned as a 'mince pie administration' (it was considered doomed to defeat after Christmas), the ministry clung to power with royal support, and in the election campaign of March 1784 — when the Plymley baby was born – Pitt turned the tables on his opponents and won a decisive majority in the Commons. He was to lead the country for most of the next twenty-two years.

In the Plymley household, of course, it was little Panton who was the centre of attention. Through the summer months he flourished, but from August on his health gave increasing cause for concern. He seemed by slow degrees to decline and on 12 November, a mere nine months old, he died. For Joseph and his wife, indeed for all the family, the joy of springtime turned to grief.

Yet Jane Josepha knew that she was already pregnant again and when, the following 13 April, another son was born he too was christened Panton. As he continued strong and healthy, his father seized the opportunity to concentrate on his studies again. As his sister recalled nearly forty years later, Joseph 'was a Commoner in the first place when he went to Oxford, but as he did not keep Terms sufficient for his degree, he entered himself upon the College again after his first marriage, and he entered a Gentleman-Commoner, as it was the most proper he should associate with the Seniors of the College in their Common Room, than with the Juniors in theirs'. On being awarded his B.A. the next year, his first thought was what he could present to the college as the customary gift on graduation. 'When he had taken his degree and finally quitted the College, he considered that a picture for the altar of the Chapel would be the best present he could make, as the College abounded with Plate [the usual gift], and he employed Cranke to paint one for it. It is a copy from Rubens, a figure of our Saviour; the original is a large picture with many figures, in one of the galleries in Flanders I believe, but this figure is a fine and pleasing picture and suits the place it is now placed in, and adds much to the Chapel'. The college historian refers to the 'pleasing marble altarpiece in which is framed a graceful copy of our Lord's figure in the picture executed by Rubens for the Petit Carmes ... it was given about 1786 by a fellow-Commoner, Mr. Joseph Plymley'.[10] The painting may still be admired in the Chapel today.

The arrival on 29 July 1786 of a baby girl, baptised Josepha, meant greater pressure than ever on the accommodation at The Bank, since Katherine and Ann, and of course their father, also lived there. Mr. Plymley snr. provided an unexpected solution. On 30 October 1786, three months after Josepha's birth, he was married again — at the age of seventy — to Hannah, daughter of Thomas Russell of nearby Lydley Hayes. Although Joseph at once volunteered to move elsewhere with his young family, his father would have none of it. He had made up his mind to settle at The Lyth, a farmhouse a few miles south of Shrewsbury which he had inherited thirty-five years before from his partner John Thornton and which he now made fit for his own residence, according to Katherine 'at considerable expense'.

When Joseph's wife gave birth to their second daughter on 19 November 1787, her sisters-in-law, who had finally moved to The Lyth only two months previously, promptly returned to Longnor to look after mother and children. The newcomer was, of course, named Jane — so the girl who five years before had been Jane Josepha Panton now had three children, Panton, Josepha and Jane. But all was not well with the young mother, whose health had always been fragile. To counter a persistent fever the doctor prescribed opiates, in spite of the misgivings of her apothecary father-in-law, to relieve her pain and to keep her rested and happy. It was in vain. Jane Josepha Plymley, aged twenty-four, passed away on 4 December 1787. Katherine later remembered that the day she died Joseph had said, 'If I had not known her I should not have believed so pure a mind could exist'. She recorded her personal memories a few years later, recalling Jane Josepha's sweet voice, gentleness and ladylike manners. 'Her countenance announced the grace and sweetness of her mind'. After the funeral at Leebotwood her body was laid to rest in the Corbett vault beneath the chancel.

Joseph was in a state of deep shock. His lovely young wife was gone and he was left with three little children aged two years, one year and two weeks. In not altogether dissimilar circumstances, except it was a wife without a husband, Sir Richard Corbett had come to the family's rescue sixty years earlier; this time it was Joseph's sisters who saved the day, for Katherine and Ann, who had run the house on and off since their father moved out, now took over responsibility for the little ones too. Katherine took a typically positive view of this, claiming that it led them to increase their own knowledge so that they could answer all the children's questions and 'provided us with honourable employment for our own time'.

For Joseph it was quite different. He was concerned to resume his clerical duties as soon as possible, but did so far too quickly. He returned from his first service at Leebotwood, where Jane Josepha was buried, his shocked sister was to recall, 'universally affected with dreadful nervous tremors and convulsive twitchings which continued with unabating violence for many months'.

In time he erected a white marble monument in the church at Leebotwood:

> In memory of Jane Josepha daughter of Thomas Panton of Leghorn in Italy Merchant and wife of Joseph Plymley of Longnor in this County Clerk, and in memory of Panton Plymley their eldest child who was born March 2nd and departed this life November 12th 1784. The infant purity of the son is the best emblem of the Mother whose sweetness of Manners and Innocence of mind more congenial to a better world ceased to adorn this at the early age of 24 years December 4th 1787.

5 THE ANTI-SLAVE TRADE CAMPAIGN

The issue that brought Joseph Plymley back to life, gave him a new interest that became a passion, enriched his faith, and added a new dimension to his church ministry was the campaign to abolish the transatlantic slave trade.

For some weeks after his wife's death it seems that Joseph was in a state of nervous prostration. His condition may have been eased by medical care and attention, but time alone could heal fully. In those dark days he was upheld by the solicitude and love of his sisters, who were also devoting them-selves to the upbringing of his children. The infants' chatter and play will have lightened Joseph's mood, while Panton, who reached his third birthday in April 1788, could have become his little companion. But what was needed more than anything was a new sense of purpose. This he was to discover through reading some of the publications of the Abolition of the Slave Trade Committee, formed in 1787; indeed, he may have been one of their earliest subscribers.

Brought up in a family that took a keen interest in what was going on in the world, and 'educated in a strong dislike of arbitrary government', Joseph and his sisters must have long been aware of the slave issue. In those years, however, it had no prominence. Even for those who thought about it there seemed no prospect of change, as it was seen as essential to Britain's commerce and the prosperity of her West Indian colonies. Yet a revolution in thought, communication and moral attitudes was even then underway. The thinkers of the Age of Enlightenment in France and Britain challenged tradi-tional attitudes: Adam Smith in his *Wealth of Nations* (1776) maintained that slavery was economically inefficient, and William Paley's *Moral Philosophy* (1785) derided the claim that slavery was a necessity. At the same time a rapid expansion of the availability of newspapers and other printed material communicated these new ideas to a greater number of people than ever before. And the Christian Church, which to its shame had not denounced slavery, was now increasingly awakened to its evils by the Methodists, Evangelicals and, above all, the Quaker Society of Friends.

Back in 1772, when Joseph was in his first year at school in Chester, the newspapers had reported the celebrated case of James Somerset, a runaway slave. Somerset's lawyer, Granville Sharp, after successfully championing another slave, Jonathan Strong, a few years earlier, had made himself an expert in the laws on slavery. He now presented his arguments so powerfully that the Lord Chief Justice, Lord Mansfield, declared that an owner had no right to compel his slave to go into a foreign country — and freed Somerset. Although the judgement did not guarantee freedom for slaves in England — even if that was the popular understanding — it generated tremendous interest throughout the country in the issue of slavery. Eleven years later, shortly after Joseph's marriage, Granville Sharp hit the headlines again when he intervened in another case before Lord Mansfield arising from the insurance claim made by the owners of the slave ship *Zong*, whose captain had thrown 132 living slaves overboard (he maintained on account of the shortage of drinking water) and who claimed compensation for the loss of 'cargo'.

Although the Plymleys had clearly known of these sensational cases, Katherine records that 'they' — and she was an even more voracious reader than her brother — had first become 'much interested in the subject' when they read Thomas Clarkson's first *Essay* soon after its publication in June 1786. Clarkson was a young Divinity graduate of St. John's College, Cambridge, whose entry had won first prize the previous year in a competition for a dissertation in Latin on the Vice-Chancellor's chosen subject *'Anne liceat invitos in servitutem dare?'* — 'Is it lawful to make slaves of others against their will?' In preparation for his essay Clarkson had read everything he could lay his hands on about what he later called 'the horrors of this bloody trade'. He became aware that the Quakers were among 'the earliest, the warmest and the most persevering supporters of abolition',[1] setting up a committee of six in 1783 to agitate against slavery and the slave trade. He drew heavily on *The History of Guinea* by Anthony Benezet, a member of the American Society of Friends and a prolific publicist for the anti-slave trade movement. 'In this precious book I found almost all I wanted' was Clarkson's verdict. He also managed to get access to the papers of a slave merchant recently deceased. Clarkson admitted that he had initially entered the essay competition with the sole aim of achieving academic honour, but the more he explored the subject the more he found himself overwhelmed with horror. 'It was but one gloomy subject from morning to night. In the daytime I was uneasy. In the night I had little rest. I sometimes never closed my eyelids for grief'. Yet when he read his prize-winning essay in Latin in the University Senate House at Cambridge it was acclaimed by the convocation of dons. On his return journey to London, however, the sufferings portrayed in his essay 'almost wholly engrossed my thoughts. Coming in sight of Wades Mill in Hertfordshire, I sat down disconsolate on the turf by the roadside and held my horse. Here a thought came into my mind, that if the contents of the essay were true, it was time some person should see these calamities to their end'.[2] For Thomas Clarkson this was an epiphany moment, a Damascus Road experience; for the anti-slave trade movement it would prove to be the decisive commitment.

What Joseph and his sister — and perhaps his wife, too — read in 1786 was Clarkson's translated and expanded version of the prize essay published by James Phillips of Lombard Street in June of that year. Joseph was only a year older than Clarkson and shared his revulsion against the horrors of the slave trade. But with his young family and his church responsibilities, Joseph was in no position to commit himself to the cause of Abolition as wholeheartedly as Clarkson. Nonetheless, it is clear that Joseph was itching to become more directly involved. Very soon after the formation of the Abolition of the Slave Trade Committee he became a subscriber and received their promotional literature, which enabled him to follow closely the development of the campaign. A brief outline of the activities of Clarkson, and soon of Wilberforce, too, is necessary to understand Joseph's growing excitement and his longing for an opportunity to play a more active part himself — an intention that had to be deferred following Jane Josepha's death at the end of 1787.

The publication of Clarkson's *Essay* had at once made him many new friends for invitations poured in from some of the leading figures of the movement. He travelled to Teston in Kent to meet the Rev. James Ramsay who had spent nineteen years on the Caribbean island of St. Kitts, and whose graphic accounts of the sufferings of the slaves provided the abolitionists with some of their most telling publicity. Ramsay in turn introduced him to Sir Charles Middleton, Comptroller of the Navy and his Evangelical wife who lived nearby. It was through these new friends that he met the renowned Granville Sharp, Beilby Porteus, Bishop of London, and Olaudah Equiano. A former slave now living in London, Equiano had been kidnapped as a child by slave traders in West Africa, had experienced the overcrowding, the putrid stench and the constant terrors of the voyage across the Atlantic, and been sold into slavery in Barbados alongside other terrified Africans torn from their homeland and now separated from their relations and friends 'most of them never to see one another again'.

As he reflected on what he had learned from his new contacts Clarkson became convinced that he had found his vocation in life. At the dinner table in Teston Hall 'in the joy of my heart I exclaimed that I was ready to devote myself to the cause'. After wrestling with himself on account of what he recognised was a public pledge, he found peace 'in obedience, I believe, to a higher Power ... On the moment of the resolution and for some time after-wards I had more sublime and happy feelings than at any former period of my life'.[3] From that summer Clarkson threw himself into the cause, seldom working less than sixteen hours a day. He arranged to meet anyone he learned had been in Africa including John Newton the former slave ship captain who was now rector of Olney, a leading Evangelical Christian, a zealous abolitionist and author of the great hymn *Amazing Grace.* Lords and ladies, Members of Parliament and others with influence were recruited. Through Middleton's influence, records at the Custom House were searched: muster rolls of men who had left London in the crews of slave ships revealed that about 20% of the men had died by the end of the voyage. That the trade was killing not only slaves but also British sailors could prove a strong political argument in a cause where moral exhortation alone, Clarkson sensed, would never carry the day.

His publisher, James Phillips, introduced Clarkson to the members of the Quaker anti-slavery committee who were able to furnish him with graphic details of the horrors of slavery and the slave trade. 'For the Quakers, Clarkson was a godsend: young, brimming with enthusiasm, skilled at persuading people to join the cause — and, above all, an Anglican'.[4] Together they decided to form a new committee of twelve, nine of whom were Quakers, including William Dillwyn, a Pennsylvanian pupil of Benezet. Clarkson and Granville Sharp, the elder statesman of the anti-slavery movement, were two of the three Anglicans. After their first meeting on 22 May 1787, they quickly made the critical decision that their aim was to end the transatlantic slave *trade*; some wanted to widen that to the abolition of slavery itself, but it was agreed that stopping the trade was a more attainable target, with the hope that in time the shortage of slaves would bring emancipation for all.

If 1786 had proved a crucial year in the history of the movement with the commitment of Thomas Clarkson to full-time campaigning, 1787 saw the recruitment of William Wilberforce as its Parliamentary general and spokesman. Clarkson had met Wilberforce when he was canvassing Members of Parliament, but it was not till some months later, in May 1787, that the historic dinner party took place at which Clarkson asked Wilberforce directly to bring forward an anti-slave trade measure in Parliament and received a positive response. Wilberforce, a year older than Clarkson, was another Cambridge graduate, M.P. for Hull in 1780 when only twenty-one and for Yorkshire since 1784. As an undergraduate, and in his early years as an M.P., he had had a reputation as an idle but witty member of the smart social set who spent much of his time at card parties, but at the age of twenty-five he had experienced a profound spiritual conversion and, influenced by John Newton, had emerged as a leading figure in the Evangelical movement with a special concern for the victims of the slave trade and for the reform of the nation's morals. He was another godsend for the cause – charming, wealthy, popular, an intimate friend of William Pitt, now Prime Minister, since their college days, and a brilliant public speaker. Pitt thought he had 'the greatest natural eloquence in England'; indeed, his melodious voice would win him the epithet 'Nightingale of the House of Commons'. The combination of Clarkson the agitator and Wilberforce the Parliamentary leader would in the long run prove irresistible. Sadly, it was to prove a very long run.

Yet for all the quality of its leaders, the anti-slave trade campaign could not have succeeded without willing supporters in the towns and counties to distribute pamphlets, organise petitions, raise subscriptions and win over public opinion. Amongst the lieutenants who emerged to take up this vital role was Joseph Plymley. It seems, indeed, to have lifted him from his grief back into an active life. 'My brother's attention was much engaged by the subject, and conscious of the goodness of the cause, it was, perhaps, of more service than any other pursuit would have been in calming his mind after the recent loss of his wife', Katherine later recorded. Early in spring 1788, she continued, 'petitions to Parliament were first agitated in several counties and towns'. It is interesting that Shrewsbury was among the places Thomas Clarkson had listed as likely to raise petitions as he made his way north from Bristol to Liverpool in September 1787 on his tour of the major slave ports, where he had interrogated informants in the dock areas.

While Clarkson went on to spend the winter writing another book, and Wilberforce gave notice in the Commons that early in the next session he would ask leave to bring in a Bill for the abolition of the slave trade, the London Committee moved swiftly to rouse local correspondents into action. They resolved to send a circular letter with their Report to the Mayor of every corporate town that had not yet petitioned. It seems very likely that Joseph saw the advertisement placed in the *Shrewsbury Chronicle* on 12 January 1788 by the Abolition Society's newly-formed Manchester Committee calling for support for petitions. In spite of the nervous disorder brought on by his recent bereavement, Joseph could not resist the impulse to become involved in Shrewsbury and the county on an issue so close to his heart. Clarkson told the Committee at a meeting early in 1788 that among the many letters he had received was one from the Rev. Joseph Plymley, 'in which he expressed the deep interest he took in this cause of humanity and freedom, and the desire he had of making himself useful as far as he could towards the support of it; and he wished to know, as the clergy of the diocese of Lichfield and Coventry were anxious to espouse it also, whether a petition to Parliament from them, as part of the established church, would not be desirable at the present season'.[5] According to Katherine he was the first to think of a petition from the clergy. Among other letters received by Clarkson inquiring about public meetings, resolutions and petitions to Parliament, was one from John Flint, Esq. — Joseph's uncle — on behalf of the town of Shrewsbury and the county of Salop. The slave trade was clearly an issue appealing to the wider family. Joseph followed up his communication by writing to the two arch-deacons in Shropshire, seeking their co-operation. Mr. Clive of the Hereford diocese readily agreed, but Mr. Leigh, of the Lichfield and Coventry diocese that Joseph had mentioned in his letter, was initially unwilling, although he complied when he saw how many clergy were signing.

'The petition campaign of 1788 fully rewarded the efforts of the London Committee. Between 1 February and 9 May over a hundred petitions dealing with the slave trade were presented to the House of Commons, more than half the total number of petitions received in the session'.[6] They included two from the Shropshire clergy and the town of Shrewsbury. This evidence of widespread public interest led to the appointment of a Committee of the Privy Council to consider the state of the slave trade. The London Committee promptly concentrated its efforts on collecting and arranging suitable evidence. The testimonies of witnesses recruited by Clarkson were corroborated by the revelations in John Newton's *Thoughts upon the African Slave Trade* published in January 1788. The old slave captain's forceful pamphlet immediately sold out; copies of the reprint were sent to every Member of Parliament. Even more telling in the long run was the Abolition Committee's

Joseph Wedgwood's iconic medallion

adopt
Wedg
It dep
togethe
I not a
Fashion
and wl ͪᵤₛper medal-
lion incorporating the same design, and marketed with all Wedgwood's commercial skill, it appeared on ladies' bracelets and gentlemen's snuff boxes, becoming the movement's most striking and popular symbol. As the campaign initiated the use of so many of the tactics adopted by later pressure groups down to our own day, it received further support from the poet William Cowper, encouraged by his friend John Newton. Cowper's verses, entitled *The Negro's Complaint*, which were even set to music and sung as a ballad, threw down the gauntlet to those engaged in the slave trade with its challenging opening:

> Forc'd from home, and all its pleasures,
> Afric's coast I left forlorn,
> To increase a stranger's treasures,
> O'er the raging billows borne,
> Men from England bought and sold me,
> Paid my price in paltry gold;
> But, though theirs they have enroll'd me,
> Minds are never to be sold.

The high hopes of supporters for a warm reception for Wilberforce's motion in the Commons faded as he fell seriously ill early in 1788. Though he began to recover he was forced to ask his friend the Prime Minister to present the motion on his behalf. Pitt's powerful advocacy on 6 May won approval for the introduction in the next session of Parliament of a bill to end the slave trade. The campaign's momentum was maintained by Sir William Dolben's introduction soon afterwards of a Bill to restrict the number of

...rried in individual vessels. It arose from his shocking findings on ...cting a slave ship moored in the Thames. The Bill came under fierce ...tack, especially in the Lords where the Lord Chancellor derided it as the product of 'a five days' fit of philanthropy'. It was finally passed, although weakened by numerous amendments. The pro-slave lobby of merchants in the slave ports and West Indian planters was seriously alarmed as the slave trade became a national talking-point.

❦

Unfortunately when Parliament re-assembled in the autumn consideration of the issue was postponed by a development that plunged the whole country into anxiety and controversy: King George III's behaviour was showing unmistakable signs of madness. While doctors argued about his treatment and the prospects of his recovery, government and opposition were locked in a combat over what should be done. The Whigs led by Fox, who was a friend of the heir to the throne, wanted the Prince of Wales made Regent, whereas Pitt saw the threat to his hold on power and played for time. The next February, just as a Regency was about to be declared, the king recovered and was able to resume his constitutional duties.

With normality restored, the anti-slave trade campaign enjoyed a further boost that spring with the publication of the plan and section of an actual slave-ship, the *Brookes* of Liverpool. Copies were sent to members of both houses of Parliament and to key supporters in the country. The publication

A view of the decks on the slave-ship Brookes *showing how the slaves were packed for the transatlantic crossing*

had a great impact for here was visual evidence of the hideous overcrowding of slave ships which had caused great loss of life, although it has been calculated that on English vessels in the 1780s the death rate had been reduced to about 6% of slaves so transported. Members of the slave lobby had been able to argue that African chiefs were responsible for the supply of slaves, and that once in the New World their living conditions were better than back in their homeland — which was hotly disputed by those like James Ramsay who had seen the treatment of slaves first hand in the West Indies — but the conditions on the slave ships were indefensible and public indignation ran high. Further valuable evidence for the cause of Abolition was produced in the report of the Privy Council Committee published in April.

Reformers' hopes were therefore once again running high when William Wilberforce rose to address the House of Commons on 12 May 1789. In a speech which lasted three and a half hours he condemned the harsh conditions under which slaves were held while waiting for the slave ships to arrive at the African ports, the even more desperate conditions in which they were packed on the ships for a voyage which typically lasted about seven weeks, and the cruelties of their sale and enforced labour on the plantations of the Caribbean islands. As his speech unfolded he endeavoured also to answer the arguments of his opponents. Slave ships, he maintained, could carry alternative cargo; plantations would become more profitable as humane treatment improved the health of slaves and increased the birth-rate; and though French slavers might initially benefit from British abolition, Britain still ought to take the lead and set an example to the rest of Europe. The evidence of Captain Norris, who had appeared as a witness for the slave merchants and praised the care given to slaves, even maintaining that they were so happy that they danced and sang, was treated with scorn. 'The truth is that, for the sake of exercise, these miserable wretches, loaded with chains, oppressed with disease and wretchedness, are forced to dance by the terror of the lash, and sometimes by the actual use of it Their songs are songs of lamentation upon their departure'. Before submitting twelve resolutions, Wilberforce concluded his speech by seizing the moral high ground:

> Sir, the nature and all the circumstances of this Trade are now laid open to us. We can no longer plead ignorance. We cannot evade it. We may spurn it. We may kick it out of the way. But we cannot turn aside so as to avoid seeing it. For it is brought now so directly before our eyes that this House must decide and must justify to all the world and to its own conscience, the rectitude of the ground of its decision ... Let not Parliament be the only body that is insensitive to the principles of natural justice.

Speaker Grenville even vacated his chair to hail 'one of the most masterly and eloquent speeches he had ever heard'.

Although Wilberforce was supported by Pitt, Burke and Fox, three of the greatest orators of the day, the fear of damaging economic and social consequences, and of French competition in particular, led the House to insist that the Privy Council report was not enough and that the Commons must exercise its historic right to conduct its own hearings. Most M.P.s, unsure how to vote, welcomed the delaying tactic; Clarkson, however, saw that the intrigue of his opponents had deferred the whole question for another year. Out in the country Joseph Plymley and other local leaders, who would have been cheered by Wilberforce's oratory, felt dreadfully deflated by the appointment of another committee of investigation.

Ironically, the fear that the French would reap the benefits if the British ended the slave trade, the very fear that had had the most influence on undecided MPs, began to look less threatening in the same month that the Commons had decided to refer the issue to a committee of the House. For the meeting of the States-General at Versailles in May 1789 triggered a succession of events that led to the storming of the Bastille two months later. These dramatic developments, which brought French abolitionists like Mirabeau and Lafayette to the fore, provided British campaigners with fresh grounds for optimism. While the London Committee opened a correspondence with the recently formed *Société des Amis des Noirs,* Clarkson himself headed for Paris. Although he remained in France till the end of the year he became disillusioned with the Society on account of its inactivity. The fundamental reason for this was, of course, the pre-occupation of the new National Assembly and the French people with the progress of the Revolution. He returned to England convinced that only the promise of speedy abolition of the slave trade by Pitt's government could induce the French to act.

Progress in England, however, was far from speedy. During the second half of 1789 and until the following April the Committee, which until January had been of the whole House, was hearing the evidence of supporters of the trade and of slavery on plantations; only then did it begin hearing evidence from those supporting Abolition. It was at this moment, according to Katherine Plymley, that her brother went to London where he spent several weeks working energetically for the campaign. Here was Joseph's opportunity to meet the movement's national leaders, and to make a contribution to the development of the campaign beyond his local sphere of activity. Dr. Baker, an Anglican clergyman and keen advocate of the cause, introduced him to members of the Abolition Committee in their rooms at Old Jewry where he became a regular visitor. 'One time when he was there he spoke a good deal and was afterwards desired by Mr. Dickson, a warm friend to the Abolition, to commit to writing what he had spoken for Mr. Wilberforce'. On one of his frequent visits to hear witnesses examined before the House, Joseph listened to Thomas Clarkson under cross-examination. He used also to go to the room set up at the Parliament Coffee House where the Abolition Committee met daily. Here he was introduced to Wilberforce, whom he wrote to tell his family was very pleasant in his manners, though insignificant in looks and person. He also met Clarkson and his brother John, an officer in the Royal Navy. Thomas, he reported, told him that for three and a half years he had led a most wearisome life, never in bed till 3.00 am and his mind so harassed by the disagreeableness of the subject that he was almost worn out. A speech by the Prime Minister made a great impression on Joseph who felt that Pitt 'seems a most decided friend to the Abolition ... His heart seemed in the business'.

Katherine, who later regretted that she had not started her journal when Joseph first became active in the cause of Abolition, tried to make amends by recording her recollections of those days in her third journal in October 1791. Her brother, she recalled, frequently dined with Dr. Baker when in London; in return he often had the doctor and other abolitionist friends to dine with him at his lodgings. At Old Jewry the Quakers were so pleased with a speech he made that they encouraged him to come there regularly and to the Parliament Coffee House. 'My brother continued from time to time doing all in his power for the cause by inserting arguments in the papers, conversing with company on the subject, and by subscribing himself and procuring subscriptions from many'.

Joseph's exertions won him many friends, but he had to return home to resume his clerical duties. In his continuing flush of enthusiasm for the abolition of the slave trade it seems certain that he made time that summer to ride out to visit prospective supporters in Shropshire and neighbouring counties. Perhaps it was on one such excursion that he met and fell in love with a young lady from north Herefordshire. Matty Dansey was the daughter of an army captain unusually called Dansey Dansey as he had, probably for reasons of inheritance, adopted the surname of the family that had provided his Christian name. Her father died when she was only two years old, an event that most likely caused her mother to move from the family residence at Brinsop Court to Little Hereford at the very northern edge of the county. It was here, in the little church with its sturdy tower on the banks of the River Teme, that on 29 December 1790 — after what seems to have been a lightning courtship — the Rev. Joseph Plymley of Longnor was married to Matty Dansey. The service was conducted by the Rev. Richard Wilding, Rector of Easthope, an old friend of Joseph who had signed the testimonial when he had applied for ordination as a priest. It was just over three years since the death of his first wife, Jane Josepha. His sister commented that Joseph had always 'a very strong predilection to a married life'. She penned no description of his second bride; all we know is that she was only eighteen years old. Katherine's comment sounds rather defensive: 'The lady was very young, and she was apprised, before her marriage, that the children of the first Mrs. Plymley were confided to the care of my sister and myself; the marriage therefore made no alteration in our situation in that respect'.

Yet the domestic arrangements at Bank House had undeniably become more complicated. As the elder Mr. Plymley no longer lived there, Joseph was the head of the family. In addition to caring for his new young wife, who had much to learn about running the household, he was the father of three young children being brought up by his sisters, Katherine and Ann, who would have become accustomed to managing the affairs of the household during Joseph's illness after his first wife's death and his more recent absence in London.

The years brought changes in the extended family, too. The death of uncle Richard Flint's wife, Eleanor, in the summer of 1788 had relieved long-existing tensions for she had bitterly resented Sir Richard Corbett's preference in his will for the youngest brother, Robert, and refused to meet other members of the family. Though they lived in Longnor, uncle Richard and his wife had studiously avoided all their relations, but when she died he had resumed contact. The next to die, in April 1791 after a lingering illness, was Anne, wife of uncle Robert who had assumed the name Corbett and moved to Longnor Hall on Sir Richard's death in 1774. Only a few months later uncle Richard himself died at the age of seventy-one. Katherine remembered him as 'a merry, joking man', who had little wealth but left £200 to his god-daughter Ann, Joseph's sister, and £50 to Joseph himself.

ℓℓ

Joseph's mind, however, was more concerned with his young family, his church duties and the progress of the anti-slave trade campaign. On that issue the Commons' inquiry ground slowly on, unchanged by the snap election that Pitt had called in June 1790. Over sixty pro-abolition witnesses, mainly recruited by Clarkson, were questioned by Wilberforce and his fellow M.P., William Smith, and cross-examined by hostile spokesmen for the other side. The Committee's work finished at last in April 1791, leaving Wilberforce and others only weeks to produce a digest of the evidence presented against the trade for distribution to M.P.s. The spotlight now turned on Wilberforce again. The long-awaited debate was on his motion 'to bring in a Bill to prevent the further importation of slaves into the British colonies in the West Indies'. He was conscious of his great responsibility, though buoyed up by John Wesley's reminder to him in almost the last letter of his life: 'Unless God has raised you up for this very thing, you will be worn out by the opposition of men and devils, but if God be for you who can be against you?'[7]

As Wilberforce rose to address the House on the afternoon of 18 April 1791, his supporters all over the country prayed for success. Katherine Plymley, who shared her brother Joseph's zeal for the cause, later recorded: 'The debate lasted two days, I feel myself incapable of saying more of it than that I believe on the side of the Abolition it was impossible for human eloquence to go higher and that the several speakers were as convincing to any not quite blinded by prejudice, when they spoke of the impolicy as when they spoke of the injustice and inequity of the slave trade'. Wilberforce had indeed spoken for four hours in masterly fashion, refuting the belief that the prosperity of British commerce was dependent on the trade in slaves. He denounced the injustice and cruelty of that trade, and concluded that his side would never desist till they had 'extinguished every trace of this bloody traffic, of which our posterity, looking back to the history of these enlightened times, will scarcely believe that it has been suffered to exist so long a disgrace and dishonour to this country'. He was supported again by the most eloquent speakers of the day, his friend Pitt, the Prime Minister, and Charles James Fox, leader of the Opposition, who scornfully contrasted the harsh penal laws of that day for petty criminals and the failure to confront the much greater evil of the trade in slaves. Fox's peroration was blistering: 'If the House, knowing what the trade was by the evidence which had been produced, did not by their vote mark to all mankind their abhorrence of a practice so savage, so enormous, so repugnant to all law, human and divine, they would consign their character to eternal infamy'.

The sad truth was, however, that the tide of events was not running in the abolitionists' favour. The more threatening developments in the French Revolution, the scare given to the propertied classes by the publication of Tom

Paine's *Rights of Man* and, most of all, news of a slave revolt in the British West Indian island of Dominica led moderate MPs to shrink from radical change, and gave new confidence to those representing slave merchants and plantation owners. Led by Banastre Tarleton, M.P. for Liverpool, they emphasised the damaging commercial effect of abolition on the employment of seamen and vessels and on Britain's export trade. The national interest must not be undermined, it was argued, by inquiring too closely into the details of the slave trade. When 'commerce clinked its purse', as the writer Horace Walpole put it,[8] the majority of M.P.s forgot the claims of justice and humanity. After the two days of debate the House voted 163-88 against abolishing the slave trade. 'The church bells of Liverpool rang and Bristol celebrated with a cannon salute, a bonfire, fireworks, and a half-day holiday'.[9]

When the Abolition Committee met after the vote, Clarkson noted that 'the looks of all bespoke the feelings of their hearts'. That same shock and disappointment were registered on the faces of the Plymley family in distant Shropshire.

6 WORKING WITH THOMAS CLARKSON

The mood of despond in both Longnor and London after the Parliamentary reverse of 20 April 1791 was soon to lift. 'A few days afterwards', Katherine wrote, 'the London Committee met and passed resolutions printed in the papers in which, after thanking the honourable minority, they declared their resolve to persevere and that they regarded the decision of the House rather as retarding the business than as a defeat'. It was the right attitude to adopt, even though the quickening pace of the Revolution in France and its impact in England would quickly replace the slave trade at the top of the news agenda.

Shortly afterwards the London Committee planned a new campaign of petitions on a much larger scale than in 1788. As Clarkson later recorded in his *History of the Abolition of the Slave Trade*: 'The Committee in order to strengthen themselves for the prosecution of this great work, elected Sir Wm. Dolben, Bart, Henry Thornton, Lewis Alexander Grant and Matthew Montagu, Esqs, who were Members of Parliament, and Thomas Harford, Esq, Josiah Wedgwood jnr., Esq, and John Clarkson, Esq, of the Royal Navy, as members of their own body, and they elected the Reverend (later Archdeacon) Joseph Plymley an honorary and corresponding member, in consequence of the great services he had rendered their cause in the shires of Hereford and Salop, and the adjacent counties of Wales'. Katherine noted how delighted Joseph was to learn of the honour in a letter from his friend Dr. Baker, since he knew nothing of it beforehand. It was indeed a signal distinction, demonstrating the high regard in which Joseph was held by the leadership of the movement.

His immediate response was to plan a meeting of subscribers in Shropshire to thank them for their support and 'to keep the subject alive in their minds'. The meeting, held at the Shire Hall on Wednesday, 13 July 1791, was reported in three successive issues of the *Shrewsbury Chronicle* in late July and early August. The newspaper headline read: 'A meeting of the

41

members of the Society for effecting an Abolition of the Slave Trade, resident in the County of Salop'. It proved to be a very well-attended meeting, since they had expected only existing subscribers to the cause. Proposed by Mr. Knight and seconded by Mr. Blakeway, the Rev. Joseph Plymley was elected chairman. The meeting passed several unanimous resolutions, the first three drafted by the chairman:

1. We observe, with infinite satisfaction, the persevering zeal of the London Committee, expressed in their resolutions of 26 April last, and beg leave publicly to add our thanks to those then given to William Wilberforce, Esq, the Rt. Hon. William Pitt, the Rt. Hon. Charles James Fox, Matthew Montagu, Esq, William Smith, Esq,, and the rest of the Honourable Minority of the House of Commons who steadily opposed the continuance of a traffic incompatible with every principle of Justice, Policy and Humanity.

2. We acknowledge the previous labourers in the cause, especially the Rev. Mr. Clarkson, whose early and indefatigable exertions have eventually given rise to an almost unparalleled junction of splendid talents, a noble dereliction of political difference in the conviction of the Truth, *That the Abolition of the Slave Trade was indispensably required, not only by Religion and Morality but by every principle of Sound Policy.*

3. That to the above declarations, spoken by such authority, and proved by evidence the most pure and impartial we thus testify our fullest belief, professing ourselves ready to co-operate in the circulation of the truths whereby it is made manifest and determined to persevere in the zealous assertion of the same.

The remaining resolutions were drafted by Mr. Blakeway:

4. Thanks were expressed to the Rev. Joseph Plymley 'for his indefatigable pains and attention in the prosecution of this humane and important business'.

5. Thanks were given also to John Flint, Esq, who became Treasurer and to 'those wishing to become subscribers who should signify their intention to him at his house in Shrewsbury'.

6. The resolutions were to be printed three times in the *General Evening Post* and the *Shrewsbury Chronicle.*

The paper listed the thirty-two present in alphabetical order:

Rev. Joseph Plymley (in the chair)	Rev. Theophilus Houlbrooke
Rev. H.C. Adams	Rowland Hunt, Esq.
Thos. Beale, Esq.	Rev. Richard King
Rev. Edward Blakeway	Thomas Knight, Esq.
Joshua Blakeway, Esq.	Rev. Mr. Lea
Robert Burton, Esq.	Rev. Edward Leighton
Edward Burton, Esq.	Rev. Hugh Owen
Rev. Henry Burton	Edward Pemberton, Esq.
Rev. Archdeacon Clive	Rev. Edward Powys
William Cludde, Esq.	Richard Reynolds, Esq.
Robert Corbett, Esq.	William Reynolds, Esq.
Rev. Mr. Dana	Joseph Reynolds, Esq.
Dr. Darwin	Rev. John Rocke
Dr. Evans	William Tayleur, Esq.
Thomas Eyton, Esq	William Tayleur, Jnr.
John Flint, Esq.	Rev. Richard Wilding

It is worthy of note that all the above were clergy or gentlemen. They included Joseph's two uncles, Robert Corbett and John Flint; Archdeacon Clive; Dr. Darwin, whose son Charles was to eclipse all of them in fame; the Revs. Blakeway and Owen, historians of Shrewsbury; and the three Reynolds, Quaker ironmasters from Coalbrookdale.

While Joseph and his co-workers in Shropshire were considering how best they could discharge their self-appointed task 'to co-operate in the circulation of the truths whereby it [the cause of Abolition] is made manifest', Thomas Clarkson was completing his compilation of the very material that would meet their need. Since his original prize-winning essay was published in 1786, he had produced his *Summary View* and essays on *The Impolicy of the African Slave Trade* and on *The Comparative Efficiency of Regulation or Abolition* of the trade, as well as a digest of letters on the subject. Now he was about to send to the printers his invaluable *Abstract of the Evidence Delivered before a Select Committee of the House of Commons*, of which 10,000 copies were to be produced. It was just what was needed for distribution to subscribers and supporters throughout the country, for Clarkson had the gifts to organise, condense and present vast amounts of factual information clearly and convincingly. No sooner had he completed the *Abstract* than he was planning another of his extended and exhausting tours. His aim was personally to meet key local figures, organise local committees and provide 'a vital link between London and the provinces, enabling the London Committee to tap a vast reservoir of public feeling'.[1]

His new tour brought him from Plymouth to Shropshire in response to a personal invitation from Joseph Plymley communicated after their meeting in the capital the previous year. The arrival of such a nationally renowned figure at the Plymleys' house in Longnor made 20 October 1791 such a red-letter day that Katherine began a journal that was to be maintained, with few breaks, for thirty-five years and that provides an illuminating record of her life and particularly of her brother's activities and family. A modern historian hails it as 'a superlatively vivid source' for the progress of the anti-slave trade campaign.[2]

Katherine's first impression of Thomas Clarkson was of a man 'amiable and courteous in manner, above the middle size, well made and very agreeable in his person, with a remarkable mildness of voice and countenance' – and utterly dedicated to the cause of Abolition. She was concerned that her notes should do justice to the 'indefatigable perseverance' with which he pursued the great object in his life; 'he seems to forget himself in his desire to promote the good of others'. The range of his personal experiences in the service of the cause carried them beyond the normal parameters of conversation in the Plymley household, and Katherine was anxious to miss nothing.

On the political front Clarkson said he was convinced that the Prime Minister, William Pitt, was 'hearty in the cause' but could act only as an individual on account of divisions in the Cabinet. As for Charles James Fox, he had known little of the subject up to a few hours before he made an impassioned speech: Clarkson had seen tears running down his face as Wilberforce's colleague, William Smith, described the horrors of the trade, and he had had to retire behind the Speaker's chair while he regained his composure. Here Wilberforce took the opportunity to speak with him and give him notes to read. On the other hand, many M.P.s — 'perhaps over a bottle' — had promised plantation owners to vote against Abolition. Clarkson admired Burke's attitude to America, but considered him wrong on the French Revolution. He was glad that Louis XVI had not escaped from France, rejoiced that Lafayette had undertaken to free his slaves in the West Indies and, as he himself was 'in favour of liberty in every respect', praised Tom Paine's *Rights of Man*. The royal family came in for some sharp criticism: 'the king is not with us' and the princes oppose abolition — 'they are all brutes, apart from the Prince of Wales'.

Joseph did his best to comply with Clarkson's wish to meet as many supporters as possible from the area. He took him across the road to meet his uncle Robert at Longnor Hall, and then at dinner, with Katherine eagerly absorbing all that was said, entertained Messrs. Houlbrooke, Alison and Adams, three clergy friends, and uncle John, treasurer of the newly-formed Shropshire Committee, who were the only ones able to come at such short notice. Over the meal the conversation ranged over the American War of Independence and the French Revolution before concentrating on the slave trade and particularly the new Sierra Leone Company, which was to establish a settlement in West Africa for freed slaves. Having stated his firm belief that the fertile soil of Sierra Leone could produce pepper and coffee, Clarkson produced some samples from his pocket. Katherine tested 'a fine spicy kind of pepper' which she found 'very warm and agreeable'. When Mr. Houlbrooke proceeded to roast a few coffee beans over the fire, she thought that the coffee 'smelt quite well'. Clarkson expressed concern, however, that the hostility of some slave traders was such that they were buying up shares in the Company in order to frustrate its aims. When the local king, Naimbama, sent his son to England to be educated his vessel was fired on by some of the slave ships off the coast. On the other hand, following Fox's emotional appeal, the Commons had voted to support the new Company which had ordered 2,000 acres to be planted with sugar and to build up trade with Britain. Even more exciting was Clarkson's news that his own brother was even then in Nova Scotia collecting the names of former American slaves, freed in reward for their support of British forces in the recent war, who were willing to accept the risks of crossing the Atlantic in winter and of settling in the unknown and possibly hostile area of Sierra Leone owned by the Company. After overcoming multitudinous and daunting difficulties, Lieutenant John Clarkson was to advise the London Committee in a letter of 15 January 1792 that he had set sail from Halifax with fifteen ships and 1,192 souls on board.

When the visiting gentlemen took their leave after dinner, Clarkson remarked that as it was only seven o'clock he would write for an hour, walk in the garden for half an hour — he said he did best thinking on his walks — and then have a further half-hour's conversation before they supped at nine o'clock.

The next morning the visitor was up early as Joseph had promised to take him to meet Richard Reynolds and his sons, William and Joseph, celebrated ironmasters at Coalbrookdale. At 7.00 am, the time they had agreed to leave, Joseph was still dressing, and his guest, who was overbearingly regular and punctual, said, 'If I had known Mr. Plymley wou'd not have been quite exact I cou'd have written some letters'. Katherine and her sister Ann, who had risen early to see that the men had some breakfast, promptly ran for a table and desk. When Clarkson sat down to write he commented that time would be gained if they would seal the letters. 'I felt elated at the thought of doing anything for him', she confided in her diary that evening. His dedication to duty enormously impressed her, but she and her brother were very concerned at his state of health, for mountains of correspondence, lack of sleep and constant travel had exhausted him. He found it particularly galling when good prospective witnesses lacked the courage to give their testimony.

Joseph duly accompanied Clarkson to meet the Reynolds family at Coalbrookdale; unfortunately, having walked two miles to Madeley, they missed Mr. Horne who had left for London *en route* for Sierra Leone to serve as chaplain. Later that day, in conversation with the elder Mr. Plymley, Clarkson, no doubt drawing on his brother's experience as well as his own, spoke of the evils of press-gangs to recruit sailors.

At breakfast the following day their visitor told of the burgeoning campaign to refrain from the use of West Indian sugar – such direct action was so novel that the word 'boycott' was not coined for another hundred years. When Katherine recalled that on a visit to the Wedgwood family in Etruria in May they had told her how they had ceased using sugar from the Caribbean, Clarkson added that many in Dorset and Devon took the same view and perhaps up to 25% in London. Joseph's children were present and clearly took to heart what the adults were saying for they eagerly joined the rest of the family in giving up sugar. Clarkson subsequently calculated that 'not fewer than 300,000 persons had abandoned the use of sugar'. In several parts of the country grocers reported sugar sales dropping by a third to a half over a few months. Some advertisers emphasised that their sugar was produced by free men, perhaps the earliest example of the modern concept of fair trade. Shaken by the potential impact on trade, for sugar was Britain's largest import, merchants began a counter-campaign to proclaim that sugar was not a luxury but a 'necessary of life'.

The Plymleys were all anxious about Clarkson's professed intention to re-visit Liverpool. On his first visit to the greatest of the slave ports, back in 1787, he had stayed at the 'King's Arms' where he learned a lot about the arguments of his opponents as he contended with locals on the slave issue. But antagonism to him had grown as his views became more widely known — on one occasion he had been close to being pushed off the end of the pier when he had been trawling for witnesses in the docks. He had since received letters threatening his life if he visited the city again. Yet he was determined to go, though he agreed with Joseph that he should stay outside the city and travel at night.

It was with anxious hearts that the family said farewell to their guest on the morning of 22 October. Katherine was impressed by the attention he paid to the little children. When he asked Panton what he would do to help end the slave trade, and received the response that he would do whatever he could, he advised him to read to build up his understanding. As soon as the visitor had left, Panton, fully six-and-a-half years old, settled down to tackle Clarkson's first *Essay*! Five year-old Josepha begged him to come to see them again, while little Jane was delighted when he put his arms around her neck. Katherine's own feelings were more complex: She had known this striking and famous man, at thirty-one only two years younger than herself, for less than forty-eight hours, but on the first morning she had confided in her diary her delight at being able to do anything for him. Her admiration of him as the champion of Abolition was unbounded: 'In his conversation is united the most perfect modesty with the noblest independence of sentiment; in short he appears to me such a man as I would wish to see engaged in such a cause'. Was she here concealing deeper feelings? If she did fall in love with him she was in good company, for years later Jane Austen, in a letter to her sister, confessed her feelings for another writer — 'I am as much in love with the author as ever I was with Clarkson'.[3]

Joseph accompanied his friend to Shrewsbury, where he made arrangements with the sympathetic editor of the *Shrewsbury Chronicle* to publish some extracts from Clarkson's best-selling *Abstracts* that appeared in ten issues between 11 November 1791 and 10 February 1792 under the simple heading 'SLAVE TRADE'. They are significant, not simply because they are Joseph Plymley's personal selections from Clarkson's *Abstracts*, but because they tell us what readers in Shrewsbury and its environs came to know about the horrific details of the slave trade, for a relatively small number will have read the original anti-slave trade literature for themselves.

The first extracts were chosen to inform readers of the atrocities committed in procuring slaves in West Africa. Captain Wilson had said in evidence: 'Kidnapping was acknowledged by all he conversed with to be generally prevalent. It is the first principle of the natives, the principle of self-preservation, never to go unarmed when a slave vessel is on the coast for fear of being stolen'. The first mate on a slave ship, Mr. Bowman, reported that armed parties would go out to capture slaves, setting fire to villages in their search. He had once been brought 25-30 men, women and children — some still at the breast. Often the captives of local native slave dealers, 'they are usually brought in with strings around their necks. And sometimes their hands tied across. He never saw any slaves that had been convicted of crimes'. Boys on the passage across the Atlantic were observed playing games in which they acted out the manoeuvres of raiding parties to round up slaves. When female slaves were asked how they came to be captured 'they answered only by violent bursts of sorrow'. No black people were safe. Mr. Bowman recalled an occasion when his captain invited two native slave traders on board, got them drunk in his cabin, and then clapped them in irons. In the view of a member of the Jamaican Assembly, Mr. Edwards, 'The whole of the greatest part of that immense continent is a field of warfare and desolation, a wilderness in which the inhabitants are wolves towards each other'.

'On being brought on board', Dr. Trotter stated in evidence, 'slaves show signs of extreme distress and despair, from a feeling of their situation and regret at being torn from their friends and connections. They are often heard in the night making an howling, melancholy noise, expressive of

'Danse de Negres'; slaves being brought up on deck to exercise, published in 1837

extreme anguish', especially the women. The conditions under which they were kept increased their suffering: 'The slaves in the passage are so crowded below that it is impossible to walk through without treading on them'. In Mr. Falconbridge's words, 'They had not so much room as a man in his coffin, either in length or breadth'. In the holds the heat became so intense and the slaves so desperate for air, especially when bad weather meant that the hatches had to be closed, that Falconbridge testified he had known men die overnight of suffocation. (There were many more black holes than the notorious one in Calcutta in 1756!) Many slaves fell ill of 'the flux', which Falconbridge himself caught. After only fifteen minutes below he was unable to get out without help. It was not infrequent in the morning to find a live man and a dead man chained together. Falconbridge said that he could not 'conceive of any situation so dreadful and disgusting as that of slaves when suffering from the flux; in the *Alexander* the deck was covered with blood and mucus, and resembled a slaughterhouse. The stench and foul air were intolerable'. There were sick quarters, but slaves had to lie on bare boards that wore the flesh away from their shoulderblades and knees.

Frequently slaves refused food because they wanted to die, and attempts at forced feeding were often unsuccessful. Some were so desperate that given half a chance they jumped overboard — twenty from the *Enterprise* on one voyage. Quarrels broke out among the slaves, others went mad and had to be chained to the deck. Some tried to end life by slashing their necks. Mr. Morley confirmed seeing slaves wallowing in their own blood and excrement, while Mr. Miller told of a woman who refused to eat being tortured with thumbscrews and then hung in the rigging. It was inevitable that there would sometimes be insurrections among the slaves on board. These were usually brutally suppressed with flogging, torture and death, but Falconbridge in the *Tower* told of occasions when they had succeeded and almost all the whites killed. The estimated loss of slaves during the crossing of the Atlantic was 20% (some modern authorities say 6% in later years),[4] although it was alleged that 50% was not unknown. Clearly it was in the interests of the slave captain and his backers to keep alive as many as possible.

As a slave ship neared the West Indies it was usual for some effort to be made to make the slaves look more healthy and presentable. They were hosed down and given more exercise. Once the ship had docked the common mode of sale was said to be by 'scramble', as plantation owners tried to grab the fittest and the strongest. Sick slaves were sold off cheaply at public auction. John Newton's sad recollection from his days as a slave captain was that 'in none of the sales he saw was any care ever taken to prevent such slaves as were relations from being separated'. So although the nightmare of capture and the horrors of the voyage were over, the sufferings of the slaves were far from being at an end. Deaths continued among those who had been most ill on the crossing; others, it was said, died of 'a distracted mind' — which meant they had lost the will to live. It is true that some went into the service of relatively enlightened owners, others showed they could shoulder responsibility and attained positions of authority on plantations or in the master's house, and others successfully escaped. But for the great majority their servitude and suffering continued.

In some quarters it was maintained that abolition of the slave trade would be economically too damaging; what was needed instead, as in Dolben's Act (see page 33), was Regulation. The extract in the *Chronicle* of 20 January 1792 had its answer to this point of view. It contended, with reference to conditions on board: 'No REGULATION of the Trade can heal the evils in this branch of the subject. It can never cure MELANCHOLY OR A DISEASED MIND. It can never prevent an INJURED people from RISING IF OUT OF IRONS, nor can it take away corrupted air, unless it reduce the number to be carried so low, as not to make it worth the while of the slave merchants to transport them'.

At rock bottom the slave trade and slavery were justified in the minds of many whites by the belief that the blacks were inferior. As the penultimate extract in the *Shrewsbury Chronicle* expressed it, according to the evidence of Dr. Jackson, 'the natives of Africa, when bought by the European colonists, are generally estimated a species of inferior beings, whom the right of purchase gives the owner a power of using at his will'. Without legal protection, male and female slaves alike were 'used with great cruelty, like beasts or worse'. Overworked and whipped for any misdemeanour, many were hurried to the grave. The view was that there were plenty more where they came from. The final extract printed in the *Chronicle* of 10 February 1792 presents a graphic description of the merciless flogging of slaves. On the wharf they could be seen hoisted up by a crane so that their feet were just off the ground and the body fully stretched. Alternatives were staking offenders out on the ground or tying them spreadeagled to a ladder. Sometimes they were given as many as two hundred lashes, followed by beating with a prickly bush.

It is no wonder that a humane and Christian man like Joseph Plymley had been shocked to the core when he had first learned of the horrors of the slave

Sir Richard Corbett, M.P.
1640-83

Sir Uvedale Corbett, M.P.
1668-1701

Builders of Longnor Hall

Longnor Hall in 1792

The entry in the register at Pentraeth church, Anglesey, of the marriage of Joseph Plymley and Jane Joseph Panton, 13 March 1783

The entry in the register of Little Hereford church of the marriage of Joseph Plymley and Matty Dansey, 29 December 1790

Thomas Clarkson at the age of about 26

1791
from Oct. 20 to 21st —
Contents:—
Mr Clarkson's first visit to my Brother, his account of Prince Naimbana; behaviour of the Factors to the Slave trade upon occasion of his going to England— Mr C. believes Mr Pitt sincere in his opposition to Slave Trade— Mr Fox's first speech upon the subject in Parliament— Mr C. sanguine in his expectations of the Sierra Leone Company, & of the speedy downfall of the Slave Trade— his account of Mr Wilberforce— Mr Wedgewood and the disuse of West India Sugar— Mr Alison, Mr Houlbrooke, Mr Adams & my Uncle Flint dine at my Brother's to meet Mr C. In course of conversation, Mr Burke, Marquis La Fayette, Genl Washington, John Woolman spoken of— Mr Clarkson sanguine upon the French revolution.

Octr 20th 1791. I had the honour of seeing Mr Clarkson, my Brother went to Shrewsbury with the expectation of meeting him & they arrived here together about 10 o'clock at night— I was prepared to see with admiration a man who had now for some years given up all his own secular interest & everything the world calls pleasure, & that too at a time of life when men think of little else, that

The opening pages of Katherine Plymley's first journal, 20 October 1791

he may dedicate his whole time to the glorious object of abolishing the African Slave trade— And, whatever his external appearance & manners had been it would not have lessen'd my idea of him, as that was founded on the qualities of his head & heart which his conduct had establish'd beyond a doubt— but I found him amiable & courteous in manners, above the middle size, well made & very agree-

-able in his person with a remarkable mildness of voice & countenance— He was at this time on a tour thro' the kingdom to converse with the friends to the Abolition on the best means to be pursued in their several counties to forward this righteous cause— he was lately come from Plymouth where he met the young African Prince who was brought over by the Sierra Leone company (of which Mr Ha

From Katherine Plymley's journal

45. I dined at Mr. Hope's with Lord Pompret, Hon.ble M & Mrs
Turnour, Mr Flyxley, Mr Meredith, Alderman Heygate,
Mr Joseph Lockley, Uvedale, Robert & Watier. I rec.d a letter
from the Bishop of Hereford. I signed a letter of attorney at Childs.

1814.
June 24. Friday. I had my teeth scaled by Mr. Parkinson. I called
of Mr. Samuel Lee at the Ch: Missionary House. I again attended
the committee at the New London Tavern. I called upon Mr. R.
Pemberton & Mr. Lyster. Mr. Malone & Mr. Williams Wynn.
I attended a committee of the House of Lords, when the Cardington
enclosure bill was committed. Thomas Davies who had
been sworn at the Bar of the H. of Lords, yesterday, was one
of the witnesses to the signatures. Ld Powis & Ld Pompret attended the committee at my request. Ld Shaftesbury, whom
I had known at Oxford, as Mr. Ashley, was the chairman.
Mr Pemberton & Mr. Coupland dined here. Uvedale dined
at Mr. Hope's & Watier at Mr. Hope's. He & Robert joined
us in the event.

25 Saturday. I called on Mr. Griffith, Mr. Pemberton & Mr. Coupland
& at Childs Bank. I saw the exhibition of pictures at Somerset House
& at the European Museum. I called at Mess. Ealey's of Grays
Inn & Mess. Hopkinsons being agent in St Albans street.
Mr. Hopkinson seems a very just & liberal man. I called
at Uvedales chambers & Roberts lodgings. Mr. Hope & Mrs
May Adams called here. Mr. Alderman Heygate
dined here, & went with my sister, Helen, Uvedale &
Watier to Drury lane to see Mr. Kean act Iago. I then
went with Robert & Mr. Wilberforce's. After our
return Robert went to the opera where he saw the Duke
of Wellington, who is just returned from abroad. I spoke
to Hanton, Joseph & Mr. Hyde. & called upon Mr Sam: Willing.

26. Sunday. We went to St. James Ch: I called afterwards
at the Chief Barons, Baron Richards, Mr. Jenkins on &
Mr. Hope. Mr. Malone breakfasted with us. Col: Goodrich
called early. Mr. William Wynn, Mr. Bennet, Mr. Hope
& Mrs Forster Leighton called here. We called on Mrs Mary
Adams. Mr. R. Pemberton called here. We dined at Mr.
Benyons No. 45. Russel Square, with Lord Sunderlin, a nephew of the
celebrated Irish lawyer Anthony Malone, a Mr. & Mrs. Smith of
Gloucestershire, a Miss Bailey, Uvedale, Robert & Watier.

A page of Joseph Corbett's diary in June 1814.
He was on a visit to London primarily about the Cardington Enclosure Bill,
but he meets a great variety of people

Woolstaston.

G. Kinlock   Co: Salop   (Vis: Nov. 24. 1792.)

Woolstaston, a village ab.t 10 Miles S. of Shrewsbury   **Name**
is in the hundred of Cundover & Co of Salop. it   **Situation**
lies ab.t 2 Miles W. of the turnpike road leading   **&**
from Shrewsbury to Ludlow, & is bounded on the   **Extent**
E. by the Parish of Leebotwood & on the N. by that
of Smethcott (both in Lichfield &C: diocese) & on
the S. & W. by Stretton Parish —— The Parish extends
2 Miles from E. to W. & 1½ from N. to S.

It is one Township

The Houses are 1 Parsonage 4 Farm Houses & another inhabi-   **N.o of**
=ted by poor people in the Village, a detached farm   **Houses.**
house on the S. E. extremity, & ten small messuages or
cottages lying at the extremities of the Parish. Within
the last 50 years five farm houses at least are re-
=membered & have been taken down. The Hall House
has been lately taken down in part & the remainder
is occupied by a farmer & there is every appearance
from the form of certain fields & apple trees growing in
them, that the dilapidation of Houses has been very
extensive. Part of the land is now let to farmers in
the adjoining parish of Leebotwood.

There are eighteen families resident in the 16 Houses within   **N.o of**
this parish consisting of 33 Men, 30 Women, & 17 Ch: the popu-   **Inhabitants**
=lation is somewhat encreased from the residence of colliers
employed in a coal & lime work adjoining. It must upon

15 Houses. 17 Fam: 53 M. 48 F. 25. a. 16 Mech: 62 other   1800.
Persons. In all 101 Persons.   41. G.

*The first page of the Archdeacon's account of Woolstaston parish,
November 1792*

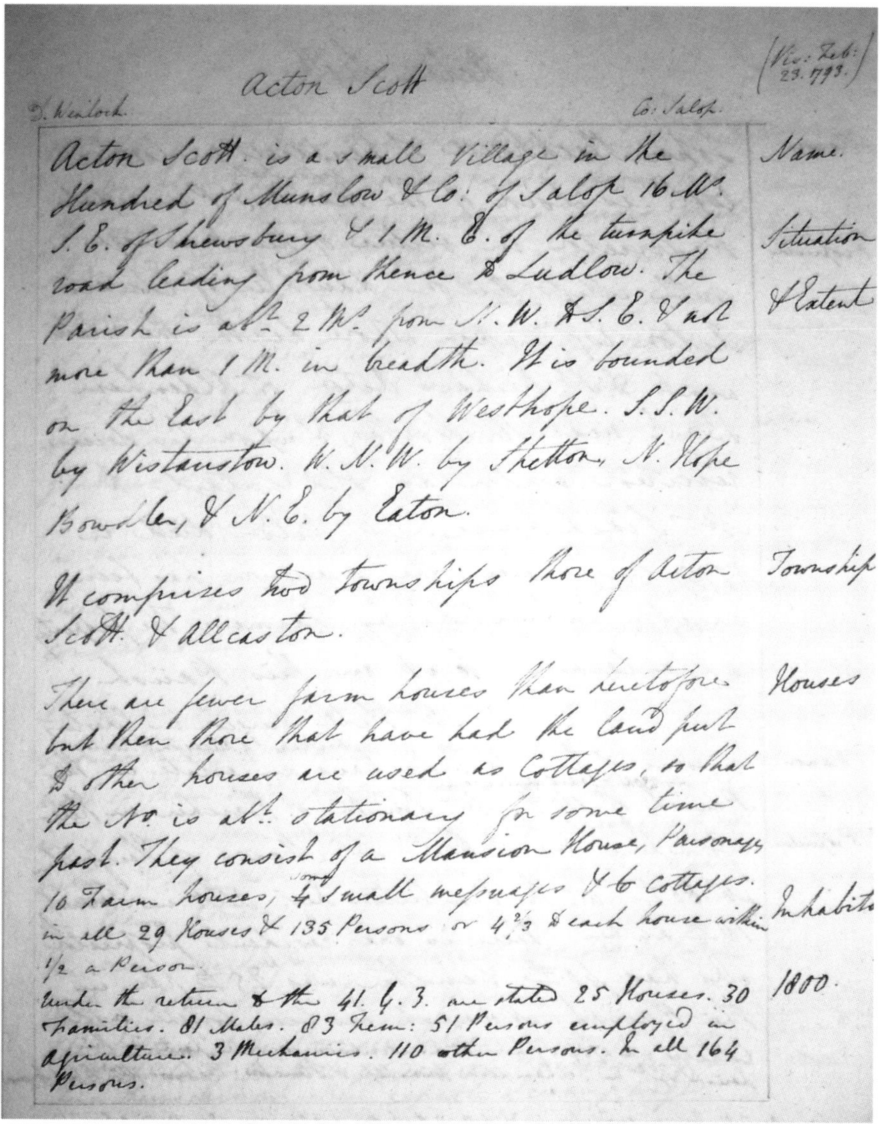

Acton Scott. is a small village in the
Hundred of Munslow & Co: of Salop 16 M.
S. E. of Shrewsbury & 1 M. E. of the turnpike
road leading from thence to Ludlow. The
Parish is ab.t 2 M.s from N. W. & S. E. & not
more than 1 M. in breadth. It is bounded
on the East by that of Westhope. S. S. W.
by Wistanstow. W. N. W. by Shetton, N. Hope
Bowdler, & N. E. by Eaton.

It comprises two townships those of Acton
Scott. & Allcaston.

There are fewer farm houses than heretofore
but then those that have had the land put
& other houses are used as Cottages, so that
the N.o is ab.t stationary for some time
past. They consist of a Mansion House, Parsonage,
10 Farm houses, 4 small messuages & 6 cottages.
in all 29 Houses & 135 Persons or 4⅔ to each house within
½ a Person.
Under the return & the 41. G. 3. are stated 25 Houses. 30
Families. 81 Males. 83 Fem: 51 Persons employed in
agriculture. 3 Mechanics. 110 other Persons. In all 164
Persons.

[Right margin labels:]
Name.
Situation
& Extent
Township
Houses
Inhabit.
1800.

The first page of the Archdeacon's account of Acton Scott parish,
February 1793

A striking statue in Barbados to mark the 150th anniversary of the Abolition of slavery in the British Empire in 1833

trade or that his mentor, Thomas Clarkson, had pledged to devote his life to the abolition of the trade. But there were others, in Shropshire too, who while sympathetic to Abolition hesitated to give their support if such a reform were to lead to revolutionary changes in society. No sooner had Joseph seen Clarkson off on his way to Chester than he discovered to his alarm that several local gentlemen 'of high monarchical principles' were shocked by Clarkson's open approval of the French Revolution and his attendance in July at a Revolution Dinner in London to celebrate the second anniversary of the fall of the Bastille. Joseph, who combined passionate commitment to Abolition with common sense realisation that many had grave doubts about the pace of reform, realised the need to pay an immediate call on several local persons of note to assure them 'how far Mr. C. was from wishing a revolution in this country'. One of his first comments to his friend, when he met up with him again the next week in Chester, was to warn him of the risk of careless talk which could make his own task of obtaining signatures for a petition much more difficult. Clarkson readily agreed, confessing that Wilberforce had warned him of the very same danger.

For his part Clarkson, never a strong Anglican though he was ordained a deacon, was eager to relate to Joseph how the Bishop of Bangor had advised him not to make himself too conspicuous on the subject of Abolition as it would hurt his prospects of rising in the Church. His immediate response had been that it was a matter of indifference to him compared with what he regarded as his duty. This led to some unpleasantness and caused him to ask the bishop why he was so angry with these poor black people. 'O', said the bishop, 'they are a disagreeable set of people, they have such ugly noses'. 'Well, my lord', he replied, 'you'll be pleased to recollect that they did not make their own noses'. Clarkson was very irritated, too, by the opposition of Dr. John Butler, Joseph's own bishop at Hereford.

A letter to Joseph from Clarkson, who had gone on to stay with Lord Muncaster in Cumberland, gave great pleasure to Katherine as he sent 'kind remembrances to your wife, sisters and little ones'. It led her to record that Dr. Darwin, a Shrewsbury physician and later father to Charles, had given Clarkson a letter of introduction to Miss Seward, 'which may produce a poem'. (Anna Seward was a friend of Erasmus, Dr. Darwin's father, in Lichfield; her verses on 'Colebrook Dale' had appeared in 1785). Clarkson's reception in Scotland was such that Joseph, who was determined to keep the cause of Abolition in the public mind, inserted a short comment in the *Shrewsbury Chronicle*: 'We have the pleasure of observing from the public prints [the *General Evening Post*] that Mr. Clarkson (whose zeal in the offices of humanity have been so conspicuous on the subject of the slave trade) was received in Scotland with that attention his philanthropy so much entitles him to, and that the gentlemen of Glasgow provided a public dinner to do the more honour to their benevolent guest'.

Another letter from Clarkson, who had moved on to York, included a commendation of Joseph as a proprietor of the Sierra Leone Company and asked if he could suggest others willing to buy shares as the capital was being increased to £150,000 and they had to prevent them from being snapped up by West Indian traders. He replied that few would be willing to travel to London to vote, but gave him the name of Mr. Wilding. In the new year Clarkson sent a copy of a printed circular entitled *An Address to the People of Great Britain on the Propriety of abstaining from West Indian sugar and rum*. Clarkson was convinced that this was a certain winner: those who so abstained were sure to sign petitions to Parliament, and even if these failed the loss of revenue would put pressure on the government. At a half-penny each the circulars sold rapidly and Clarkson claimed thousands had already given up sugar. Advised to order a thousand copies, Joseph sensibly decided to go for five hundred for a start. He assured his friend that 'this family have left off the use of sugar and the little people were the first to wish it'.

A further communication from Clarkson on 23 January was in effect a starting-pistol for the race to get signatures on petitions. Joseph was advised in confidence that notice would be given in Parliament on 6/7 February of a motion six weeks later to abolish the slave trade. The pressing need was for petitions, because in 1788 they had impressed the Commons enough to have the issue referred to a committee for detailed examination, and it was now believed that an avalanche of petitions could influence sufficient numbers of wavering M.P.s to gain a majority for Abolition. Clarkson begged Joseph to act early and set an example 'as he has so many places under his care'. He moved at once into over-drive. The Mayor of Shrewsbury, Mr. Eyton, agreed to call a public meeting whenever requisitioned to do so; the Sheriff declared himself ready to do the same for the county. Wherever he went Joseph carried letters asking for the calling of a public meeting to hand to prospective supporters. On 27 January he was in Ludlow with a draft petition for Mr. Knight to send from there; on the 28th in Shrewsbury, posting letters on to Bridgnorth and Wenlock; on the 30th he went to Mr. Eyton at Wellington, calling on Mr. Pemberton of Wrockwardine and Mr. Cludde of Orleton. From Wellington Joseph rode to Shrewsbury, Worthen and Montgomery, where the Rev. Mr. Powel was keen to raise a petition. Back home on 3 February he found a letter from the Rev. Mr. Fewtrell at Bridgnorth saying that 'the business seemed in good train there'. Encouraged by another letter from his friend Mr. Houlbrooke telling how well things were going in Scotland, he returned to Shrewsbury the next day and obtained many more signed letters. On 6 February he visited Bridgnorth, taking time to write an account of his activities for Granville Sharp of the London Committee, as Dr. Baker had reminded him that he was a corresponding member. On the 9th Katherine, proud to record her brother's valiant efforts for the cause so dear to her own heart, noted his return from Bridgnorth, happy that all was going well with Mr. Fewtrell and Mr. Corser, and that the High Sheriff, Mr. Pardoe, a very steady friend to Abolition, had given him a mandate to the Under-Sheriff to call a meeting to consider a petition from the county.

After a fortnight of almost incessant activity Joseph could look forward with confidence. He shrugged off the report that Mr. Forrester at Wenlock had set his face against Abolition. More worrying was Mr. Reynolds' disclosure that Clarkson was talking of raising £100,000 for the French National Assembly. 'My brother heard about this with great concern', recorded Katherine. 'He was convinced that should it be talked of it would be of infinite disservice to the cause of Abolition'. Joseph agreed with Reynolds that it would prompt a counter-subscription for the emigrant French princes. It was not that Joseph was hostile to the developments in France, for he and Katherine had rejoiced at the end of autocracy and the prospect of greater liberty, but that the achievement of Abolition was his primary aim. Katherine herself was confident that while Clarkson had strong sympathies with the French revolutionaries, and favoured reform and greater freedom for the individual at home, he would oppose any resort to violence in this country. The Priestley Riots in Birmingham the previous July, when the house of Joseph Priestley, celebrated chemist, Unitarian and radical, was burnt down, had shown that too close an identification with the French Revolution could unleash the fury of an ignorant populace.

As he prepared to advertise the promised meetings, Joseph dashed around to get more signatures on the letters requisitioning them. Two new names were added at Atcham, and Mr. Eyton was convinced that when the renegade Mr. Forrester heard that Mr. Pemberton, Mr. Cludde, Mr. Edward Harries and himself had signed he would quickly change his mind. The names and numbers make clear that Joseph believed that it was gentlemen of some standing in the county whose views would carry weight in Parliament and perhaps influence their own M.P.s' votes in the division. The mass Chartist petitions were still fifty years away, and where attempts were made, as in some large cities, to cast the net more widely, opponents were quick to denounce intimidation and unfair influence. Joseph also visited Moreton to see Archdeacon Clive — 'very unwell but always a most hearty friend to the cause'. Clive had just had a call from Josiah Wedgwood who was playing a very active part in the campaign in Staffordshire.

The moment had now come. The *Chronicle* of 10 February 1792 carried an advertisement of meetings one week later, at 11.00 am for the town and 12.00 noon for the county. Eager to fire others with his own enthusiasm, Joseph invited a large number of friends to dine at Longnor. 'Receiv'd company at home', Katherine noted on the 10th, and added, 'Not only the party he made today but almost all the company he has seen for some time past, as well as every visit he has paid, have been subservient to the cause, either by informing those who were ignorant, showing the necessity of exertion to the many who in this as in every other public evil, are contented to lament without endeavouring to reform and, where there was any chance of success, endeavouring to convert those adverse to the Abolition'.

Four days later Joseph drew up petitions for the county, Shrewsbury, Ludlow, Bridgnorth and Wenlock in case they had not done so. Excited at the prospect of the imminent meetings, but wearied and saddle-sore after the punishing pace of recent weeks, Joseph had what Katherine saw as a Providential escape in a riding accident. 'As he was riding to Shrewsbury his horse fell with such extreme violence as to roll over, as it were, and alight on his back. My brother was necessarily thrown; as the horse was rising one of his spurs, which was entangled, came off. This probably saved him from being dragged ... He escaped entirely without hurt'.

Joseph may have been uninjured in his mishap, but the cause itself suffered lasting damage from the slave insurrection in the French island of San Domingo. White planters were quick to blame the campaign for Abolition in Britain. Clarkson was nearer the truth, however, when in a letter to Joseph he blamed the deprivation of liberty, their treatment 'as creatures of another species', and the impact of the Revolution in France. The island Assembly of planters used torture and death to suppress the rising, although the French National Assembly acknowledged the rights of the black people. The situation led Clarkson to appeal for re-doubled effort, an appeal that Joseph relayed to the supporters he entertained at home on the eve of the meeting to launch petitions.

The resolutions carried at the gathering in the Guildhall at Shrewsbury on 17 February, together with the wording of the petition, were published in the next issue of the *Chronicle* and for the following two weeks:

ABOLITION OF THE SLAVE TRADE

At a meeting of the Mayor, Aldermen, Burgesses and Inhabitants of the Town and Liberties of Shrewsbury, held at the Guildhall the 17th February 1792,

It was UNANIMOUSLY RESOLVED that a PETITION be presented to the House of Commons, praying an ABOLITION of the SLAVE TRADE.

RESOLVED, that the Petition now read is approved of, and that the Representatives in Parliament of the Borough, be desired to present the same.

RESOLVED, that the Thanks of the Meeting be given to the Mayor for his Conduct on this Occasion.

RESOLVED, that the above Resolutions, with a Copy of the Petition be inserted in the *General Evening Post* three times and in the *Shrewsbury Chronicle.*

Loxdale, Town Clerk.

To the Honourable the Commons of Great Britain in Parliament assembled:

The humble PETITION [of the people of Shrewsbury] sheweth,

That your Petitioners have long beholden with great CONCERN the traffick [*sic*] for Men carried on in Africa by the Subjects of these Kingdoms, and have felt additional Grief from a more particular Necessity appearing to have been disproved by incontrovertible Evidence, whilst the Oppression and Injustice with which it has been charged have been too fully substantiated. They therefore beseech this Honourable House to put a Stop to the Evils inseparable from the Slave Trade, by such an Abolition of it as to their Wisdom shall seem meet.

This Petition will remain a few days at the Guildhall for the Signature of those Friends to the Measure who were prevented from attending the meeting.

Katherine's journal adds extra detail. Her verdict was that both meetings were 'very respectably attended' — but almost wholly by those whom Joseph had contacted in person or by letter. She encouraged her brother with this judgement and added that had he attempted more his health would have suffered. Mr. King proposed the motion for the county, seconded by Mr. Eyton; for the town Mr. Corbett (Joseph's uncle) and Mr. Blakeway were the spokesmen. Support for petitions was unanimous and between fifty and sixty signatures were obtained for each, with many more expected as sheets of parchment were carried to different parts of the county and town.

At Bridgnorth 150 signatures were obtained; the signs were promising in Ludlow and Wenlock where the meetings were to be held later. Joseph hesitated about little Shifnal but went along with the view of Dr. Beddoes, 'the chymical lecturer at Oxford' and his old college friend, that it would 'show the universal voice of the nation'. He squeezed in another visit with his wife and sister to Archdeacon Clive, now 'in a declining state', collecting a few more signatures in Shrewsbury on the way.

Wherever he went in the following days Joseph tracked down more signatories — and Katherine kept almost daily running totals. Bishop's Castle at last began collecting signatures, news came from Hereford, the last county to organise a petition, that the Mayor had finally called a meeting, and Joseph ordered hundreds of his friend Houlbrooke's pamphlet-sized summary of Clarkson's *Abstract* to be posted in Shrewsbury and one to be enclosed in every copy of the *Chronicle* sent into Montgomeryshire. When news came from Clarkson that Wilberforce was to present his motion on 27 March, and that therefore all petitions must be in by the 23rd or 24th, Joseph began his final tour to whip up support. In Shrewsbury, after opening a few more minds to at least a dislike of the slave trade, the petition was dispatched with upwards of 300 signatures; Ludlow's went off, too. On 6 March Joseph was at a gathering in Wenlock where more than a hundred — including Mr. Forrester — signed. The list of county petitioners grew daily. A hundred and fifty names came in from Shifnal and Wellington. Joseph took the county petition to the Under-Sheriff for dispatch to the House; it contained 464 signatures, including fifty-seven clergymen, and was over nine and a half feet long! Wenlock's petition grew to 450 signatures, and there were over 200 on Bridgnorth's when it was finally sent off. Montgomeryshire was proving the hardest nut to crack. Joseph had visited Pool (Welshpool) on 28 February and conferred with a young apothecary called Jones who had been on the African coast. He could not be persuaded to support Abolition, but provided Joseph with some useful facts. Support was stronger in the Newtown neighbourhood. The Sheriff at last on 7 March approved a meeting for Montgomeryshire. The very next day Joseph was there again to meet Mr. Brown, his chief backer in Newtown, and Arthur Owen, an attorney from Berriew and a man of influence as agent to several landed gentlemen; the Rev. Powel of Montgomery also saw him. Joseph sent off to the *Chronicle* an advertisement of the county's meeting on 15 March and in a letter urged Owen to get powers of proxy for those who did not want the personal trouble of attending the meeting. He was there again on the 14th preparing for the next day's gathering in Pool. In seeking to counter the rumour that

Jamaican slaves were ready to revolt, he made shrewd use of a letter from Mr. John Watkis, a planter in Jamaica, to his father in Shrewsbury and dated 11 January, asserting that 'Since I have known the island the Negroes were never more peaceable and quiet'. Moreover, a local clergyman, the Rev. Daniel Williams, who owned an estate in the West Indies but had signed the petition, went to the Pool meeting and promised to liberate his slaves when the legislature thought proper. In the end the Montgomeryshire petition contained 260 signatures, 'gentlemen freeholders of weight and credit', some former opponents and one whose nephew was captain of a slave ship.

All this incessant activity took its toll of Joseph's health. On 9 March his sister noted: 'The fatigue my Brother has lately gone thro' has been great and he is in consequence of it very unwell today'. He was well enough the next day, however, to attend a General Board meeting at the Shrewsbury Infirmary, and the day after, as it was Sunday, 'he did the duty of his churches and wrote many letters'. Both he and Katherine would have been heartened by the praise of others in the cause. Dr. Baker 'and everyone of my Brother's friends who are sincerely interested in the object of his unwearied pursuit, have a just, that is a high, sense of his merits'. Still more to be treasured was the tribute from William Wilberforce himself, whose letter 'begs my Brother never to apologise to him for applying to him for information relative to their common cause, as he shall always think it a duty as well as a pleasure to aid so active a fellow labourer. His expressions are full of respect for my Brother's character whose zeal and indefatigable exertions he mentions to have heard of from various quarters'.[5] In response to an account of the progress made locally, together with signatures obtained, and copies of all resolutions and petitions, Dr. Baker, on behalf of the London Committee, said he 'cannot sufficiently congratulate my Brother on the successes of his glorious exertions'. And Wilberforce again, after receiving Joseph's account of the Montgomeryshire meeting, hailed it as 'proof of how much may be done by proper exertions'.

On 23 March Joseph set off for London to hear the debate and, more pressingly, to ask Wilberforce to present the Montgomeryshire petition as he feared that Mr. Alfred Owen, M.P., would shamefully desert his duty, like Mr. Kynaston, a Shropshire M.P., and many others. As he reflected on the coach taking him first to Oxford, he regretted his failure to persuade those who had said that their support would be worthless, feeling that 'their situation of privacy and obscurity precludes all possibility of serving the cause'. He remembered, too, individuals who, as his sister lamented, failed to give their support as 'the love of pleasure and the love of ease make it too formidable'. Even Dr. Baker seemed 'hopeless of success at this time, but thinks the majority [against Abolition] will not be nearly equal to the last'. It was the response of M.P.s that was now crucial, as Dr. Baker told Wilberforce: 'Let the friends to the cause do and say all they can, we shall not succeed this time unless the minister will give some good votes as well as good words'. Dr. Baker's comment was to prove both perceptive and prescient.

Perhaps, as his next coach rolled towards London, Joseph's own hopes rose at the thought of meeting up with his fellow-labourers in the sacred cause and of the great Parliamentary occasion that was now imminent.

7 ABOLITION GRAVELY DELAYED

On his arrival in the capital at the end of March 1792, Joseph found supporters of Abolition agog with excitement. Petitions to Parliament were being continually presented, Edinburgh's with over 9,000 signatures, Glasgow's with over 13,000; even the Livery of London were trying to get up a last-minute petition 'to wipe off the stigma of the City'. When Joseph had left for London, Katherine noted that the papers were announcing 154 petitions; ten days later her figures had risen to over 510. Further encouragement came with the remarkable news that the king of Denmark had announced the abolition of the import of slaves into his country's three little West Indian islands, the ban to be effective from 1803.

Joseph met up with Clarkson whom he found full of hope for Monday, 2 April, the date now fixed for Wilberforce's motion in the House. Wilberforce himself, he discovered, was staying with the Thorntons in Clapham. When he visited the Committee at Old Jewry Joseph was given, his sister recorded, 'a very flattering reception'. They went on to tell him of a recent incident in which some slave captains had bombarded Old Calabar on the African coast merely in order to secure lower prices for slaves. Joseph thought that this news broke at a good time for the cause. He breakfasted at Wilberforce's house with Mr. Gisborne and was introduced to Lord Muncaster, another committed supporter. One of Josiah Wedgwood's sons, whom Joseph had met at Old Jewry, came to dinner with him along with Clarkson. His letter to his wife dated 2 April advised the family that he had again just breakfasted at Wilberforce's house, although their champion did not put in an appearance before late afternoon, as Pitt had visited him at Clapham in the morning. Joseph had heard that one of the M.P.s for Montgomeryshire had been looking for him as he wished to present the petition, but then he learned that the members for that county and Denbighshire had dined with the Speaker — which he feared might be bad news.

The tension was building on that Monday as Joseph made his way to the gallery of the House of Commons with the ticket that Clarkson had obtained for him. Back home three days later he was to amaze his sister by his detailed account of the debate: 'Extraordinary as I know his memory is, I was yet surprised that he could retain so much'. The gallery, he told them, had filled immediately it was opened at 11.00 am, so he had a long wait before William Wilberforce rose to speak in the early evening. 'Africa, Africa', he began, 'your sufferings have been the theme that has arrested and engaged my heart — your sufferings no tongue can express, no language impart'. He went on to argue that if Denmark had abolished the slave trade, Britain could not be far behind. When he referred to the Calabar incident members demanded names of the ships and captains involved — which he eventually disclosed. After a speech of more than three hours, whose conclusion his latest biographer considers to have been less effective than on previous occasions,[1] he moved 'That it is the opinion of this Committee [it was a Committee of the whole House] that the trade carried on by British subjects for the purpose of obtaining slaves from the coast of Africa ought to be abolished'. If the motion were carried, Wilberforce asserted that he would move to bring in a Bill.

Joseph listened intently as others joined in the debate. A plantation owner talked of 'the wild, impracticable and visionary scheme of Abolition'; he maintained there was more wretchedness in the parish of St. Giles in London than in the colonies, and claimed that it was the talk of Abolition that had sparked the revolt on San Domingo. Robert Jenkinson, the future Prime Minister Lord Liverpool, argued that no other major slave-trading nation had shown any sign of following the British example. Their old opponent from Liverpool. Bamastre Tarleton, denounced the folly of allowing 'a junction of sectarians, sophists, enthusiasts and fanatics' to destroy a profitable trade employing 5,000 seamen and 160 ships. Joseph must have been tempted to protest when Tarleton went on to accuse petitioners of fraudulent signatures, claiming that in some villages and towns 'mendicant physicians and itinerant clergymen have exercised almost unexampled zeal and industry to extort names'.[2] But four other M.P.s spoke up for Abolition, among them Robert Milibanke, Lord Byron's future father-in-law, who maintained, in Adam Smith vein, that wherever slave labour was used 'every operation was performed in a rude and unworkmanlike manner'.

What proved at the end of the night to have been the decisive contribution came from Henry Dundas, the Home Secretary and a close confidant of the Prime Minister. He conceded that the trade should be ultimately abolished, but not so suddenly as to endanger the country's commerce and colonies.

He therefore proposed that the word 'gradually' should be inserted into the motion. He was immediately challenged by Charles James Fox who contended that slavery was only tolerated because the slaves were of a different colour from Europeans; his view was that if the plantations could not be cultivated without slaves they should not be cultivated at all.

The debate concluded with William Pitt making what was widely regarded as the most eloquent speech of his career. He described the trade as 'the greatest practical evil which has ever afflicted the human race'. It would never be terminated if every nation waited for the concurrence of the whole world. In a peroration so inspired that it is unsurprising that Joseph could remember it almost word for word, Pitt took his cue from Wilberforce's remarks to him in the morning and his moving words about Africa when the debate began. If, as some maintained, Africa would never be civilised, Pitt argued, could not the same view have been taken of ancient Britain by a Roman senator? He called on the House to restore Africans to the rank of human beings. The danger of gradualism, he believed, was that year after year there would be some reason not to proceed and so the most enormous evil would go unredressed. It was on the future of Africa that he brought his speech to a brilliant climax:

> We may live to behold the natives of Africa engaged in the calm occupations of industry, in the pursuits of a just and legitimate commerce. We may behold the beams of science and philosophy breaking in upon their land which, at some happy period in still later time, may blaze with full lustre; and joining their influence to that of pure religion, may illuminate and invigorate the most distant extremities of the immense continent. Then may we hope that even Africa, though last of all the quarters of the globe, shall enjoy at length, in the evening of her days, those blessings which have descended so plentifully on us in a much earlier period of the world.

Just as the first rays of sunlight shone through the windows above him, Pitt chose two lines from Virgil's *Aeneid* to illustrate the coming of dawn to Africa:

> And when the rising sun has first breathed on us with his panting horses,
> Over there the red evening star is lighting his late lamps.

Windham, Fox and Grey walking home together agreed it was 'one of the most extraordinary displays of eloquence they had ever heard'.[3]

The family in Longnor was desperate to know the result of the debate. The girls asked that they should only be told in the morning if the vote was good, but Panton said he was not afraid to hear. They scanned the papers for news, with Katherine noting on 4 April that the debate had not finished until 6.45 am on the previous day and that the result was favourable to Abolition. But on Thursday, 5 April, Joseph arrived home and was able to give them a full account of all that had happened.

Pitt's speech winding up the debate was followed by a motion to adjourn, ending all further consideration of the issue. That was defeated 234 to 87. Dundas's amendment, 'that the slave trade ought to be gradually abolished', was voted through 230 to 85. For most M.P.s this was the most acceptable outcome. In the face of all the revelations they found it difficult to defend the slave trade, but they recoiled from anything remotely radical when there was so much unrest in the country.

Hours later, when Joseph joined the London Committee members at Old Jewry, the question in all minds was: had the cause gained victory or suffered defeat? Wilberforce, who was not present, grasped the significance of what had happened. He wrote to a friend: 'I am congratulated on all hands, yet I cannot but feel hurt and humiliated. We must endeavour to force the gradual Abolitionists in their Bill (for I will never bring forward a parliamentary licence to rob and murder) to allow as short a term as possible, and under as many limitations'.[4] In spite of their misgivings about the vote in the Commons, members of the Committee first proposed a vote of thanks to those M.P.s who had voted with Wilberforce in all divisions. Joseph, however, pointed out that the motion for Abolition had never been put — Wilberforce had left the House to decide when a Bill should be introduced. Joseph thought the proposed vote of thanks might take some members further than they wished to go. The Committee disagreed but no vote was taken. That same evening, however, when Joseph met up with other friends to the cause, Wilberforce told him that he agreed with the point he had made. At the same gathering Joseph expressed his indignation at the conduct of Dundas. Wilberforce, expressing himself more gently, said he would no longer bring in a Bill, but would only support Dundas if he proposed Abolition within a short time; anything distant he would oppose with all his power. The next day Joseph was pleased to hear from the M.P.s for Montgomeryshire and Denbighshire that they had voted with Wilberforce, although they favoured regulation rather than Abolition. Joseph clearly understood the significance of the Commons' acceptance of a gradual approach, for a letter to his friend Thomas Gisborne in Staffordshire told how indignant he felt about Dundas's treatment of Wilberforce.

With Joseph back in Longnor, the family had to follow subsequent events through the press and correspondence with friends. The news was not encouraging. When asked by M.P.s when he would introduce a Bill, Wilberforce replied that the matter was now out of his hands. When Dundas was asked the same question he announced that he was not yet ready, but under attack from Fox agreed to bring forward a resolution. Fox then demanded a date for Abolition and, when his motion was passed, Dundas had to concede that he would lay his ideas before the House in two weeks' time.

A letter to Joseph from the London Committee urged that Abolition must be kept alive; further petitions could be received up to the 18th. Three resolutions of the Committee asserted that the vote in the House confirmed that the trade was cruel and unjust, that gradual Abolition would not satisfy those who had signed petitions, and that any delay would mean that more Africans would suffer. Joseph would have supported these wholeheartedly. Thomas Gisborne produced a timely pamphlet, published without approaching Wilberforce so that he could not be blamed. It called for *immediate* Abolition to avoid further suffering and to stop the slave traders from re-doubling their efforts in any further term set: 'Woe to the inhabitants of the earth, for the Devil is come down to you, having great wrath, *because he knoweth that he hath but a short time*' (Revelations 12:12). M.P.s were challenged to put themselves in the position of captured Negro slaves: 'Let him do as he would be done by'.

When the slave trade debate resumed on 23 April, Dundas said that the anti-Abolitionists would not hear of a shorter time than ten years before the trade was abolished, whereas the advocates of Abolition rejected anything above five years. He therefore suggested seven years as a compromise. Pitt, Fox and Wilberforce demanded immediate Abolition, but Dundas was able to remind them that the House had voted for a gradual approach. On the resumption of the debate two days later Dundas proposed Abolition from 1 January 1800. An immediate amendment to substitute 1793 was defeated. After a subsequent amendment to substitute the year 1795 was also voted down, the House voted by 151 to 132 to accept 1 January 1796, three years on, for an end to the trade. When Dundas spurned the proposition because it would ruin merchants with contracts already agreed, it was remitted to a Committee of the whole House. The issue then went to the House of Lords where the Duke of Clarence, the future William IV, who had seen service in the West Indies as a midshipman, maintained in his maiden speech that slaves lived 'in a state of humble happiness'. In spite of his opposition to any Abolition, the Lords supported Dundas's amendment — but then voted to hear evidence at the bar of their own House! Dundas, who had clearly been playing a devious game to maximise delay, saw that his stratagem had triumphed. 'The most brilliant orators in British history had been outmanoeuvred, as had the parliamentary leader, Wilberforce, of the most powerful movement of agitation which any country had experienced'.[5] Thomas Gisborne hit the nail on the head when he wrote to Joseph to express his opinion that the Lords were protracting the business in the hope that something would turn up to impede the cause or that the people would lose interest. Both were to happen much sooner than anyone expected.

✢

While the two Houses of Parliament wrangled during April and May, Joseph was still active in Shropshire. With the help of Mr. Brown of Newtown his first task was to draw up a full list of signatories from Montgomeryshire. Next an appeal from Granville Sharp for financial help for the London Committee prompted him to make a collection among supporters that produced seventeen guineas for London and one guinea for his uncle John's clerk, John Jones, who had been keeping the local committee's accounts. Wilberforce expressed his concern in a letter that Joseph had taken his suspicions of Dundas too far — Wilberforce was always a gentlemanly opponent — but assured him that he would always pay attention 'to anything my Brother writes'. Joseph responded that he did not harbour suspicions of Dundas, but believed that anything that Dundas accomplished would take the initiative from Wilberforce.

When he received a supportive letter from Sir Richard Hill of Hawkstone, a leading Evangelical, Joseph gained his permission to publish it in the *Chronicle*. It appeared in the issue of 20 April. The Shropshire M.P. wrote that he was 'not a little flattered in seeing so many respectable and judicious names coinciding with me in the great Question in favour of an *immediate* Abolition of that most infamous, most disgraceful, and most inhuman Traffic'. He praised the speeches of Pitt and Fox, but condemned Tarleton's exaggerated suspicions of the veracity of signatures on the petitions. The impact of Hill's letter was diminished by the appearance in the same issue of a letter from 'A Convert to the Truth', who believed the testimony of an army chaplain who had been based in Jamaica that 'he wished our labouring poor [in Britain] were half as well off as the Negroes: they have each a little snug house and garden, with plenty of pigs and poultry', clothes found for them, and a five-day week. A third letter published on 20 April and signed 'Late a Chaplain in the Army' — presumably the same one quoted in the previous letter — was more substantial for it quoted from evidence given before the

Committee of the Council in Jamaica and the testimony of others who had lived in West Africa and witnessed the cruel despotism of local chieftains. Nevertheless his picture of the slave living among his children 'who share his labours in the vigour of his life and are a comfort and solace in his age' till he dies 'surrounded by his friends and relatives, to whom he bequeaths in confidence and security the earnings of his industrious life', defied belief.

The *Chronicle* carried a sharp riposte to 'The Convert' and the 'Army Chaplain' three weeks later over the name 'Salopiensis'. This was almost certainly the work of Sir Richard Hill who had agreed with Joseph to publish an anonymous reply to what he called 'an artful performance ... an entire forgery to serve an iniquitous purpose'. He maintained that many plantation owners did not even feed their slaves and that great cruelties were practised.

On 8 June the *Chronicle* published the last of a series of letters from a correspondent calling himself 'Oronoko' which had begun after Joseph's series of extracts from Clarkson's *Abstract* had come to an end. In his first letter in March 'Oronoko' told how he had lived in both Antigua and St. Vincent and was well acquainted with the work and life of slaves. His principal contention was that nothing had done more to increase the hardship of Negroes than 'that cruel, that inexorable act, by which they are excluded from giving evidence in foreign courts of English law'. This restriction meant that owners who used barbaric methods of control could not be brought to justice or punished in a legal way. He believed that the Negro 'is capable of the highest degree of civilisation and that he is grateful and affectionate'. In his third and final letter in June, 'Oronoko' ridiculed Tarleton and those doctors who claim from the study of their bile and bodies that Negroes 'partake more of the Baboon than the Man'. He went on to tell of the suffering of slaves from cruel punishment, impure water, and bites on the feet from an insect known as the Chigger.

The disappearance of the newspaper correspondence after June was the consequence of Parliament's rising for the long summer recess with no decision reached in the Commons and the hearing of evidence in the Lords only just beginning. Katherine even suspended entries in her journal for four months, noting when she resumed on 26 October: 'Little could be done during the summer months towards the abolition of the slave trade'. Joseph had corresponded with friends about accumulating evidence to put before the House of Lords, but on their journey to Anglesey for a holiday he had encountered a general lack of interest in the cause in Cheshire and north Wales. 'But such is often the case among good and even well-meaning people who have accustomed themselves to take things as they find them, who have a certain dread of innovation, who have not turned their thoughts to these kinds of subjects, who are accustomed to treat as visionary and romantick [sic] every great endeavour to promote human happiness'. Katherine had a good understanding of human nature!

Joseph had even found himself involved indirectly in the trial for murder of John Kimber, the slave captain named by Wilberforce in the debate in April as having flogged to death a fifteen-year-old pregnant slave girl. One of the two witnesses in the trial, Mr. Dowling, a ship's surgeon, wrote to him inquiring about a certain Mr. Ford of Shrewsbury, whose son he believed would be able to corroborate the evidence he had given in court. Katherine recorded that upon inquiry the father said he had 'heard from his son the very same account of the murder of the girl as they gave in court'. It seems almost certain that it was the ever-active Joseph who located Mr. Ford in Shrewsbury, but the son had gone to London and could not be found. Katherine's comment was unusually cynical: 'I fear his being found is very uncertain as anyone who had knowledge of that affair has been carefully concealed'. The trial was conducted with the Duke of Clarence (the future William IV) having the effrontery to clap his hands when anything favourable to the accused was expressed. Not surprisingly Kimber was acquitted and went on to pursue Wilberforce with such threats of violence that he had to have an armed bodyguard. The two chief witnesses were committed for perjury in their evidence against the slave captain, Dowling being found guilty, but Devereux, the surgeon's mate, released.

The development that prompted the resumption of Katherine's entries in her journal was the imminence of a second visit by Thomas Clarkson. In the event the family was at church when he arrived at Longnor. On their return their first impression was that he looked ill, as indeed he had been. In consequence he was behind his schedule and anxious to press on, but he exclaimed, 'I could not bear the thought of coming to this house and not staying a night'.

Clarkson was eager to tell them first of his brother's voyage to Sierra Leone. There had been much illness, with his brother himself pronounced dead by the surgeon and his coffin prepared before it was noticed he was still breathing. He went on to make a full recovery, but of the 1,100 former slaves a number succumbed because of the lack of fresh food. The good news was that, though the cultivation of sugar presented problems, coffee and cotton flourished in the new land. There was also rejoicing that certain blacks who had acted as priests on the voyage had emerged as influential religious leaders; the Sabbath was strictly observed, with Sunday Schools for adults as well as children. Sierra Leone, Clarkson told them, took its name from the range of mountains called The Lion. Its flag, a beautiful green in colour, portrayed a lion and, below, a white hand clasping a black hand. Without doubt Clarkson, who had heard from Joseph that the children were 'zealous in the disuse of sugar', asked them to tell him more. Little Jane had declared that she would eat no more sugar till it came from Sierra Leone, while Panton refused to have his shoes blacked because he understood that sugar was used in the manufacture of the polish.

The purpose of his new tour, their visitor told them, was to find the best witnesses to go before the House of Lords. Fortunately many who had given evidence to the Commons were still in the country. This was particularly true of those who could testify on the treatment of slaves in the West Indies, but evidence from Africa was more of a problem because so many slave ships had sailed that captains were not available. He looked to Joseph for help.

Clarkson was more aware than most, however, that all these efforts might be in vain on account of the dramatic events in France and their effects in Britain. He had been in France, though not in Paris, on 10 August when King Louis XVI had been arrested and imprisoned, the victim of his country's involvement in war. France had declared war on Austria in April when threatened by the efforts of Austria and Prussia to form a counter-revolutionary alliance with Russia and Britain. The situation had become critical in July with Prussia's declaration of war on France and the publication of an inflammatory manifesto by the Duke of Brunswick who was preparing an army of invasion. It was the end of the monarchy, with real power henceforth in the hands of the Convention (National Assembly) and the Committee of Public Safety. Clarkson believed that the Convention would soon abolish the slave trade, but was concerned for the safety of Lafayette, whom he thought had been hasty in condemning the imprisonment of the king. Joseph and his guest agreed that they would not talk in company of the revolution in France for fear that it would harm the cause of Abolition. Because of the tense atmosphere created in Britain by events across the Channel, neither man had read Burke or Paine, respectively hostile to and supportive of the Revolution, so that they could honestly deny it if questioned. Katherine listened intently, considering it a privilege to have sat in on their conversation conducted 'in a strain of calm wisdom and true goodness'. She felt proud 'to call one of these my Brother'. Clarkson she held in the highest esteem for his greatness, goodness, sweetness and 'true dignity which can only be derived from the mind'. She added, 'I know none with whom I am more unrestrained in conversation'. In turn he felt free to say that he believed there would be great commotions in Britain in a few years unless the government made prudent concessions. If the French Revolution succeeded, low taxes there would enable them to undersell British goods in all markets. Although it was known that Paine's *Rights of Man* was widely read by the common people, especially in the manufacturing towns, the government showed no signs of conciliation.

At this point in the conversation their friend Archibald Alison from nearby Kenley arrived. Katherine gathered that he was 'a very warm well-wisher to the French Revolution and, I believe, to the republican form of government'. Clarkson was pleased to tell them that the Bishop of St. David's was an able and zealous supporter of Abolition who would be very valuable in the House of Lords.

When Joseph and Alison rode off after breakfast the next day 'to look at some roads which my Brother is much engaged in improving', Clarkson chatted to the children about Africa. As they were putting a wooden 'dissected map of Africa together', he marked on Sierra Leone and told them of the discovery of Timbuktu. When they then looked at a map of Europe, he said he thought France would become the leading country — and noted the children's aversion to Russia. 'He looked kindly and pleased at Jane who pointed out his native county of Cambridgeshire on the map of England'. He also promised to send them some Sierra Leone coins (they arrived six months later). On Joseph's return, Clarkson kissed the children good-bye, as he had the previous evening when they had run into the garden in moonlight to wish him good-night. Panton insisted on giving him his whip as the two men rode off towards Oswestry.

On their way Joseph took Clarkson to meet several gentlemen in Montgomeryshire including Mr. Vaughan, a surgeon on several slave voyages and now a prospective witness before the House of Lords. Some of the gentlemen belonged to 'the aristocratic party', which Katherine had told Clarkson was also very strong in Shrewsbury. Joseph reported that they were very impressed with his friend, in spite of his views on the French Revolution — Clarkson had apparently broken his self-imposed rule of silence on the subject. He said to one of them, 'Take the New Testament in one hand and the French constitution in the other, compare them, and you will see it comes nearer to the general tenor of it than any government that has yet been established'. When they parted, Clarkson told Joseph that after visiting Chester he was going on to stay with the Bishop of Bangor because he was an old family friend — and in spite of his views on negroes and Abolition. He would then be heading off on another extended tour.

⬱

Joseph continued to correspond with and meet Clarkson occasionally, but it was to be two years before he came to Longnor again. In that time much was to change in his life but sadly very little in the progress of the cause of Abolition.

In June 1792, just before Parliament rose for the long summer recess, the House of Lords had voted to postpone its consideration of the slave trade question and the hearing of evidence until the next year. The Commons had agreed that the trade should be abolished from 1 January 1796, but few believed that this would happen. As Katherine was later to observe: 'Now the novelty has ceased and it is no longer, if I may use the term, fashionable to think and talk about the Abolition, many who appeared forward in the cause show their real indifference, and it is seen how few, in comparison, took it up on fixed principles'. Locally this trend was disheartening to Joseph; nationally it weakened the campaign just as other major political developments were to seize centre stage. By the time Parliament met again in December, recalled early by Pitt who, with French troops poised to invade the Netherlands, was facing a possible war, the prospects for Abolition looked bleak indeed. Worse was to come. The execution of Louis XVI on 21 January 1793 was followed within days by the French declaration of war on Britain and Holland. Every mention of abolishing the slave trade could now be represented as an attack on Britain's ancient constitution and flirting with revolutionary ideas from France. In a Lords' debate in April, one speaker asked: 'What does the abolition of the slave trade mean more or less in effect than liberty and equality?' Moreover, the war came to dominate Pitt's thoughts and led to an estrangement from Wilberforce who opposed the war – for which he was denounced in many quarters.

To the added dismay of all supporters of Abolition, the slave trade was flourishing more than ever: in 1793 Jamaica imported a record number of 23,000 captives and exported record amounts of sugar and coffee. The cause made almost no progress in Parliament: in the whole of 1793 the Lords examined only seven witnesses, and only two in 1794. They also rejected a Bill to impose a ban on British merchants selling slaves to foreign markets that Wilberforce had succeeded in piloting through the Commons. The reverses did not damage his faith. 'Let us do our duty, trust in Providence, and be prepared to resign ourselves to His will', he wrote to Joseph. His motion in 1795 to end the trade the next January, as had been agreed in the earlier debates, was defeated 78 to 61 in the Commons, which led Joseph to observe: 'It will be as Mr. Clarkson said, the Almighty had taken it into his own hands, and the Abolition will be accomplished by means we have not foreseen'. Wilberforce's Bill the following year to effect Abolition from the beginning of 1797 got as far as a third reading in the Commons, but was then voted down. His motions on Abolition now became annual events, yet by 1800 nothing had changed. Even worse, the trade was still profitable in spite of the activities of privateers in the war at sea. Indeed as British troops conquered French and Spanish islands in the West Indies, the market for slaves expanded. At the end of the century British ships were transporting 50,000 slaves a year.

Long before this, Clarkson's health had cracked. Letters from him to Joseph in March and April 1793 had been upbeat about progress in Sierra Leone and Wilberforce's plans for a renewed campaign in Parliament. He also sent the promised Sierra Leone coins to the children. A letter in June, however, related that he was unwell, agitated and depressed by the defeat of Wilberforce's Bill, although he was still asking Joseph to push on with the campaign to dissuade people from using West Indian sugar and inquiring if he knew any possible witnesses who had been in Africa. The news in August was worse. He was writing, he explained in his letter dated 27th (reproduced in full by Katherine), to a few trusted friends to seek their advice on whether he should retire from the Abolition campaign. Joseph was included, he said, out of respect for his friendship, character and judgement. It was the letter of a man on the verge of a breakdown. He told how he had dedicated himself totally to the cause for the last seven years. He had travelled constantly, covering 35,000 miles, working often till 2.00 or 3.00 in the morning. Vexations and disappointments had added to the physical and mental toll. His whole nervous system had been affected. 'I am often suddenly seized with Giddiness and Cramps. I feel an unpleasant ringing in my Ears, my Hands frequently tremble. Cold sweats suddenly come upon me. My Appetite becomes all at once ravenous'. His condition, he said, was daily getting worse and if he went on he would be 'killing myself by inches'. He was also in a bad way financially. For years he had met his expenses out of his own pocket and even paid fares for seamen to travel from Bristol and Liverpool to London to testify before committees of inquiry. The London Committee had no funds for such purposes. He calculated that he had spent £1,500 in seven years. He foresaw his ruin if the campaign continued for another two or three years, whereas he would have enough to live on if he retired at Christmas. He was in anguish because he did not want to desert the cause, but felt his health and independence threatened if he went on.

Joseph's response was swift. He met Clarkson for supper in London the next week. He found him rather better than expected, and felt able to assert that if he retired the cause was absolutely lost, for he knew far more about it than anyone else and was the link through which the whole campaign was managed. With Clarkson's permission Joseph disclosed his money problems to Sir Richard Hill, the Shropshire M.P., who said he would join others in a delegation to the Prime Minister to request a reward to Clarkson for his public services. Joseph feared he would not accept this. It was clear that Clarkson needed a period of complete rest, but instead he set off on another tour. Joseph joined him at Bishop's Castle in November and accompanied him into Wales. He found his health somewhat improved though he quickly became fatigued, and he was happier about his finances because of the response of his friends. Clarkson was delighted to be presented with 'a sweet bag' that Josepha had made for him. At heart he was probably relieved to hear that Joseph and others were privately raising a fund for his assistance, although he maintained that he was beginning to regret ever having sent the letter. In fact Joseph had corresponded with Wilberforce and had approached some trustworthy friends on the subject of financial help for Clarkson. He heard from him a few days after their parting: he wanted no approach to Pitt and asked that the whole idea of recompense should be dropped. Clarkson was also deeply hurt by the news of the guillotining of Brissot and the Girondin leaders, moderate republicans, in France. Wilberforce wrote to invite Joseph to a meeting in London of half-a-dozen close friends of Clarkson to discuss what they should do. Joseph told them of Clarkson's recent letter but believed that they should not be deterred by his reluctance. This proved a wise judgement, for in January 1794 Clarkson wrote to Joseph to say that seven of his eight respondents thought he should carry on so long as his health did not suffer, and that he accepted the private initiative of key friends to seek donations of at least £50 from sympathetic individuals. Katherine recorded that her brother secretly approached Sir Richard Hill, the two Mr. Reynolds and Mr. Houlbrooke for contributions in addition to his own. Joseph appears to have donated over £100 which led his sister to enter in her journal: 'His conduct has been great and worthy of him, his family have to rejoice in their near relation to such a character'. Clarkson, aware of Joseph's energetic approach to problems, wrote to ask him to hold back his friends' subscriptions for the moment so that more

71

pressure could be put on some wealthy supporters reluctant to contribute. In May he wrote saying that he wished others could organise like Joseph: 'It's not Wilberforce's *forte* — and he's very busy'.

Clarkson's letter in July contained the welcome news that he was planning to spend most of the summer of 1794 near Penrith. Wilberforce wrote two months later with the even more pleasing, and surprising, information that Clarkson was to marry 'a very amiable and sensible young lady at Bury'. Clarkson himself wrote to confirm that he had a lady friend, though marriage was not imminent, to say how much better his health was and to suggest a visit to Longnor in November. When he arrived for a four-day stay at the end of that month he was clearly much improved in health and launched into a vivid description of the Lake District. His latest news was that he had purchased 'Woodside' and thirty-five acres on the north shore of Ullswater where he would retire when the slave trade business permitted. He was keen that they should visit and persuaded Joseph there and then to use his skill in drawing up plans to show what the cottage he envisaged should be like; Katherine herself was 'lucky enough to draw the elevations of the different sides in a way that exactly met his ideas'. Was the subject too sensitive for Katherine to record anything about his lady friend other than that he said he had not yet made up his mind whom to marry?

They spent a lot of time discussing the situation in France and Britain. Clarkson's view was that if the French invaded they would find support in Scotland and the industrial north of England. Shropshire he considered 'remarkable for its aristocratical principles'. The slave trade and Sierra Leone featured much less prominently in their conversation than on his previous visits, but he had hopes of Wilberforce's new Bill. Joseph invited his guest to preach at Longnor; he declined but accompanied the family to church. In the evening he went with Joseph to Leebotwood, where Panton told him he would see his mother's memorial. Josepha made him a new lavender bag, while Mrs. Plymley (Matty) wanted to know if he had had his portrait painted. On his departure he again pressed them to visit him at Ullswater, though he had to concede it would not be easy with a family of young children.

The family's plan to make the visit in the summer of 1795 fell through in the end because Joseph was too busy, but when in London the following January the two men dined together and attended a meeting of the London Committee. After that news came by post — Clarkson's resignation as an Anglican clergyman (he was drawn to the Quakers), his marriage to Catherine Buck in 1796, his new house by the lake, his experiences as a novice gentleman farmer, his growing friendship with the Wordsworths and Coleridge, and the birth of his son. Clarkson was to spend ten years in the Lake District before returning to London in 1804, just in time for the revival of the slave trade campaign.

For Joseph, too, there was the threat of ill-health on account of overwork, but the grave delay in the progress to Abolition meant at least that he no longer had to dash hither and thither gaining signatures or distributing literature against the slave trade. Instead he was pre-occupied with his new responsibilities in the church, with a fast-growing family, and with his roles as landowner and magistrate in what were to prove very difficult years politically, economically and socially. Of course he remained true to his convictions on the slave trade, convictions strengthened when, in 1797, on his way back from the long-postponed visit to Clarkson in the Lakes, he went on board some slave ships in Liverpool, heeding the warning not to ask too many questions.[6] He kept in touch with Clarkson, with the Committee until it ceased operations in 1797, and with Wilberforce. His relations with the latter were most cordial, as is apparent from a letter sent by Wilberforce in August 1797 in response to Joseph's congratulations on his recent marriage:

> Many thanks for your kind letter. Your intelligence however respecting the slave trade has really moved me so much that I can scarcely turn to any other subject with proper composure. Surely Providence will not suffer such wickedness and cruelty to go unavenged. One is strongly tempted to wish not merely that the sufferings of the Africans may cease, but that some signal mark of the Divine displeasure may desolate those abhorred islands. However, we are to bear in mind that 'the wrath of man worketh not the righteousness of God', and strive to retain that spirit of love which should bleed for the offender while it prevents or punishes the offence ...
>
> Your intelligence concerning Clarkson amuses me. My time is here so much occupied that I can scarcely get a vacant half-hour for the most pressing business. But for this impediment I would gladly discuss with you for a sheet or two, but I must lay down my pen – not however without thanking you for your friendly congratulations on my marriage. I hope sometime to have the pleasure of introducing Mrs. W. to your family circle.
>
> I remain, my dear Sir, with very sincere regard,
>
> Yours always, W.W.[7]

Over time Wilberforce consulted Joseph widely on matters of poverty in the countryside, agricultural improvements and the impact of new taxes – and welcomed Joseph's opposition to the war.

His involvement in the slave trade issue over several years had profoundly influenced Joseph's attitudes, character, ministry and life. And it was his liberal, humanitarian instincts as well as his Christian faith that had made him so active a champion of the cause of Abolition. A recent historian of the period acknowledges that 'there can be little doubt that the evangelicals were sincere. This does not mean, however, that they were motivated by humanitarian feelings'. He believes that, like Mrs. Jellyby in *Bleak House*, they were more concerned with the natives of Africa than poverty at home. In both cases, he maintains, 'it was the souls of the downtrodden and not their material well-being which signified'.[8] This may well be true of many in the Clapham Sect of Evangelicals and their adherents in Parliament, but it was certainly not true of Clarkson, nor of Joseph, nor of thousands of signatories of petitions in the provinces without whose support the campaign would never have had the same impact in Parliament. Joseph's heart and head were engaged in his campaigning for Abolition, though he was also deeply concerned about poverty in his own country and area. He emerged from these years a more mature person, a leading figure in the county of Shropshire, highly regarded by national leaders like William Wilberforce and Thomas Clarkson, and with a faith now imbued with a burning sense of justice.

8 THE YOUNG ARCHDEACON

Katherine Plymley had first begun her journal on the day in October 1791 when Thomas Clarkson had arrived at the family home in Longnor. She renewed it, after the first substantial break in her regular record, twelve months later when the second visit of their celebrated friend was imminent. The four-month gap since her last entry on 9 June 1792 is explained by the loss of impetus in the anti-slave trade campaign after the Parliamentary rebuffs and by the family holiday in Anglesey which she detailed in a separate journal.

In the intervening period two major developments occurred in the life of her brother. The first was the pregnancy of Joseph's second wife, Matty. His three children by his first wife and named directly after her — Panton, Josepha and Jane — were now respectively seven, six and four years old. The news of a baby expected in November created great excitement in the family. The second significant change in Joseph's life had for some time been predictable as the health of his friend Archdeacon Robert Clive was in visible decline. They had first met four years earlier when Joseph was canvassing support for the 1788 petition. The ageing cleric, who was finding his role as treasurer of the Archdeaconry Fund for Clergy Widows and Children increasingly arduous, saw in his vigorous new acquaintance the answer to his prayers. Joseph duly became assistant treasurer, demonstrating his usual zeal and efficiency by 'riding hundreds of miles to visit all in receipt of relief to satisfy the charity of the justice of their claims' and, one hopes, the adequacy of the charity's response to their needs. Before the old archdeacon died Joseph had taken his place as treasurer. His friend had greater plans for him, too — no less than to succeed him as Archdeacon of Salop in the diocese of Hereford. Though the bishop declined to offer the post to Joseph while its holder was still alive, it seems that he had the move in mind and that other clergy were also in favour.

It was surely no coincidence that Joseph was the one invited by the bishop to preach the sermon at his Triennial Visitation at Church Stretton on 5 July 1792. This is the only one of all Joseph's sermons to have survived;

unfortunately, perhaps, it belongs to that special genre associated with such formal occasions. It is a learned discourse, deploying his knowledge of the classics as well as of the Bible, especially St. Paul's epistles. He took his text from 1 Corinthians 1:21 — 'The world by wisdom knew not God'. His aim was to examine 'the causes of present infidelity'. He looked back to ancient Greece, concluding that 'the nations best instructed were unable to establish any one commanding idea of the universal parent — any one integral account of that almighty Being who made heaven and earth'. But he paid tribute 'to their honour, and to the honour of reason be it mentioned, that under the disabilities of their situation, they preferred doubt to decision'. The scepticism natural in the pre-Christian age 'is much more optional in ours'. Why then the lack of faith in his own day? He believed many were too indolent seriously to study the Scriptures, while others approached them with pre-conceived ideas. For him the Bible was God's revelation: 'It is the fact thro' which we are to know God', and internal evidence confirms its authenticity. The Christian religion, he believed, is the basis of morality for it has replaced contention by mercy. Since the spread of the Gospel, 'we find in the general conduct less asperity of carriage, more mild manners and kindness of consideration'. In spite of his recent heroic commitment to the anti-slave trade movement, there is no direct reference to the cause, but perhaps it is hinted at in his conclusion on the civilising impact of the Gospel:

> If it is observed that the general well-being of society has improved in conformity with the extension of Christian principles, how much is it our duty, and how much is it the duty of all mankind to whom the knowledge of it shall come, to represent both by precept and example the advantages that have thus obtained, which we hope are obtaining, and which we hope will obtain, till man 'shall not hurt nor destroy', the blessed consequence of that promised era, to the establishment of which all our labours should be directed, and which by the blessing of God, they may tend to approximate, the time when 'the earth shall be full of the knowledge of the Lord as the waters cover the sea'.[1]

The optimism with which the sermon closed, with its echoes of Isaiah, will have brought comfort to Archdeacon Clive when Joseph spent a day or two with him in the week before he died. The bishop, who had opposed Abolition, nonetheless recognised leadership talent when he saw it and at once offered Joseph the post. He was just thirty-three years of age. As Katherine noted, it was 'an honourable office, but of very little profit', though her pride led her to add: 'It is very pleasant that the wishes of the clergy met and indeed anticipated the appointment of the bishop'.

It is surprising and intriguing that in 1792, that year of change in Joseph's life, he should have found time to organise yet another alteration in his status. Katherine makes no reference to it, but the records of Cambridge University are quite clear. On 26 March, the Rev. Joseph Plymley, son of Joseph, gentleman, of Condover, Salop, was admitted a member of Emmanuel College.[2] His matriculation at Pembroke College, Oxford, on 28 March 1776, at the age of sixteen, is confirmed; so is the degree of Bachelor of Arts awarded at Oxford in 1786. Why then did he seek admission to Emmanuel to be awarded his Master of Arts degree and why at this time? One notes that it was almost exactly sixteen years since he had been admitted to Pembroke, but that hardly seems significant. Was it that he wished to have his Master's gown before, as perhaps he anticipated, being made Archdeacon? But why Cambridge and why Emmanuel College is a mystery. It is noteworthy that on his return journey from attending the great slavery debate at the beginning of April, he sent a letter to the family from Cambridge. It seems likely that on that visit he was granted his Master's degree, having perhaps written to the college beforehand and received confirmation of his admission, but why Cambridge? — since he had stayed in Oxford on his way to London!

It is worthy of note that as the challenge of campaigning to abolish the slave trade had helped Joseph recover from the shock of his first wife's death, so just as that campaign lost its momentum a new challenge presented itself to him on his appointment as archdeacon. At a time when communication was slow, and the bishop normally resident in Hereford, the position of Archdeacon of Salop[3] made Joseph the senior Churchman in south Shropshire though, of course, subordinate to the bishop.[4] In those days before the creation of 'rural deans' in the six deaneries within the archdeaconry, his was a position of significance and authority. One of his principal duties was to conduct annual visitations, first in Ludlow and then in Church Stretton, in the two years out of three when these were not conducted by the bishop. At the visitations he had to deliver a 'charge' to the local clergy — setting out what he saw as the priorities for the year ahead — and to swear in the churchwardens of all the parishes. He had, as archdeacons have today, special responsibility for the maintenance of church buildings and parsonages, and general pastoral over-sight of all the clergy within the archdeaconry.

Joseph threw himself into his new responsibilities with his customary enthusiasm and thoroughness. He planned to pay a personal visit to every one of the churches in his charge. It was to be much more than a fleeting visit to meet the incumbent, if present, and to cast an eye over the church building. His aim was to compile a full account of each parish, complete with a description of the church and parsonage house, details of clergy and income, and a statistical survey of the parish and its people. In a letter to Wilberforce in 1800 he explained a further intention; 'In the account I took of the state of each parish in my Archdeaconry some years ago ... it was my object to get first at the fact of what our civil and ecclesiastical state was; then to see how far existing laws were adapted to meet existing evils'. It is small wonder that in April 1793 his sister confided in her journal:

> For some months past my brother has been much engaged in a very useful but laborious undertaking, a personal survey of all the churches in his Archdeaconry which is a very extensive district and contains nearer two hundred than one hundred churches; he has now gone through I believe upwards of sixty. When finished it will show a more compleat [sic] statement of the ecclesiastical, civil and natural history of this district, I believe, than has ever yet been made of any part of England. It is a work worthy an enlightened mind ... We are much deprived of my brother's company by this undertaking for he is generally engaged in making his surveys one part of the week, and in arranging the materials he has procured the other; but though fully sensible of the value of his conversations, we are not selfish enough to regret that he should use the talents he possesses for the public good and for his own, engaged as he always is in benefiting by some means his fellow creatures; we look beyond this world and consider that he is increasing his future glory when, as a good and faithful servant, he shall enter into the glory of his Lord.[5]

Few sisters would describe their brothers in these terms, but Katherine was the greatest admirer of his ability, activity, quickness and zeal. She also gives us valuable insight into his organisation of his time. That we are able to fill in the details of the whole exercise is possible because the material he compiled has most fortunately survived and is now held at Shropshire Archives.[6] Joseph appears to have determined from the outset that he would allocate one large volume to each of the six deaneries that made up the archdeaconry. At the beginning of each he listed all the churches in alphabetical order. That is also the order in which they appear in the volumes, although he did not visit them in that sequence. The fact that one of the pages for Wentnor is out of order tells us that his practice was to write up his findings on loose leaves that were bound when all a deanery's parishes had been visited. Nor did he complete one deanery at a time, probably because he did not wish some areas to feel neglected, and because as the new archdeacon he wished to make himself generally known as soon as possible. Detailed letters to him from Neen Savage and Stottesdon were incorporated in the Report.

Joseph's *modus operandi* becomes clear as one peruses his accounts. Having decided which churches he would visit next, perhaps over a month or more beforehand, he would send a detailed questionnaire to the parish clerk, churchwardens or incumbent requesting its completion and return as soon as possible — relying, perhaps, on the wish to create a favourable impression with the new archdeacon! A letter from the rector at Hopton Castle dated 4 May 1793 — Joseph visited two weeks later — provided, the writer believed, 'a pretty exact account of the inhabitants now resident in the parish'. On the other hand, the archdeacon noted the absence of the parsonage house from the list that the incumbent, James Woodhouse, had sent him from Culmington. Indeed, he told his sister that he often received more accurate information from clerks than from clergy. He would presumably advise parishes by post of the date of his intended visit and then, armed with their written response, he would ride out there, meet the people concerned, make a careful survey of the church building and advise what repairs were necessary, and finally have a look at the village or town area, speaking with local folk as opportunity offered. More detailed information about landholding and income was probably available from the incumbent's tithe accounts.

The information he gleaned from his respondents and his visit was written up under a standard set of headings. He dealt first with the parish, setting out its name, its precise geographical location and its extent. If it comprised separate townships these were detailed, too. There followed the number of houses and of male and female persons, the average size of families and the average number per house. After the first national census in 1801 he updated his initial figures to the now official population. He then gave details of the parish, listing the principal proprietors with their holdings and income, together with purchases and alienations where appropriate. There followed the number of cottages, the poor rate, the rental of the parish, any land enclosures completed, farms and resources like timber. He noted if there was a school, a local constable, the number of alehouses, the conditions of the poor, any legacies for the poor, and if there were any almshouses. Where there was some industry he gave details of manufactures, mines, labour and apprentices. He recorded if there was common land, what crops were grown, and the existence of a stone quarry.

Beginning a new page in his final copy, he then turned to the church — its situation, the names of the patron and incumbent, the parsonage house (or other residence), any terriers (inventories) with dates, the glebe, tithes, and whether there was a curate and where he lived. Also noted were the frequency and times of services and Holy Communion, the catechising of children, the size of the congregation and the amount in the offertory. Church plate was listed, and the state of the fabric described including any improvements made. His account concluded with dates of incumbents and curates, dates of his own subsequent visits, details of repairs completed or still outstanding, and finally the keeping of the Register with its record of baptisms, marriages and burials.

⁓

The size of the parishes in the archdeaconry ranged from the large to the very small. Ludlow and Bewdley, with nearly 4,000 inhabitants, were being overtaken by the increasingly industrialised towns of Broseley and Madeley in the east of the county. Much Wenlock and Pontesbury just topped 2,000; Rock, Tenbury, Bishop's Castle, Clun, Chirbury, Meole Brace and Westbury, a parish of ten townships, all exceeded 1,000. At the other end of the scale was the tiny hamlet of Sneade with a total of just 47 people, and several others like Easthope, Hope Bagot, Highley and Preen had populations of less than 100. Most of the parishes were wholly rural in character, with scattered farmhouses and a few cottages near the church.

In recording demographic, economic and social details of the 168 parishes (some were only chapelries) he visited, Joseph did future local historians a great service. As a pastor what concerned him most in their social composition were the varied occupations and the living standards of the poor, for although he had so far demonstrated his ardent opposition to the slave trade, he now showed his deep and increasing concern for the poor in his own area and for education. In Barrow parish he found about a hundred engaged in the manufacture of 'Shropshire China' at Caughley. Industry was much more advanced in Broseley where the mixture of forges, furnaces, factories, lime works and shops were connected to Coalbrookdale by the iron bridge over the Severn. The principal works there were foundries where the iron ore was smelted into 'pigs' and sold in that state. He was concerned that the labourers spent so much in the alehouses that their homes and personal appearance were neglected; their only saving was through 'benefit clubs'. The workhouse at Broseley had 30-40 inmates, chiefly the elderly and orphans. The children of the poor were bound apprentice at ten years old. There was no endowed school, but dame schools took infants and there were two taught by men. At Cardington he felt that the poor were getting poorer. As at Broseley, so in Madeley the furnacemen — who earned 11-12 shillings a week, sometimes up to 40 shillings — spent too much, to Joseph's thinking, in the alehouse instead of on home comforts, although occasionally they enjoyed 'dainty living' especially at Sunday dinner. There were three schools and a Sunday school in Madeley, but, Joseph noted and underlined, <u>'some more education than they already have is necessary to make them understand their real interest'</u>. At Rushbury he observed, 'I have known aged labourers who had saved money formerly forced to employ it in aid of their earnings latterly. I am afraid none save money now; daily subsistence is all their object and parish relief all their resource'. Much Wenlock had many decayed houses. The declining numbers receiving poor relief at Woolstaston were explained by new employment in collieries and lime works nearby. The labourers there lived chiefly on bread and potatoes; there was very little butter and scarcely any cheese, which once was plentiful. High rates of pay were noted again in the collieries and lime works at Coreley, where Joseph himself would become incumbent a few years later as his uncle Robert had purchased the advowson. At Clungunford he was again constrained to lament the popularity of the alehouse: 'I have always wished to inspire labourers with an attachment to their house and garden as a lively principle of good behaviour and prosperity to them'. This was always his guiding principle: the poor would be best helped not by relief in hard times — though that would sometimes be necessary — but by being educated to lead an industrious, sober and self-disciplined life. It was the same principle that today suggests that the world's hungry benefit most not from emergency aid but by being given the means and the skills to provide for themselves.

As an archdeacon, of course, Joseph had a particular concern for the state of the church buildings. At Barrow he was critical of the state of the church floor and the 'indecent forms'; when he visited again in 1797 the benches were properly ordered but the floor still poor (on his last recorded visit in 1834 the church was in good repair, with two stoves installed — one, he was pleased to note near the seats for the poor). At Broseley the floor and ceiling needed attention and the south wall of the chancel was dangerously cracked; by 1797 the repairs and improvements had been carried out. The cracks he had observed in the steeple at Cardington had also been attended to. The tower at Eaton-under-Heywood where the north side was not perpendicular, was in so dangerous a state that the repairs were carried out by November 1793, only eight months after his initial visit. The working of coal seams within twenty yards of the churchyard boundary at Jackfield (Broseley's new church) threatened the whole future of the building. Linley's problem was much less serious — 'the rubbish under the belfry should be taken away'. Major repairs were done at Cleobury Mortimer, and approval granted to moving the choir from the north aisle gallery, which was considered unsightly and inconvenient, to the front of the gallery occupied by the school. The request of the patron, Mr. Botfield, at Hopton Wafers to take down the north wall and add two aisles and three rows of pews — at his own expense — was also approved. Though the church at Bishop's Castle was in generally good condition, 'great awkwardnesses pervade the fabric both inside and out'. Major repairs were needed at Brampton Bryan, where by 1831 the tower was being repaired and the church enlarged to 306 'sittings' — for a population of 404! Clun church was described as 'a venerable old fabric, but very infirm'; some restorative work had been achieved by 1818. Leintwardine was praised for the magnificence of its original architecture, but was judged by the archdeacon to be in need of repair and cleaning. Repairs requested at Bromfield and Caynham in the Ludlow Deanery were carried out promptly. The archdeacon failed to gain entry to Hope Bagot church, 'the clerk being gone out and taken the key with him'; the view from the outside revealed cracks in the walls and the need for a new roof. St. Lawrence's at Ludlow was, of course, in a different league: it was accorded a lengthy description and praised for its 'very beautiful fabric'. Here there were pews for 1,200 as well as benches. At Silvington the archdeacon ordered the replacement of the Bible and Prayer Book. Visits to Wistanstow in 1793 and 1797 led to the recommendation for new pews throughout the church. When re-visited in 1804 there were forty-eight handsome oak pews and benches with backs for the poor, as well as a gallery for the children of the Sunday School; the new resident rector put a ceiling over the chancel and re-laid the floor. Developments at Chirbury were even more impressive after criticisms of irregular pews, uneven floor and a gallery that needed to be removed. In 1797 an apology was received for the delayed response, but advising that agreement had been needed for the proprietors to pay for re-pewing and the tenants for other repairs. The archdeacon happily recorded the next year that Chirbury church was uniformly pewed, with a hundred oak pews with numbers japanned on each, a new gallery over the west door, and a new pulpit given by the patrons. On the other hand, the church at Shelve — which Joseph remembered from his early days as a curate — was 'in a most indecent state', while the church at Cleobury North was 'in general dark and very dirty', with irregular pews, and floor and roof needing attention — although the rector claimed it was much better than when he came!

Within the same Stottesdon Deanery, only a few miles from each other, and both boasting Saxon arches, Ditton Priors church had still failed in 1834 to complete the repairs to floor and ceiling called for in 1794 and 1797, whereas Morville church was commended for its good state, especially its new tiled roof and its tower, 'a respectable one for the district'. At Chetton he found on a later visit that a gallery had been added, paid for by fifteen inhabitants — 'I scarce know a church where there is less cause for complaint than this'. At Stottesdon itself, an anonymous correspondent lamented 'the sad, mutilated and neglected edifice', where the 'elegant part of the exterior of this mouldering pile has been most sacrilegiously destroyed'; the archdeacon noted, however, that repair had recently begun. The archdeacon's report on St. Mary's Church at Bitterley, on the western slopes of Titterstone Clee Hill, is of particular interest for it contains his draft of a letter to the churchwardens and the rector's subsequent reply:

> Archdeacon Plymley's service to the Church Wardens of Bitterley; and as he is forced to notice the state of their Church, begs leave to remind them that the season is approaching wherein it may be conveniently repaired. He fears the steeple will become ruinous if not attended to, and that the floor of the Nave is already too bad for safety or decency. The desks both for the Clergyman and Clerk he apprehends also to be infirm, and the pews in general rather unseemly. Indeed the whole of the Fabric is susceptible of great improvement, and as he has the pleasure of hearing from the Rector that he is desirous of doing his own repairs to the Chancel, it will certainly be best that the whole building be examined at the same time. The great respectability of the Parish of Bitterley makes the Archdeacon confident that the necessary work will be properly gone thro' with, (and he has indeed the satisfaction of knowing that some of the worthy landlords will readily concur in making all due provision for the decent administration of religious worship). He hopes also that the parishioners in general will not only think that he is discharging his own duty by pointing out these defects, but he consults also their present interest in doing it, as the longer repairs of any kind are delayed the more burdensome they become.

The Rector soon replied to this wise and circumspect letter:

> In consequence of the letter you favoured me with and the one addressed to the Church Wardens of Bitterley, a parish meeting has been held for the Purpose of taking under consideration the State of the Church. Mr. Telford the architect had previously surveyed it and his Report is that the State of the Church is extremely dangerous and that nothing short of taking down and rebuilding is advisable. The Farmers are unanimously against the measure. I mentioned to Mr. Probert a

> subscription in aid of a Parish Rate and wished to know whether Lord
> Clive as Proprietor of one of the Hamlets in the Parish would lend us
> his assistance. His reply was that His Lordship would give whatever
> was proper on the occasion or you might think so.
> Ludlow, 23 March '94. I am respectfully yours, Jas. Hastings.[7]

There are no further notes on this issue, but the building today is clearly the original one. In 1796 John Walcot, LL.B., Rector, purchased the advowson from Hastings and resided in the parish till his death in 1834, to be succeeded by his son and then by his son.

The visit to Madeley on 15 December 1792 is of special interest for three reasons – the rapid growth of industry and population, the continued influence of the former Swiss rector, Jean Guillaume de la Flèchere (but better remembered as Fletcher of Madeley), and the pressing need for a new church building. Fletcher, a close friend of John Wesley and who had been seen as his possible successor as leader of the Methodist revival, had died in 1785 worn out by his labours. Methodism was strong among the working class families, but there were only a few Methodist meeting places in the area and most of its adherents worshipped with the Anglicans. The dilapidated church was packed on Sundays with perhaps three hundred at the morning Communion. The curate, Samuel Walters, preached twice every Sunday and at least two evenings a week in special rooms in Coalbrookdale as had been Fletcher's practice. Joseph noted that Fletcher's 'zeal for the propagation of Christianity was much adorned by his charity and benevolence'. The archdeacon had a good word, too, for the Quaker ironmasters he had met when campaigning against the slave trade. As the people with the greatest influence in the area they encouraged the evening preaching 'perceiving the good effects it has upon their workmen'. The faith may have flourished but old St. Michael's did not. There was general agreement on the need for a new church but much dispute over the best site. On his second visit only two months later the archdeacon, who favoured two new churches, found opposition because of the trading recession. And although Thomas Telford had already submitted a design, argument continued over the best situation. 'After much further cavil and delay', Joseph recorded in 1794, 'I was forced to send a peremptory message to the parishioners of Madeley, and accordingly a new church was begun to be built' — and the old one demolished that same year. The project received welcome backing from the Quaker Reynolds family who believed all should have the opportunity to worship God in the way they wish. Telford's new church, an octagonal design in white stone, was completed for £2,000 and could seat 1,800, with benches for the poor. As at Church Stretton, the archdeacon called for the removal of two 'abominable' wall paintings of a skeleton and a representation of Time — but they were still there when he called again in September 1800.

᪻

As with the buildings, so with the clergy, the archdeacon encountered both good and bad examples. Non-residence was very common, chiefly because stipends were so small that clergy — Joseph Plymley himself among them — held more than one living. At Badger 'no resident rector is remembered', and the curate lived at Shifnal; the congregation was said to be largest when the patron, Mr. Browne, M.P. for Bridgnorth, was at home as he had such a large family! At nearby Beckbury, where Mr. Browne was lord of the manor, 'the present rector scarce ever comes near the parish', and the curate lived at Albrighton. Yet the church was tolerably full in the mornings as Mr. Browne 'bestows weekly bounty on many of the poor families' — so long as they attended church. At Cardington, on the other hand, with an average congregation of two hundred, the farmers attended better than the poor. 'No resident rector in living memory', Joseph was told at Hol(d)gate, but there was a curate and a subdeacon, Dr. Goodrich, rector of Cound, who was entitled to a small emolument for reading the second lesson! Joseph was himself presented to Holgate by the bishop in 1800 'to defray the expenses of the archdeaconry'. At Munslow the patron was also incumbent and lived in the house he himself had built; in time he was succeeded by his son. Abberley was served from 1733 to 1865 by four generations of the resident Severne family, one of whom was to tutor the archdeacon's sons. By contrast, an Oxfordshire clergyman appointed to Edgton in 1783 had, ten years later, 'not been seen since'. The living of Lydbury North was in the hands of the headmaster of Shrewsbury School who had bought the patronage for 1,000 guineas but paid his curate only £40 per annum. At nearby Mainstone that was the maximum salary that the infirm eighty-two-year-old incumbent, whose own stipend was £100, was prepared to give his curate who had complained that his £35 was inadequate. The rector of Diddlebury, who was Chancellor of the diocese of Bristol, lived in his other living in Worcestershire. Similarly, at Stanton Lacy, where there had not been a resident vicar for forty years, Joseph Pickering resided on his living in Hampshire; he had another in the Peak District. Although his predecessor at Wistanstow had lived in the parsonage house for twenty-four years, in 1793 the Rev. Robert Johnson lived in Kenilworth. Joseph's friend, Lewis Williams, lived in his rectory at Woolstaston but also personally served his other parish of Longden. Oxford colleges owned some advowsons, Worcester

College presenting the incumbent at Neen Sollars, New College at Worthen, and Christ Church at Wentnor. The Roman Catholic patron at Ditton Priors usually left it to others to make presentations to the bishop. The Rev. Charles Tucker, rector of Hopesay and Morville, chose to reside in the former.

That the Anglican Church in the late 18th century was at a low ebb — a state that prompted the rise of Methodism and the Evangelical movement — is borne out by Archdeacon Plymley's notes on the parishes he visited. The demoralising effects of pluralism, non-residence and poorly paid curates were compounded by problems with individual clergymen in some parishes. At Hopton Wafers a dispute over patronage dragged on in the Court of Chancery after the violent death of the rector, and the living was void for several years. The vicar of Rock, who was uncle to the patron, suffered fron occasional mental disorders and had lived in London for six years before the archdeacon's visit. There was general dissatisfaction with the rector at Bucknell: the archdeacon did not consider him fit to preach at his visitation; the patrons of the living, the Grocers' Company of London, would not build a new parsonage house because of his failings; and in three years numbers at Holy Communion fell from fifty or sixty to ten. In nearby Clun the arch-deacon had to hold an inquiry at the 'Buffalo's Head' inn 'upon complaints against Mr. Chapman, the new resident curate, whose piety and zeal are not balanced by sound judgement and who, in attempting to do extensive good, has overlooked plainer duties'. St. Lawrence's at Ludlow was shaken by the suicide of the rector, Richard Baugh, who put a gun to his head. The death in 1799 of David Hemus at Broseley came as a relief, for after fifty-two years as the incumbent he had almost lost his faculties. The same parish suffered another shock some years later when a curate was found guilty of forgery and transported to New South Wales. Two other neighbouring parishes in the Wenlock Deanery encountered acute problems. At Rushbury services became irregular when the elderly vicar, sometimes deranged in his mind, appointed curates and then dismissed them. Hope Bowdler's rector, George Marsh, was in prison for debt for five years.

The position of archdeacon was no sinecure!

To fulfil his ambition to visit all the churches in his charge the new arch-deacon had set himself a punishing schedule. Nor did he systematically work his way through the parishes of one deanery at a time, although Wenlock and Pontesbury figured large in his early visits, and Burford churches were gener-ally left towards the end of his programme. Unsurprisingly, he did not begin his round of calls immediately; he needed to write requesting information from the first parishes on his list, and then he would have wished to support his young wife, Matty, who was nearing the time of her first confinement. In the event the baby — a boy named Uvedale after the 17th-century head of the Corbett family — was born on 15 November, and only eight days later Joseph was off to visit St. Laurence's at Church Stretton, where he praised the 'elegant' parsonage house that Rector Mainwaring had erected 'at very considerable expense'. Stretton was followed shortly by Woolstaston and Longden, also nearby. He managed to fit in another thirteen fairly local parishes before the end of the year, even riding out to Habberley on Christmas Eve.

With great determination he began the new year of 1793 by going to Ratlinghope and Norbury on 1 January; altogether that month, in spite of wintry weather, he visited twenty churches, including nine in the three days ending 30 January! This was possible only because he stayed overnight in the western area of Pontesbury Deanery, reducing the riding time involved with single visits. Busy times followed in the next three months; several times he stayed away from home to reach a number of parishes in the same vicinity on one day, actually visiting six villages in the Stottesdon Deanery on 23 April. There followed, in May, the most hectic month of the whole exercise. He managed to call at no fewer than twenty-six churches, with a record seven on 15 May, again in the south-eastern reaches of the archdeaconry, and six in Clun Deanery in the west on 23 May.

After this burst of activity the summer of 1793 was much quieter. Only twelve churches were visited in the next three months. Joseph probably had a lot of recording to catch up on, he needed rest, and he must have recognised the need to spend more time with his young family. In July he conducted his first archidiaconal visitation — occasions when he, or every three years the bishop, met the clergy of a large area — on the 16th at Ludlow and two days later at Church Stretton. The bishop wrote to praise his 'charge' to the clergy, encouraging him to publish it. Katherine was moved to record that when Joseph read the bishop's letter aloud to his father, 'little Panton took his Papa by the hand, looked very attentively at him for some time, and at last the tears came into his eyes. I thought it was an uncommon instance of sense and feeling at his age'.

In September Joseph needed to go to London to deal with some property affairs of his father. Recognising the need to concentrate in his church visits on Burford Deanery, where he had not set foot before going to Witton in July, he determined to go to as many parishes as possible at the start of his journey to the capital. His temporary headquarters were at The Nash where his wife joined him for part of the time. No fewer than eighteen churches received the archdeacon in six days between 7 and 12 September, with Burford itself on the last day. After his return, only two expeditions were made in the last three months of the year, but in the space of three days he appeared at eleven churches in four different deaneries. Altogether in 1793 he had visited 129 churches!

With only twenty-two churches still to visit in the new year of 1794, he limited himself to one busy day in each of the first two months. At this time of year he found the roads around Bewdley were very bad. His task was virtually completed by a marathon tour of eight villages in the Burford Deanery on 25 June when Katherine recorded in her journal that he was out from 5.00 in the morning till nearly 11.00 at night. His final goal was the little hamlet of Westhope at the southern end of Wenlock Edge on 7 July. Katherine rejoiced that he would have no more fatiguing journeys, although there was still much arranging of materials to be done. In well under two years he had achieved the remarkable feat of paying a visit to all 168 churches and chapelries in the archdeaconry. Occasional visits were made to individual churches in subsequent years to check on progress with repairs. This was particularly true of 1797 when Katherine recorded that he had 'had the satisfaction to find many repairs done in consequence of his former visitation, but much yet remains'. He was still making entries in 1838, the last year of his life.

Just as daunting in a different way was the task of collating, systematising and writing up his detailed reports in the way already explained. What is still more astonishing perhaps is that the six volumes of hand-written reports, one for each deanery, now in possession of Shropshire Archives, are partnered by six volumes of illustrations held by the Corbett family. These include miniature water-colour paintings of all the churches he visited, sometimes with illustrations of the parsonage house, too, and neat representations of the coats-of-arms of patrons and incumbents where appropriate. Although some of the illustrations have not been completed, it is a mystery how he found time for all this work, but as he will have visited the parishes alone he must have made the initial sketches. And we have Katherine's authority for concluding that the finished illustrations were also the work of her brother: 'He embellishes his work by taking views of the churches in different situations and of the parsonage houses'. It is clear from these beautiful volumes that he had inherited some of his father's artistic talent.

What is indisputable is that the diocese of Hereford had found an energetic, gifted and dedicated archdeacon to succeed his aged predecessor. And all who are interested in the local history of the area are hugely in his debt for an invaluable source of information.

9   LIFE AT LONGNOR

AT THE CLOSE OF THE 18TH CENTURY

The start of Joseph's marathon visitation of the parishes of his archdeaconry was delayed by the expected arrival of his wife Matty's first baby; before the visitation was completed another child had been born to the young mother. Uvedale, whose unusual Christian name had been the maiden name of the wife of Sir Richard Corbett in the 17th century, was born in November 1792. His brother, named Joseph, after his father and grandfather, was born on 7 February 1794. At this time Joseph's children by his first wife, Panton, Josepha and Jane, were respectively eight, seven and just six years old, still in the care of their aunts, Katherine and Ann. With five young children and four adults in the home, the accommodation at the Bank House in Longnor was in need of extension. Only a week after little Joseph's birth, Katherine was recording that her brother 'had been and still is making convenient alterations and improvements about this house and premises'.

The family, however, continued to grow rapidly, with Matty, only twenty-one when her second child was born, regularly conceiving three months or even less after giving birth. Her first daughter, baptised with the name Helen at only two days old, was born on 18 February 1795. Less than a year later another son, christened Robert, entered the world on 9 January 1796. Before that year was out Matty gave birth yet again, this time on 23 December, to a baby boy who was baptised on Christmas Day by his father and given the name Waties, the maiden name of the wife of Sir Edward Corbett, the first baronet in the mid-17th century. In this case, extensions to the house preceded the new arrival, for Katherine noted that her brother had carried out enlargements 'not with a view to show or entertaining company, but merely making bedchambers and family conveniences for we have grown, like the statue of Alphonso the Good in the Castle of Otranto, too large for our habitation'.[1]

The size of the establishment had grown not only through the births of children — and as the new year of 1797 began their number stood at eight, with the oldest, Panton, still only eleven years old — but in consequence of the return to his former home of Mr. Plymley senior. Back in 1786 he had insisted on moving to the Lyth after his second marriage to Hannah Russell, a near neighbour, and before the birth of his second granddaughter Jane. But the new Mrs. Plymley fell seriously ill in 1793, causing Katherine and Ann to divide their time between caring for their father and his sick wife at the Lyth and educating their brother's children by his first wife at Longnor. Mrs. Plymley senior suffered great abdominal pain and at the same time became confused, finally losing the power of speech. She died at the end of June 1793. The elderly widower came to stay at the family home for a time before returning to the Lyth with Ann, who periodically exchanged roles with her sister. At the end of 1793 old Mr. Plymley's move to Bank House became permanent, the best of the furniture at the Lyth brought to Longnor and the remainder sent for auction.

A crowded house was far from ideal for Joseph, who had to use it as his office for carrying out the administrative aspects of his many responsibilities and for the daily demands of an increasing correspondence. The naming of two of his sons, Uvedale and Waties, after past members of the Corbett family, suggests he was upheld by the prospect of inheriting the Corbett estates and Longnor Hall. Under the will of Sir Richard Corbett (who had died as long ago as 1774) he was now the heir since none of his mother's brothers had had male offspring. Of Joseph's three maternal uncles, Richard had died; John, in his seventies, had only a daughter; and Robert, who had inherited the estates and taken the name Corbett, was widowed and had no children. But Robert re-married in 1792 and the next summer, according to Katherine, his new wife Anne, in her early forties, 'is, or fancies herself, with child'. The new prospect 'makes it more difficult for my brother to determine his plans ... Should she have a son, the will of Sir Richard Corbett ... by which he entailed his estates upon him in default of issue male of my uncles, who were all of them married and not likely to have children, will be defeated — and having then no reversionary interest in Longnor it will become imprudent in him to sink additional sums upon his house there, which is only leasehold, and which is still too small for his growing family. Whatever money he can lay out upon houses it will clearly be more advantageous for him to employ in building upon property that will descend to his children'.

For these reasons the condition of Mrs. Corbett was of great concern to Joseph's family. It aroused wider interest, too, for wagers were laid on whether the lady would have a child — with the odds increasingly against it! The Corbetts went to Bath for the summer of 1793, but Mr. Corbett hinted to his brother and Katherine that he thought his wife was mistaken. Great uncertainty continued in the Longnor family, however, although Katherine put her trust in God: 'We are fully persuaded that whatever happens is under the direction of Providence and is for the best. We have been accustomed to extend our views beyond this world, my brother says, and I am confident unaffectedly that he has much more reason to be thankful for what he enjoys than to repine at what such an event may deprive him or his family of'. In October uncle John reported over dinner at Bank House that his brother's latest communication informed him that all hope of an increase in his family was at an end. Katherine's response was: 'As we had seen the prospect of his having a family without depression, we received this account I can truly say, without any undue elevation — yet we may allowably rejoice in the present circumstances as it enables my brother to look forward with more pleasure to the future provision for his growing family'.

From the pages of Katherine's diaries emerge fascinating vignettes of family life. She was always proud to write of her brother's good and active life and of the children of his first marriage in whose upbringing she and her sister Ann had played a leading part. The children had displayed their early social maturity when one day in May 1793, with their father away on a parish visit and Katherine at The Lyth, Gustavus Vasa, or as he is now better known Equiano Olaudah, on a tour to publicise his memoirs, called at the house to see Joseph whom he had met in London. When he was invited to dinner, 'the little people, though they had never been accustomed to blacks, immediately went to him offering their hands and behaved in their pretty, friendly way'. He gave Panton a pamphlet against the use of sugar. When Ann assured him that they had long left off its use and strongly supported Abolition, he presented Panton with a signed copy of his *Memoirs* telling of his life as a slave. Asked if they would like to go to Africa with him, Panton and Josepha replied that they would if their Papa gave his approval. When Joseph returned later he sent letters to Bridgnorth encouraging his acquaintances there to buy copies of Equiano's book, although he had reservations about the publicity tour.

Life at Bank House, where the family gained another member on the birth of Matilda in August 1798, bringing the total to nine children and five adults (apart from nursemaids and any live-in servants), could have become chaotic had it not been for a regular routine. The youngest children must have been largely confined to the nursery supervised by Joseph's wife,

Matty. After the rest of the family had breakfasted there would have been morning prayers, led by Joseph when he was at home. Dinner was the main meal eaten in the late afternoon, with supper at 9.00 pm. This routine was, of course, broken by outings and holidays. One day in May 1794 the Plymley family set off for Coalbrookdale, visiting the iron bridge, the Rotunda on Lincoln Hill which afforded 'a night view of the furnace fires in the Dale and towards Broseley and Madeley', and the works at Coalbrookdale 'of which I am too ignorant to speak', confessed Katherine. In complete contrast, on their return journey they looked over Lord Berwick's magnificent house at Attingham. On another occasion there was an outing to Hereford, stopping on the way at Leominster and Hampton Court where old Mr. Plymley had some property. While Joseph visited the bishop who was elderly and ailing, the family walked round Hereford, which Katherine found 'in general old and dull'. She was disappointed that there was no service at the cathedral as she wished the children to hear the choir. The next day the bishop received them all. On the return journey they called at Ludlow Castle, and were received by Lady Clive at Oakley Park. Longer holidays included visits to Plas Gwyn on Anglesey, where Joseph had met his first wife, and in 1796 a six-week stay in London for Joseph (with much business to attend to), his wife, Panton and Katherine.

Joseph had strong views when it came to the children's education. He was firmly convinced that public schools tended to corrupt the young. Writing to Wilberforce in 1800 he counselled deliberation on the issue of national education for poor children. 'The discipline of a public school weakens, or suspends or destroys all the best feelings of the mind'. He conceded that it might be different for those in humbler conditions, but he objected to large school societies of boys because of the corruption of morals. As his own children were therefore to be taught at home, initially by Joseph's sisters, he was determined that they should receive a broad education. Panton was first introduced to Latin and Greek by his father, whom Katherine adjudged 'an excellent master'. She herself was able to teach the older children French until M. Pelletier, an émigré priest, began to come twice a week. The older Mr. Plymley would have loved opening their minds to the wonders of nature and imparting some of his artistic skills. Their general knowledge and grasp of current affairs would have been daily enhanced by family conversation and the company of gifted visitors invited by their father. In addition, as they grew older, the boys in particular sometimes accompanied their father on visits. When Panton was thirteen the two of them went to Plas Gwyn, and then on to Yoxall Lodge in Staffordshire, home of Joseph's fellow abolitionist

Thomas Gisborne. The next year father and son stayed with Lord Muncaster in the Lake District and visited Clarkson and his wife in their new home on Ullswater. On their way back they walked across the sands of Morecambe Bay at low tide, stayed with the Rathbones — 'very superior people' — near Liverpool, and 'sailed for about a dozen miles on the Mersey to join the canal that joined it to Chester'. By his fifteenth birthday Panton was considered ready by his father to be entered at Pembroke College, Oxford — Joseph's old college — although he did not take up residence at once. From Oxford they went on to London to visit the Houses of Parliament, the Board of Agriculture (that Joseph had been corresponding with) and several exhibitions, and to dine together with the Wilberforces.

Panton, accompanied by his father and Matty, went up to Oxford at the start of term in October 1800. He was entered at Pembroke as a 'gentleman commoner', which allowed him access to the society of the Senior Common Room for, although Joseph considered the college better regulated than in his own day, he was still concerned to protect young Panton from the worst excesses of student life. While his son was left to make his own way in what for one who had never attended school must have been the frighteningly new world of the university, Joseph immersed himself in the familiar but demanding responsibilities that he had accumulated in the previous few years.

Joseph's first responsibility was to his family, primarily for the care and upbringing of his nine children. In addition, his wife, sisters and ageing father looked to him as the head of the household. Although the prospect of inheriting the Corbett estates lay before him, he had decided to purchase landed property at Woodbatch near Bishop's Castle a few years earlier, land on which trials for lead ore at Sadler's Wood were underway within months. The improvement of this estate necessitated frequent journeys. He had also to give substantial amounts of time to his father's financial affairs which involved sometimes lengthy visits to London — in February 1796 he had written to say he would be there till summer if he waited for the business to be finished. He felt obliged to assist his uncle, John Flint, who had been so supportive at the height of the anti-slave trade campaign, but whose neglect of his wife's family's affairs had embroiled him in an interminable case in the Court of Chancery. Another claimant he met at the court told him he had been waiting eighteen months for an interview with the

Attorney General! An unexpected, and unwelcome, call for support came from his uncle Robert at Longnor Hall who, although approaching seventy years of age, put himself forward in 1795 as a candidate in a by-election in Montgomeryshire. Joseph accompanied him to (Welsh)Pool where he made two speeches on his behalf. Suddenly Mr. Corbett got cold feet and withdrew from the contest, only to enter again and then withdraw a second time. Joseph was relieved that his uncle had not 'taken in others' even if he had been 'taken in' himself.

Even after he had completed his visitation of all the parishes in his archdeaconry, and the task of writing up his copious notes and making his miniature illustrations of each church, Joseph's ecclesiastical responsibilities remained demanding. Katherine wrote in 1794: 'He reads prayers and preaches at two churches every Sunday and is very attentive to the duties of his profession'. In 1799 he was invited by Mr. Baldwin, who had another living in Gloucestershire, to purchase the advowson of the parish of Coreley in Burford Deanery. Joseph could not afford this, but his uncle Robert bought it for him. Though he preached there occasionally, he would have had to appoint and pay a curate to take the regular services. However, the additional income, helping to offset the cost of the archdeaconry, would have been welcome. He was soon in demand as a guest preacher on special occasions. When he gave the address at the Annual Anniversary service on behalf of the Shrewsbury Infirmary in 1794, Katherine was so impressed that she doubled her intended donation. Matty and Katherine accompanied him the next year to the Three Choirs' Festival at Hereford where his sermon to the Charity Meeting led her to double her gift again! In 1796, on the annual Fast Day for the war with France (which had begun in 1793), she applauded his excellent address on the text: 'Except ye repent ye shall all likewise perish', when perhaps his anti-war stance was apparent. On his way back from Lord Muncaster's in 1797 he visited the son of his old schoolmaster at Chester and was prevailed on by his widow to preach in the evening, having had to snatch a few minutes here and there during the day to make his preparations. Katherine later hailed his sermon at the Infirmary Anniversary as 'a model of true pulpit eloquence', listened to with rapt attention for thirty-five minutes as he expounded the injunction in Acts 20:35, 'Ye ought to support the weak ... it is more blessed to give than to receive'. The £158-19-3 collected at the door at the end of the service was the largest ever known.

'The common business of the archdeaconry when duly performed requires considerable attention', Katherine observed, especially as Joseph was such an able and active person. When it was one of Joseph's years to conduct the visitation, he called all local clergy to one of two meetings held each July at Ludlow and Church Stretton, at which his 'charges' to the clergy were so admired that he was pressed to publish them. The bishop wrote of his 1796 address: 'I am full of admiration at your excellent charge, which ought to be read in every parish of the kingdom. It does lasting honour to your administration'. His initial visit to each parish on his appointment was followed by repeat visits where there were pressing problems or where he wanted to check on the progress of repairs. And always there was correspondence over vacancies, buildings or pastoral issues. Joseph was confronted by an unsavoury problem when most of the clergy in Shrewsbury and the neighbourhood, as well as several gentlemen, received anonymous letters warning them to be on their guard against two clergymen, Mr. Roche and Mr. Adams, 'whom the letters accused in the grossest terms of an unnatural crime in several instances'. Joseph himself received such a letter, which also accused his sister of stealing a cloak. A watch on the Post Office in Shrewsbury led to the identification of the Rev. George Scott as the culprit. The clergy named brought an action for damages against Scott in the Court of King's Bench. Joseph went to London to meet counsel before the case was heard at Shrewsbury. Damages were awarded to the two clerics, whilst Scott left the county to live near London and was struck off the list of magistrates. Joseph and Mr. Corbett, out of sympathy for Scott's wife and family dropped their action against Scott — they had filed criminal informations against him in the Court of King's Bench — on condition that he published a confession in the press and paid £100 to the Shrewsbury Infirmary. Some time later Bishop Butler wished to compensate Joseph for all the expense he incurred as archdeacon by presenting him to the living of Holgate, but Joseph declined. The bishop expressed his delight at his comment that he did not wish to take a position if a more needy candidate was available.

Another unwelcome task had landed on the archdeacon's desk when the bishop, in response to the king's request to all bishops to assist refugee French clergy, asked him to send circulars throughout the archdeaconry and to receive subscriptions. Three months later he was able to send off £360. His friend, the Roman Catholic Edward Smythe, welcomed a group who had fled from a college at Nancy. Joseph was also still working hard as treasurer of the Clergy Widows' and Orphans' Fund which flourished under his care with additional subscribers and benefactions under the wills of many clergy. Joseph was shocked to find, in the service of a wealthy rector, a curate with a wife and seven children — and a drink problem! — paid only £30 per annum. Although as archdeacon Joseph gave his full support to the clergy and knew them personally, he was not blind to their faults. He confided to Katherine in 1794: 'The behaviour of the clergy was not, in general, such as would procure them respect. The people must observe that instead of considering what good they could do in their parishes, their attention was engaged by the common pleasures of life, and their object seemed to be to enjoy the revenues of the church as little encumbered with its duties as possible'.

This damning verdict was occasioned by Joseph's awareness of the growing prejudice against the clergy as the economic privations following the outbreak of war with France in 1793 deepened the gulf between the better-off and the poor. It was also influenced by his own increasing nervous exhaustion as he responded to more and more requests for assistance and assumed ever more responsibilities in the community. His journeys on horseback around the archdeaconry had made him painfully aware of the bad state of the roads in the county; he recognised, too, their importance for economic development. As early as 1793 Katherine was writing: 'For a year past he has been employed in improving the turnpike roads about us, and in some private roads he has made considerable alterations and improvements, as well as about his own house and grounds'. Only a year later she could report: 'He has taken the care of the turnpike road for many miles and by his exertions great improvements have been made not only in repairing but widening, and turning the course of some streams. The roads in this village have been greatly mended, causeways have been raised for foot passengers and footpaths through many fields stopped'. On the family visit to Hereford in 1795 they found the road between Ludlow and Leominster so bad that their carriage could go at only walking pace. The next month he was at Ludlow for meetings called to plan improvements to the turnpike road. Katherine worried about how much he was taking on but mused: 'It is the active and busy that alone can find time to be useful'. He had already become involved in the group at Ludlow discussing a proposed canal to come by Bishop's Castle.

At that same time, as a Director of the Shrewsbury Infirmary for several years, his presence was needed at Saturday meetings; it was he who drew up their annual report. When Wilberforce inquired about the degree of hardship in the county, he wrote to tell him that at the Infirmary the previous week he had invited subscriptions of five shillings each to a charity to provide clothing or a conveyance home for the convalescent poor, knowing that if he had asked more the scheme would probably have failed. As the preacher invited to the Infirmary's anniversary in 1794 and 1800 he was, as already noted, both eloquent and able to generate record-breaking collections.

Already he was devoting more and more hours to drawing up a new report on Shropshire's agriculture (see next chapter). His clergy friend, Archibald Alison, forecast that 'by the time he is fifty he will have all the burdens of the county on his hands'.

That prophecy seemed likely to be fulfilled even earlier when, at the age of only thirty-seven, Joseph began to take a very active part in the plan for a lunatic asylum, drawing up the necessary papers. And two years later he agreed to become one of the acting magistrates for the Condover hundred (a sub-division of the shire) as Sir Thomas Edwards had died and Mr. Corbett was aged seventy-one. Soon he was carrying the whole burden for the hundred, answering innumerable inquiries about the incidence of the new taxes and taking his turn as a visiting magistrate at Shrewsbury Gaol (see Chapter 13). It was inevitable that he should be invited to join a committee when it became clear that abuses that had crept into Shrewsbury School demanded reform. He had already, when in London, met with a gentleman from St. John's College, Cambridge, which had the right to make appointments to Shrewsbury School. Now he was to the fore as a Trustee when the masters were asked to resign. Dr. Samuel Butler became First Master, and an old friend of Joseph's from Pembroke College days, Mr. Adams, was appointed Second Master but withdrew before taking up the post. Unfortunately the problems were not at an end, for the man who took his place was for years at loggerheads with the First Master. The following years, however, were to prove that they had made a good choice as headmaster because under Dr. Butler's leadership over the next thirty-eight years the school became renowned for its classical learning and the number of scholars rose from 20 to 295. The classical bias, however, did not suit the school's most famous scholar, for Charles Darwin later wrote: 'Nothing could have been worse for the development of my mind than Dr. Butler's school'.[2]

Joseph's increasing responsibilities were assumed in years when nationally and locally the strains of war were adding to economic hardship, social unrest and demands for political reform. The war with France had begun in February 1793, a war in which, Katherine noted, when commenting on a gloomy letter Granville Sharp had sent to Joseph, 'I believe we have nothing to gain and much possibly to lose'. War caused the further disruption of trade, already in decline as the long economic boom came to an end, leading to the suspension of payments by several commercial houses and country banks. The sudden recall of Parliament in the previous December and the call up of militia had led to rumours of plots to subvert the constitution, fears already aroused by the impact of Tom Paine's *Rights of Man*, of which within weeks nearly 200,000 copies were in circulation. The response of loyalists was to form Associations in large and small towns to declare their allegiance to the crown, to aid the government in the suppression of seditious writings, and even to report dangerous opinions expressed in private conversation. This threat to a free press prompted the formation of the Friends of the Liberty of the Press, with crowds attending the meeting at the Crown and Anchor Tavern in the capital. This in turn provoked 'Church and King' mobs to collect in the streets, denouncing all friends of Reform and well-wishers to the success of the French Revolution. Katherine's view, no doubt reflecting Joseph's too, was that 'every sentiment favourable to liberty and the general good is labelled seditious'. But she lamented the way the revolution in France was turning 'the freedom we hoped they had acquired, and so honourably, so peacefully acquired in the first instance, into licentiousness'. She was shocked by the execution of Louis XVI and the beginning of the Reign of Terror, yet still clung to the hope that 'the darkest night is sometimes succeeded by the brightest day', going on to quote the words of Jesus: 'Ye shall know the truth and the truth shall make you free'. She feared, however, 'the time is yet at some distance when men shall be sufficiently virtuous and enlightened for the enjoyment of true national liberty'.

The heated atmosphere in the country, with some demonstrating for reform and others parading their loyalty to the king and the constitution, penetrated even as far as the village of Longnor. A loyalist publication claiming that if all the land were divided up it would give only a paltry one and a half acres to each, was posted up at Longnor Forge. In response a local champion of reform echoed the popular sentiment, 'Let the French come — then we cannot be worse and may be better!' Katherine recorded that some local gentlemen — 'violent aristocrats' she called them — 'had the folly to make a bustle about this', but her brother's wisdom stopped it going further. Nonetheless, 'the present is a very disagreeable time for those who live in the neighbourhood', especially if they were related to the aristocratic party.[3] Loyalist diehards maintained that silence was not enough; gentlemen were expected to express their support for the government. Accusations were made against her father, brother and family and other good and wise men, not against their character but against their political opinions that were regarded as disloyal to the landed classes. Even Katherine and Ann were subjected to the same criticism but they held firm. She said she was proud to stand with principled men who believed in the need for reform to remedy abuses. Divisions appeared among men of property in Shrewsbury: their friend Mr. Adams' address was answered by Mr. Blakeway's jibe: 'I perceive, Sir, in your speech the cloven hoof of reform'. She stated Joseph's position clearly: 'My brother, as a good and wise man, would rejoice in any constitutional measures that tended to avoid anarchy and confusion, but he is among the number of those who apprehend no danger unless it springs from the Proclamation of last summer [against seditious writings] and from the subsequent Associations'. As ever, in a time of polarised attitudes, the position of the moderate was extremely uncomfortable.

French military successes on the continent tightened the screw still further on international commerce: a letter from Mr. Panton in Leghorn reported sixty ships in the port awaiting a convoy escort. Mr. Houlbrooke, who had visited Liverpool, told of record numbers leaving to settle in America. In his view, 'the affairs of this nation wear a serious, if not a dismal, countenance'. Even large commercial houses figured among the bankruptcies, many iron forges stopped production, and there was the threat of factory closures, throwing thousands out of work. 'Bankruptcies continue every day to be more alarming', Katherine recorded in the summer of 1793, 'even in Shrewsbury, a town of no great trade, they have been numerous'. The previous week, to general astonishment, Mr. Blakeway had failed with debts of £63,000. Complaints about the stagnation of trade and the shortage of credit were heard on every side. In September of that year Joseph noticed a marked change of mood in London: everywhere he saw written on houses 'NO WAR' and 'POOR POLAND' (Poland was threatened with dismember-ment by Russia, Prussia and Austria). In the coffee houses there were copies of new opposition newspapers denouncing the war. Joseph himself was opposed to the war: 'I disliked the war myself politically because I thought peace would much more certainly ensure the advantages its advocates meant to obtain by it; for with respect to foreign enemies I deemed a defensive posture the strongest we could stand in; and if discontent was apprehended at home, you lost the power of repelling it by sending your troops abroad and increased the cause of discontent by the additional taxes necessary to defray so expensive a mission'. He regarded self-defence as the only ground for war, refusing to contribute when a subscription was raised for what it described as the just and necessary war. By the end of 1793 there was increasing talk of the risk of invasion. Katherine admitted that she had never had 'the smallest apprehension of invasion', but Clarkson thought it likely and two other respected friends, Reynolds and Houlbrooke, were anxious.

Across the Channel the execution of the Girondist leaders — Brissot had been called 'the Clarkson of France' — was for the Plymleys dreadful news. 'No public event has ever shocked me so much', Katherine wrote. 'I have rejoiced at the overthrow of despotism in France. I lament for human nature and learn to dread its weakness and the triumph of a wicked and desperate faction over liberty'. The Plymleys were upheld through these dark days by their trust in God. It was Katherine who expressed this in writing: 'Amidst the most cloudy scene there is always one bright spot on which the eye may rest. The belief in an over-ruling Providence is admirably calculated to dispel the gloom. He who makes the wrath of man to praise him, and by ways to us unsearchable bringeth good out of evil can, from the ruins of despotism and anarchy cause order to arise, and to the darkness of this political night may succeed a brighter day than the world has yet witnessed'. Quoting from Paul's Letter to the Romans she declared that 'all things will work together for good to those who believe'.

As the new year of 1794 opened, however, the situation seemed darker than ever. News came of the Allied evacuation of Toulon under the barrage directed by a young artillery officer named Napoleon Bonaparte, Mr. Panton wrote expressing fear of a French invasion of Italy, and the Reign of Terror in France gained momentum. Mr. Alison sent newspaper cuttings of riots in Edinburgh after the authorities closed down the so-called 'National Convention' where calls had been made for citizens to divide into sections and elect committees on French lines. The Plymleys avidly scanned the papers for the latest developments, noting the sentence of transportation to Botany Bay for two leading Scottish radicals and lamenting the setback to moderate reform that they favoured to ease hardship and reduce unrest. The government crackdown continued with the suspension of the Act of Habeas Corpus and the imprisonment in the Tower of several radicals on charges of High Treason. Joseph disapproved of those government supporters who 'guard the people against the doctrines of Paine and those who have written on his side'. The consequence was that, unable to read the writings of the radicals for themselves, the populace paid heed to rumour and thereby gained a partial but dangerous grasp of these ideas. Instead of reforms proceeding in Parliament, he believed that the people would be tempted to seize power for themselves. He would have agreed with Clarkson who wrote to express his shock that membership of moderate organisations like the Society for Constitutional Information and the Society of the Friends of the People should be considered treasonable; both men would have seen as a victory for democracy the acquittal at the end of the year of Thomas Hardy and Horne

Tooke, London radical leaders, who were alleged to have been involved in a revolutionary plot.

In a letter to Sir Richard Hill in January 1795, when the news from the war-front was that the French had over-run Holland, Joseph made clear his personal attitude to the war, which he opposed because it was not 'just and necessary'; a position of defence, he thought, was much to be preferred. He also wrote to Wilberforce praising his opposition to the war, though this had strained his personal friendship with the Prime Minister. Wilberforce replied; 'I believe your expressions of approbation came from the heart and there-fore they are truly valuable'.[4] Katherine's general view in March 1795 was that 'all the public war is disastrous', with French ships even bombarding the little colony in Sierra Leone, destroying several buildings at a cost of £40,000; the only silver lining was that Liverpool's slave merchants were suffering even more. On a visit to the capital Joseph heard how the king on his way to prorogue Parliament had been greeted with hisses and cries of 'Give us bread! No war! No Pitt!', and he himself saw 30,000 assemble at St. George's Fields and overheard one demonstrator remark, 'The soldiers all think as we do'. Britain could do little in 1796 when Napoleon, now an army commander, in a brilliant campaign over-ran north Italy and forced Austria to make peace. There was a renewed threat of invasion when Napoleon assem-bled an army on the other side of the Channel, before changing his mind and leading an expedition to Egypt. Unfortunately Katherine was having one of her periodic breaks from writing her journal when Nelson destroyed the French fleet at the Battle of the Nile on 1 August 1798. The century ended with Austria on the eve of making peace again with Napoleon, who had returned to France and in a *coup d'état* become First Consul.

While the war had continued on the continent, the government at home clamped down on all movements for reform. Joseph was in the Commons gallery in November 1795 to listen to the debate on the Treasonable and Seditious Practices and the Seditious Meetings and Assemblies Bills, Pitt's 'gagging bills', limiting meetings to no more than fifty people. Joseph and Katherine thought they went too far in suppressing freedom of speech and would promote rather than prevent revolution. 'The only method to repress discontent is surely to reform real defects and to suppress real grievances'. In general, of course, Joseph was extremely busy with his responsibilities as archdeacon and his active involvement in many local issues, not to mention his growing family. But as the disruption of trade and the cost of war led to increasing privation in the country, he could not but be concerned at the suffering in his own village and district. According to his sister, 'he never sees a poor person without wishing at least to befriend him ... and is desirous to contribute to the comfort of the poor whenever he has the power'. The immediate problem was the sharp increase in the price of necessities. Katherine was told by her hairdresser in Shrewsbury in 1795 that his children would have died the previous year but for potatoes, as they could not afford meat, butter and even bread at times. Even the better-off were under pressure with corn at ten shillings a bushel and taxes rising, although some generously sold on corn and coal to the needy at reduced prices.

Katherine was outraged by her brother's information that price rises were partly the result of rich farmers storing grain. She exploded in the privacy of her journal: 'Taken in a body, with no doubt many exceptions, they are unfeeling, overbearing and purse proud'.[5] As corn prices rose still higher, reaching eighteen or nineteen shillings a bushel even in Shropshire where, 'as an excellent corn county we suffered probably less than many others', there was widespread rioting. Wolverhampton ran out of bread for four days; in other places there was rationing. It was in that same year of 1795 that the magistrates at Speenhamland in Berkshire inaugurated the 'Speenhamland System' by which poor relief was tied to the price of grain and which was widely adopted especially in the southern counties. Fortunately a good harvest brought grain prices down sharply; it also revealed that farmers had indeed been storing grain with the intention of selling at a higher price. The vicar's wife at Worthen in Shropshire managed to persuade a body of five hundred miners to disperse by promising that she would urge farmers to sell at 10/6d per bushel and that her husband would meet a deputation — though she needed to treat some to a pint of beer each to get the last ones to go home! Her husband, the vicar, also met the farmers who said they were down to the last ten bushels in the district (later another 1,000 were discovered!); he bought some at 21/- (shillings) to sell on at 10/6d per bushel. Katherine noted that Joseph preached an excellent sermon at Leebotwood at harvest time 'with a few extempore words directed at the farmers present'. It was not only grain that was dear: butter, cheese and meat were beyond the means of poor labourers who depended on the potato. Some like Mr. Corbett tried mixing barley with wheat, but that pushed up the price of barley; the Plymleys were mixing one-third potatoes with two-thirds wheat, which made 'uncommonly good bread', whiter than Mr. Corbett's and preferred by the servants to ordinary bread. Later Joseph commended a mixture of three pounds of wheat with two pounds of potatoes with their skins on which produced a loaf of over 5 lbs. both nourishing and enjoyed by themselves as much as the servants. The problem, of course, was that the price of potatoes went up from 2/- a bushel to as high as 4/-.

Joseph, who had just been invited by Sir John Sinclair, chairman of the newly formed Board of Agriculture, to compile a report on Agriculture in Shropshire (see next chapter), attended a meeting of experts and interested parties in London where seventy different types of loaves were on display. He wrote to Wilberforce to keep him informed on the state of affairs in the county. But he was also seeking ways of giving immediate relief to the local poor. He drew up a scheme for 'broth shops' — we would call them soup kitchens – in the larger centres of population throughout the county. He did not intend this scheme to be charity: there would be small payments, small enough, he hoped, for poor housekeepers to be attracted to purchase. But Joseph believed that the sullen mood in the country had deeper causes than the current inflation. In a letter of November 1795 to Wilberforce he wrote: 'The bulk of the people have their minds alienated from the present state of things, not through any political reasons but from the circumstance of that ... interchange of good will and benefit that existed between the different classes being in a great degree destroyed and by the largest class of persons now feeling the pressure of distress, unsoothed by those feelings of attach-ment they formerly entertained for their superiors'.[6] He regarded the loyal Associations as a dangerous restraint on society. The insults to the king had made persons of property wish to overawe the poor who, in turn, felt they could not be worse off and therefore could support any external or internal enemy of the constitution. The poor were kept quiet by fear and sullen hope-lessness, though colliers and miners were encouraged by their 'combina-tions' (unions) to seek redress; the soldiers shared this dissatisfaction but were restrained by fear of the consequences if they rebelled — which the sailors were to do in the mutinies at Spithead and the Nore in 1797.

Widespread poverty was a feature of the closing years of the century. Weekly collections for the poor were made in Birmingham. Katherine commented on 'the hardships sustained by the poor even in this village'. Her brother regarded his own labourers 'as his peculiar care', giving away rice and broth thickened with vegetables. But the system of poor relief was not working properly. In 1799 six people were sent to Shrewsbury gaol for stealing provisions; the next year that figure had risen to sixty-three. But when Joseph became a magistrate in 1798 (see Chapter 13) he gained the power to regulate help to the poor. 'He has been very liberal in his orders to parishes for poor relief', Katherine observed approvingly. Yet the compassion he felt, and urged, as a pastor, and the more generous response to the needs of the poor that this attitude demanded, were not shared by all his fellow magistrates. Joseph, as we shall see, had a very high conception of what was required of him as a landed gentleman, and he certainly influenced others that he was close to, but there remained many who were more concerned at the effect higher poor rates had on their own finances, at the maintenance of their own standards of living, and at the long-term interests of their families. As a result, Joseph, with his liberal ideals and genuine Christian concern to help those in greatest need, was often at odds with the outlook of the propertied classes.

It was not just the poor who were under pressure. Higher prices, rising poor rates and new taxes meant that those on middling incomes were increasingly feeling the pinch. Joseph was himself forced to consider where he could make economies. 'Now I am living upon the income of a landed estate, with eight children to educate, and which income is barely equal to the demands upon it', he confided to Wilberforce in 1797. This was the year in which the sharp fall in the value of government stocks, on account of the war, led the Bank of England to suspend payments. The doubling or even trebling of assessed taxes was under consideration. Joseph went on, 'I have no luxuries to lop off. I cannot go lower in my scale of living here without giving up that decency of appearance my situation requires, and on which my usefulness may in some measure depend'. How then, he inquired rhetorically, was he to raise £100 or any large sum for the extra tax. Some possibilities were rejected: 'I may withdraw my subscription from all public charities, and withhold my assistance from private distress, but this would be a vile way of providing for the tax. I may make a sinecure of my Archdeacon's office, the proper execution of which costs me much more than the income, but this is also highly objectionable. I keep more horses than I want because some of them are old and would be ill-treated if sold. I must not be cruel though taxes are high'. What then was the answer? 'Now comes the grand temptation, I may desert my post in the country and live in a town and then I keep my situation in life'. He thought it wrong for Parliament to hold out a temptation that would lead to a deserted countryside, for already some had taken this option to save money on carriages, horses and servants. Not Joseph Plymley, however. 'I will not at present yield to any of these temptations'. What he did do was to cancel his London paper and cut down on visitors. 'Though my house is open to passing friends or persons coming upon business, I have never kept the general miscellaneous visiting of the country, but I will lessen the neighbourly intercourse of that kind I did keep up'. He favoured taxes on the activities of those who wanted to maintain their place in society — duties on opera and theatre tickets, higher-priced licences for London coffee-houses, taxes on cards and dice. 'You would thus get either morals or revenue or a mixture of both'. The alternative, he suggested, was a tax on all property to avoid evasion.[7]

Pitt's first move, however, in 1798 was to treble assessed taxes, those levied on windows, houses, servants, carriages and horses. The calculation of the new tax, which was graduated so that the better-off had to pay more, meant that the state had to know more of an individual's circumstances. This, as much as the extra payment, made the tax very unpopular. Joseph, who had only just become a magistrate, was involved in many meetings at Pitchford (a meeting place for the local justices) to settle the taxes because the business for the Condover hundred fell almost wholly upon him. Katherine was concerned at the number asking him to calculate and explain their tax liability. He agreed in the same period to take the chair at meetings of those who had subscribed to the internal defence of the county four years earlier. He had been unwilling to subscribe then, but the rise of Napoleon now offered a different threat. Sir William Hill and Mr. Thomas Eyton offered to raise troops of yeomanry cavalry. Early the next year, 1799, as his knowledge of economic affairs and his standing in the county became known in government circles, he agreed to be one of the commissioners for setting the new land tax. The 'triple assessment' of taxes proved to be so subject to evasions, alternative explanations and exemptions that it raised far less than originally planned. Pitt therefore turned to a less complex and more reliable method of raising about £10,000,000 a year: he introduced income tax. It was applied on a sliding scale, so that those with incomes below £60 a year paid nothing; those with £60-£200 a year were taxed at 5% of their income; and all with incomes over £200 were taxed at 10%. The tax authorities were given the power to require an itemised schedule of income. Predictably, Joseph Plymley was named as one of the commissioners for the new tax. He saw the new powers as very inquisitorial and likely to provoke altercation; Lord Muncaster told him he thought the Bill 'abominable'. Many local farmers and freeholders came to see him seeking help in making out their income tax returns.

The continual increase in Joseph's responsibilities throughout much of the 1790s, though willingly accepted by a public-spirited man, was bound to put a strain upon his health. His sister noted as early as 1794 that his health was 'very indifferent, his nervous complaints have been worse than usual'. He was worst when casual visitors arrived or he found himself in mixed society. As he admitted in a letter to Archibald Alison, 'I feel myself daily contracting more and more against that idle commerce with the world, which under the names of society, company etc. is urged on by one simple vice or folly, vanity'. This sounds a harsh attitude, but one can understand why a very busy man resented time being spent on paying purely social calls or competing with others in the entertainment of guests. 'The pride of giving good or better dinners than this or that person seems to me', he went on, 'the principal motive on which that round of visiting is kept up, the *Dramatis Personae* whereof neither advance by practice or in theory any one given truth subservient to the purposes of their creation'. Joseph was irritated by pointless chatter or social pretence when he had pressing matters to deal with. Conversation with close friends he enjoyed, business meetings he thrived on, but the social round he did his best to escape. Yet on occasion he could shine in high society: when visiting Mrs. Montague, whose house in Portman Square he declared the most elegant he had ever seen, he had so impressed his hostess that she wrote to thank her friend Mrs. Alison for effecting an introduction to 'so agreeable and respectable a person as Mr. Plymley, from whose conversation, whenever he will indulge me with it, I shall derive great instruction and delight'.

His respectability meant that, for all the good that he did and his natural generosity, there was always a distance between him and those from humbler backgrounds. That his older sister shared the same attitude is apparent in her account of the tracts written by the Evangelical author, Hannah More. Joseph had been asked to contribute to the cost of these publications 'intended to amend the morals of the poor' and to counter the improper ballads and irreligious stories usually sold by hawkers and pedlars. Katherine's father and brother subscribed, but their hopes were not high because, she wrote, 'nothing appears more difficult than to write properly and acceptably to the uneducated part of the community'. She considered some tracts good but others should not have been printed. 'In our [earlier] attempts among our servants we have apparently been particularly unfortunate', and they were fearful of repeating the experiment for the servants had shown themselves disgusted by books written for their improvement. 'Yet surely we must try!' The best of the new simple tracts, which the children were delighted with, were casually left in the kitchen where John Hotchkiss, one of the servants, read them aloud. Katherine's own general reading was serious and weighty, though it is interesting that in one journal entry she quoted from Fielding's *Tom Jones.* Her brother was too busy to read a great deal, but if he did have some spare time he liked to pick up a book – in February 1795 he enjoyed Burns' *The Cottar's Saturday Night.* And if he struggled to find the way to reform the morals of the poor, he reached them with his kindness. He could always find time for a youngster in need, like the Shrewsbury grocer's son whom he helped to get a job on a merchantman, or to give a helping hand to his poor next-door neighbour whose cottage he improved and whose garden he extended (though the man did not develop it in the way that Joseph approved!).

Only rarely was Joseph too unwell to discharge his clerical duties. In March 1797 Katherine returned from a visit to Bath to find him with a swollen face and a fever which caused him to miss his church duties for four Sundays and, church apart, not to leave the house for seven weeks. The children's health naturally gave cause for concern from time to time. In 1794 there was an outbreak of smallpox in Longnor. Joseph had his youngest children inoculated, a precaution that he and Mr. Corbett at their own expense extended to all in the village who had not had the disease. An epidemic of scarlet fever two years later saw old Mr. Plymley, nearing eighty years of age, 'active as ever in benevolence and employed as usual in making and dispensing medicines for the poor'. The young members of the household were not affected on this occasion, but were not so fortunate in 1800 when they went down with whooping cough and then chickenpox. By then there was a new baby to care for, Matilda, born in 1798.

As the eighteenth century drew to its close another chapter opened in Joseph's life: his eldest son, Panton, (as mentioned earlier) went into residence at Oxford in his father's old college. Joseph stayed four days and saw Panton settled in his rooms at Pembroke, 'which are very good ones'. Joseph welcomed the establishment since his day of a Junior Common Room which was intended to contribute to the sobriety of the students, although Panton, at only fifteen, initially found it lively but not agreeable. This was hardly surprising since he had never left the family before, owing to his father's concern over the corrupting influence of public schools.

As the year, and the century, drew to an end, Joseph and Matty celebrated their tenth wedding anniversary, perhaps gazing proudly at their own four boys and two girls (the three eldest children had been born to Jane Josepha), and perhaps reflecting how in these years Joseph had risen to a position of authority in the Church and the county. Two days later, according to the custom at Longnor, the church bells rang out the old year and welcomed the new.

10 THE REPORT
ON SHROPSHIRE AGRICULTURE

Joseph had first corresponded with Sir John Sinclair, President of the newly-formed Board of Agriculture, in the autumn of 1793. With his first year as archdeacon completed, he was then in the midst of his survey of his 168 churches, a survey which was developing his views on countryside issues, the needs of the poor, the role of the Church in rural society, and changing agricultural practice. He had, of course, been brought up in a village surrounded by fields and the Corbett estates, which he knew he might one day inherit. It was the receipt of a copy of Joseph's first 'charge' as archdeacon that prompted Sinclair to invite his views on the subject of the tithe. Their exchanges continued until, in September 1795, Sinclair asked Joseph to undertake the preparation of a detailed report on agriculture in Shropshire, which was to be part of a county-by-county survey aimed at promoting scientific farming. An earlier report had been drafted by John Bishton, but he had not had the time to give an in-depth account. Joseph yielded to the entreaties of Sir John Sinclair and agreed to undertake the project. In the later stages he had the encouragement of Sinclair's successor, Lord Carrington.

In the two years since the correspondence with the Board had begun Joseph's own opinions had become more focused. His survey of the archdeaconry had given him a comprehensive knowledge of the southern half of the county and he had seen for himself the crippling effects on the poor of the inexorable rise in the price of necessities on account of the war. Only weeks after he accepted the invitation to write the report for Shropshire, he took advantage of a visit to London on his father's business affairs to talk with Wilberforce and Lord Muncaster about rising grain prices and how best the poor could be helped. No sooner was he back home than he was asking local gentlemen about the composition of their bread: Mr. Corbett at Longnor Hall was using one-third barley to two-thirds wheat, while the Plymley household was trying one-third potatoes with the wheat and was pleased with the quality. Back in the capital, Joseph went, at Sinclair's request, to the Board's display of seventy sorts of loaves available; he was able to contribute to the discussion from his knowledge of what was happening in Shropshire. In a subsequent letter to Wilberforce he calculated that if the population of the country was eight million, and on average one person consumed six bushels of wheat a year, six million quarters of wheat per annum were required. He compared the harvest of 1795 with that of 1794, using information from farmers, threshers, country gentlemen and clergymen to calculate the shortfall. By December his own household had increased the proportion of potatoes in a loaf to nearly half, and other people of property were setting a similar example. The effect, however, was a sharp rise in the price of potatoes — and that for barley followed. Privately Joseph was complaining, as Katherine noted angrily, that some farmers were hoarding supplies to push prices still higher. Early in 1796 he was elected, at Wilberforce's instigation, as an honorary member of the Board of Agriculture; and he felt able to suggest to Sinclair a clause to be added to the draft Bill on Enclosures. His sister wrote: 'The report for Shropshire now occupies him considerably'; late in the year it had become 'a very laborious undertaking as the Board proposes the queries which extend to every possible minutia'. By May 1797, when he was still busy on the Report, he learned that the withdrawal of government support meant that the risk of publishing would now lie with the authors. But Joseph believed that its value lay in the fact, as he told Wilberforce, that his archdeaconry was 'an epitome of the kingdom at large'.

Late in 1799 the Board of Agriculture solicited Joseph's views on 'the present scarcity' of grain and whether he considered it worse than in 1795. His long and reasoned reply was dated 26 February 1800. At the same time he was composing three lengthy letters to Wilberforce on the question of poor relief. His analyses were therefore based on detailed knowledge, wide consultation and deep reflection. He agreed that the situation was critical because grain prices, after falling back in 1797-98, were rising rapidly again (and would peak at 119/- per quarter in 1801, more than double the price four years earlier). He made several suggestions for immediate action to ease the position before the next harvest. They included local associations to regulate bread consumption, perhaps limiting it to one meal a day; a temporary cessation in formal dinners; a halt to hunting for the rest of the season to reduce the consumption of oats and to protect wheat crops in the fields; a temporary ban on hair powder made from grain (already applied in the army) and on distilleries; and the planting of early potatoes and white peas that could be ground into flour. Above all, he urged an increase in imports. To assist the destitute he proposed the extension of the soup kitchen system.

For the longer term he advocated an examination of current deficiencies in the production of and trade in grain and of the Corn Laws. He believed higher prices resulted not just from the effects of war but also from rising demand. Further, there had been a movement of capital from the land into commerce because of the attraction of higher returns, just when investment in agriculture and the rural infrastructure was required to feed the growing population. At a time when imports needed to be increasing, they had fallen because of the war on the continent where the presence and movement of large armies took labourers off the land, damaged crops and consumed more. At home, heavier taxes were discouraging the extension of cultivation and raising unemployment among labourers. He proposed the accelerated enclosure of waste land and action to provide steady returns for dealers to dissuade them from holding back supplies. These last ideas would feature prominently in the prolonged debate on the Corn Laws.

In the same month, February 1801, that he sent his reply to the Board, Joseph received the congratulations of Lord Carrington, Sinclair's successor as President, who wished to meet him to discuss any updating and the preparations for the publication of his Report. The next month, while visiting London with Panton to get his son's name on the books at Lincoln's Inn, he met with Carrington who pressed him to finalise his Report. In the event, his preface was dated 25 May 1801 at Longnor, and *A General View of the Agriculture of Shropshire* appeared in 1803.

In his preface Joseph justified the use of his time as a clergyman on the project, arguing that it was concerned with the living conditions of labourers. In earlier papers he had sought 'to gain the attention of [Board] members to subjects connected with the moral improvement, as well as the outward prosperity, of a large class of our fellow subjects, and whose welfare was closely linked with matters of an agricultural nature'. There were bishops on the Board, he pointed out, and his friend, the Rev. Thomas Gisborne, had contributed to the report on Staffordshire. His visits to the parishes of the archdeaconry had provided him with factual knowledge of the cultivation of the countryside. He included a list of all the 262 church buildings in the county.

His general introduction referred to a number of the county's valuable resources. On the climate he admitted that his general observations were short on accurate statistics. It was the same with measurements of altitude. His comparison of the heights of the Wrekin and the Longmynd is amusing: 'It is said that the Wrekin has been ascertained to rise no higher than the top of the glass door at the east end of the parsonage house in Woolstaston. How far this is strictly accurate I do not know'! He was on surer ground when it came to describing the mineral resources of the county as he was assisted by some of his scientific friends. William Reynolds furnished details of the strata beneath five collieries in the east where, according to his new acquaintance Dr. Robert Townson, 260,000 tons of coal were raised annually. Most of it was used in the iron works, but some was exported down the Severn to neighbouring counties. Some coal was mined in the Stottesdon and Clee Hill areas, and also close to Joseph's own home in Longnor. As regards lead, there had been mining since Roman times in the west of the county; production continued in the parish of Wentnor and at Snailbeach. Shropshire was plentifully supplied with lime in Lilleshall, the Wrekin, Wenlock Edge, the Clee Hills, and near Leebotwood. According to Mr. Reynolds there were iron ore deposits at Billingsley, but they were not worked. The county had good building stone at Grinshill and red sandstone near Bridgnorth. Dr. Townson had found a stratum of Bath and Portland stone at Orton Bank between strata of common limestone. Stone slates were produced at Bettws in the south-west, stone flags for floors at Soudley.

Friends at the Salop Infirmary provided valuable information on sites with water containing medicinal properties. The well of 'mineral water that purges those who drink it' found near the parsonage at Moreton Say by Archdeacon Clive was valuable, in the opinion of Dr. Darwin, as a strong chalybeate. Dr. Evans had tested the water at Sutton Spa on Lord Berwick's property two miles south of Shrewsbury and, helped by 'my ingenious friend', Dr. du Gard, had found that it had a purgative effect like sea water. It was also good for the treatment of glandular 'affections' and for the cure of scrofula. Joseph's judgement was that it would benefit the health of the poor of the county. In addition, a medicinal oil extracted from red sandstone at Pitchford resembled Friars Balsam, while a spring at Brolley Moor on the west side of the Longmynd contained some salanites, sea salt and muriated lime.

When he turned briefly to waterways it was the navigability of the Severn throughout the county that he recognised as of first importance. Perhaps 50,000 tons of coal was transported annually from Coalport by river to Worcestershire and Gloucestershire in barges of 20-50 tons. The return cargoes included wines, soap and grocery goods. From the wharf at

Shrewsbury cargoes as varied as flannels, grain, cheese and lead were sent down river; there was another wharf at Bridgnorth. Remarkably, there were no locks or weirs on the Severn from Montgomeryshire to the mouth of the Avon. Fishing was important, with twenty-two different species identified in the Severn including flounder, pike, trout, grayling, perch, eel, chub, roach, dace and, above all, salmon, which sold for 1/6d to 2/6d per lb. and was destined mainly for the London market.

-ℓℓ

It was when he turned, in chapters 2–4, to people and property that Joseph relied more on his own observations. He had been surprised, during his visits throughout the archdeaconry, that there were generally more landed proprietors, and of more varied character, in a parish than he had expected. Men who had enjoyed success in industry, commerce, the armed forces or the law were able to purchase the estates of others, while some of hereditary fortune had to sell off parts of their domains. Thrifty farmers, too, were able to buy up the land that others alienated in order to increase their investments or try their fortune in manufacture. 'The number of gentlemen of small fortune living on their estates has decreased', he wrote. 'Their descendants have been clergymen or attorneys, or shopkeepers in the towns of their own county; or more probably in this county emigrated to Birmingham, to Liverpool, to Manchester, or to London'. The number of opulent farmers who were able to buy up their rented property and add to it had increased. The annual value of land and houses in Shropshire he estimated at £600,000. He had the same message on non-residence for landowners as he had had for his fellow clergy. 'I would offer to landed proprietors a consideration of how much their own good, and that of the community, may be often times promoted by a residence upon their estates'. He firmly believed that they lost out by living in London, spending weeks in watering places like Bath, or frequently attending balls or horse races. On the other hand, he commended visits to one another's homes which promoted 'more decency of behaviour and more room for rational and improving conversation'. Speaking from the heart, he continued: 'Let them cherish true hospitality, in a degree suited to their fortunes, but let them discountenance all exhibition or show, all competition in luxury, all frivolous entertainments; let them guard against excess in any species of entertainment. They will not want employment for their time: they can attend to the state of their poorer neighbours, and, in giving them employment, they afford them the means of self-support, and serve them effectually, at the least expense to themselves'. He could not have expressed more clearly his personal attitude and morality, though his words may have fallen mainly on deaf ears.

Joseph had clear views on the siting of farmhouses which, he believed, were best in the middle of their farms, and of cottages, preferably in the centre of the village. He included a village plan he had submitted to the Board in 1794 to illustrate the saving on roads. Cottages, he argued, should be detached, with two bedchambers, and be surrounded by sufficient land — up to six acres — for their own livestock and produce. Sub-tenancies were not in the best interests of labourers: they should be tenants of the landlord and charged a fair rent. Their wives, as well as running the household, could tend the livestock, while the menfolk would work on their own land in the evening — 'when it is six o'clock'. If wives went out to work — and some Shropshire countrywomen sought summer work in the market gardens round London — the house and children were neglected and the husband tempted to go to the ale-house. Once again his moral seriousness is evident. 'Before men can be made good, they must be made serious, and this is best done by giving them an idea of property'. He quoted with approval Archibald Alison's successful experiment at Kenley where he divided the thirty acres of former common land, allocated to him as glebe, into ten three-acre holdings let at 7/- an acre to the poor people of the common with the largest families. A jury of farmers inspected the holdings annually and the tenant who had improved his land most was excused the year's rent. With such developments the number of married labourers would grow, total production increased, and 'a greater proportion both of the necessaries and comforts of life should be the lot of all'. He thought farms should be of 30-40 acres as a minimum, with 100-200 acres as the most desirable, but not larger than one man could direct.

He quoted some instances of improved farming: Mr. Childe at Kinlet Hall near Bridgnorth was praised for improved breeds of livestock imported from other counties and for the use of the latest farming implements; Walcot Hall was an example of good management, with the cultivation of turnips encouraged by Lord Clive's annual distribution of six silver cups for the best and second best holdings of 25, 15 and 8 acres. But he was critical of the excessive drinking of some affluent Shropshire farmers at their gatherings. Too much time spent in public houses was also a consequence in the north-west of the county of neglecting farms to make quicker profits by carrying for hire on the roads — with refreshment on the way!

Property values were influenced by the state of the roads: rents per acre could be as low as 8/- to 12/- when the roads were bad, rising to between

15/- and 20/- when good, and as high as £2 to £6 near towns. Tithes, rarely collected in kind, averaged 2/- in the £ as a money payment. A greater burden on the land was the poor rate which had approximately quadrupled in the previous thirty years to between 1/6d and 2/6d in the £, swelled by special levies for the new gaol, the new County Hall and several bridges. Shropshire had been quite generous, he thought, in granting temporary 'outdoor' relief (in their own homes) to the poor. The 'House of Industry' or workhouse at Shrewsbury was very well run by Isaac Wood; similar institutions had been opened at Oswestry, Ellesmere and near Welshpool. Joseph much preferred trying to raise the living standards of the poor through education and the inculcation of better ways of organising their lives. The office of 'overseer of the poor' was often not discharged well as all better-off males had to take a turn. In small parishes they managed better than in large, where he considered there should be either a paid overseer or one per township. The attitude of the magistrate was all important: 'The salutary power of a country magistrate who has time, fortune and inclination is incalculable'. Unfortunately, not all were as committed as the archdeacon himself.

Tenants, Joseph maintained, needed the security of a lease, especially where landlords took little interest in the cultivation of an estate, but shorter leases were becoming increasingly common. Tenants also needed safeguards to ensure that they benefited from improvements made. *The Victoria County History* in its analysis of wage rates that appear in the archdeacon's visitation records[1] concluded that by 1793 'the average daily wage for ordinary work on south Shropshire farms seems to have been 8d. if the farmer provided meat and drink, 14d. if he did not'. But there were seasonal variations and considerable differences between parishes, sometimes because of proximity to industrial areas, sometimes because some large landowners like Isaac Browne at Badger (see reference to him in Chapter 8) were more generous. By the time Joseph's Report on Agriculture was published in 1803 wage rates had risen sharply but not as quickly as prices. Hours were from 6.00 am to 6.00 pm. At harvest, hours and payments were extended and beer allowances of five to eight quarts were given, which the archdeacon said led to excessive drinking.

As a landowner himself, a compassionate clergyman and a public-spirited magistrate, Joseph took a keen interest in the improvements in farming that constituted the latest phase of the Agrarian Revolution. Enclosure had been proceeding for hundreds of years and by the late 18th century Shropshire was no longer a county of open fields. It may be contended that Joseph's support of the further enclosure of common land is in contradiction of his image as a 'compassionate clergyman', for in their book *The Village Labourer* the Hammonds exposed the hardships suffered by many of the poor when they lost their common rights. And there were probably families in Longnor who still re-told tales of how their forebears had lost their cottages when the Corbetts of the late 17th century had cleared the land for the construction of Longnor Hall. But this does not do Joseph justice. He was anything but a harsh landlord and, as we have seen, gave special care to his tenants in hard times, was to the fore in organising 'broth shops' in the county when things were at their worst, and as a magistrate was generous in the provision of poor relief. His stance on the enclosure of the commons was clear and consistent: he believed that though short-term relief might well be necessary, in the long run enclosure would lead to improved standards of farming and higher wages. He did not want to perpetuate the life-style of the poor labourer scratching a living from his small plot, and keeping his pig on the common where he could also collect wood for his fire. He wished to see the labourer with his family in a neat, detached, two-roomed cottage, on a long lease, with six acres of land where he could grow crops and keep his livestock, enjoying the improvements he could make on his holding, sending his children to the local school, and spending more time with his family rather than in the ale-house. Economic and moral improvement, he believed, would go hand-in-hand, and as archdeacon and magistrate, as well as agriculturist, he sought to urge, and to set an example to, his fellow landowners to take the necessary practical steps to realise this vision.

When Joseph referred to the largest area of common land in the county, the 12,000 acres of Clun Forest, as open to development, he was willing to concede that enclosure could sometimes spoil the beauty of the country-side: 'It must be owned, a great deal of beauty is lost by enclosures, and it seems a pity to lose some of pure Nature in a country so artificial as that of south Britain'. To those who also argued that enclosure was too costly, he told how he himself had enclosed a small area of common land a few years earlier without the expense of posts and rail by planting a hedge in a deep trench. His friend, the Rev. Richard Wilding, had just enclosed part of the Longmynd. They both opposed the planting of trees in hedges for a number of reasons including the perceived effect on the taste of butter made in the autumn. Some farmers erected fencing while a hedge grew and then moved it to another area.

'Enclosure of land and rational consolidation of estates were essential prerequisites for the advancement of arable and livestock-breeding techniques. Without convenient field boundaries the progressive farmer could neither improve his livestock nor derive any advantage from new crops or crop rotations, underdraining schemes, or the expense of applying fertilisers', is the judgement of a modern historian.[2] Joseph's 'General Survey' provides a snapshot of the state of development in the county at the beginning of the century that was to see the triumph of scientific farming over outmoded methods.

One of the key ways to raise productivity was the rotation of crops. When Arthur Young had visited Shropshire twenty-five years before Joseph completed his Survey, he found turnips cultivated in some areas in the east (though others preserved the traditional fallow year) but not yet the Norfolk four-course rotation of turnips, barley, clover and wheat. By the 1790s John Bishton, author of the first Shropshire Survey, was using it on the eastern border and it even appeared in the hilly parish of Hope Bowdler. Various patterns of rotation were increasingly used as the new ideas were disseminated. Joseph noted the popularity of peas, claiming that they were 'more grown upon our sound soils than in any other county'. He described ways of storing turnips and of using them fresh for animal feed. At Longnor Hall, which he knew well and was shortly to own, 'turnips have been given successfully as winter food for deer'. He gave details of letters that John Cotes of Woodcote had sent to the Board of Agriculture advocating the growing of potatoes on wheat fallow. Cotes maintained that growing potatoes would actually enhance the wheat crop, not loosen the soil; nor would it cause delay in planting the wheat as the potatoes could be turned up by the plough. Although many of the poor almost subsisted on potatoes when grain prices were at their highest, farmers were generally slow to introduce them, except near towns and industrial areas, on account of the heavy 'dunging' required. The opinions of Messrs. Harries, Pritchard, Tench and Rowley were all quoted on successful rotations of crops, the use of lime and manure, times and quantities to sow, and yields. Mr. Wilding at All Stretton had experimented with potatoes, producing starch and sago from them, and (as we have seen) mixing them with grain for bread. Joseph himself had the pleasure of producing some light cakes of mixed wheat and potato at the Board of Agriculture in London 'and witnessing the approbation with which they were received'. Wheat remained the most important cereal crop, but oats were grown widely in the south, and barley was important in central, east and north Shropshire. The war years encouraged the development of mixed farming, with the cultivation of cereals combined with the keeping of sheep and cattle.

Joseph's Survey was published in the early days of farm mechanisation. Ploughing in 1801 was still widely done with oxen, though these were slowly losing out to the more versatile horse. The common practice was still to harness four or five horses in a line to pull a single furrow plough; the use of two horses abreast came later. The original report noted that with a 'single plough' and two horses a boy could plough an acre and a half in a day with ease. Arthur Young did him the favour of procuring for him 'an improved Suffolk swing-plough, made by the blacksmith he employs'; he judged that it would require a skilful ploughman but he preferred it to the single-wheel plough generally favoured in the county. Like his ancestors, the Shropshire farmer of this time used implements made in the workshop of the village blacksmith and wheelwright — hay rakes, pitchforks, spades and wheelbarrows, as well as ploughs, rollers and harrows. The first mechanisation was in threshing and winnowing corn. George Ashdown believed that his father had had the first threshing machine at Hopesay in 1790. Joseph noted that there were such machines of various designs across the county, but they were in the early stages of development. Winnowing fans were in increasingly general use. There had been experimental seed drills since the 17th century, but in Joseph's day the time-honoured methods of broadcasting seed were still generally practised. Harvesting remained the last area to be mechanised. According to Joseph's survey, wheat was still generally reaped with broad hooks or saw sickles; barley and oats were mown with a scythe which was quicker and less tiring. Farming therefore continued to be labour intensive.[3]

Included in the Survey were substantial sections on other means of improvement. The importance of drainage was still not widely recognised: Joseph recommended brick arches of six-inch diameter, and advocated teaching and publicity to achieve more general acceptance. Manuring, using farmyard dung, lime and marl was advised by a number of improving landlords; Joseph's advice was not to bury it too deep. Lime was considered more effective than burning to get rid of scotch (couch) grass. He lamented the failure to combat weeds: 'The advantages from weeding ground seem not sufficiently attended to'. Farmers cut off thistles between ridges but left them in the hedgerows; he favoured cutting them down twice a year before the seeding stage. Meadows were often not weeded at all with the result that good grasses were swamped. He had not seen long-handled thistle tongs used anywhere in Shropshire. Watering was also important: streams could be used, but sluices were needed to control deep flooding.

When he turned to livestock, Joseph described first the varieties of cattle in the county that resulted from crossing the original Shropshire Longhorns with better animals from Cheshire and Lancashire. Numbers of the Herefordshire breed were rising in Corvedale, the Severn Valley and on the border with the county's southern neighbour. He mentioned a prize Shropshire bull bred at Botvyle close to where he lived. Of another prize bull shown at Shifnal in December 1800 he wrote: 'He appears to me to combine many of the favourite points of Mr. Bakewell's breed with those in which the old Herefordshire breed were thought to excel'. Lord Clive at Walcot Hall was one who had imported the Alderney breed. More common were the Leicestershires that were good beef producers but often too fat as they were less adapted to work than the Herefordshire and Devon cattle. Cross-breeding also improved milk production, although he admitted that 'this county is not famous for dairying'. The largest dairies were close to the Cheshire border, smaller ones prevailed in the south-east and south-west. He spent some time outlining different methods of slaughtering, describing a new method introduced by Thomas Clarkson's brother and Dr. du Gard's reservations about its failure to eliminate pain. Finally he quoted in full a letter from Everard Home Esq. of London to Lord Carrington at the Board identifying the precise spot where the spinal marrow needs to be divided if death is to be both instantaneous and painless.

Because Joseph's archdeaconry covered the generally hillier southern half of the county, sheep were far more numerous than cattle. His conclusion was that the county contained most of the breeds found in England, from the smaller, nimble Welsh to the large Leicestershire. What he called 'the old Shropshire sheep,' found in the southern hills including the Longmynd, he described as hardy and horned, with black or mottled face. Nearer Wales they had no horns, white faces and heavier but coarser fleeces. He judged that they made excellent stock when crossed with the Dorset. Go-ahead landowners experimented with other cross-breeds, Lord Clive at Walcot importing Cheviot sheep and even Spanish rams. 'The farmers in different districts have tried at one time or another almost all the improved breeds'. Coming into favour in the hill country, as he wrote, was a cross of the Southdown breed with Longmynds, which improved the wool and carcass weight of the local sheep without loss of hardiness.

When he moved on to pigs he quoted the opinion of Mr. Edward Harries that 'perhaps no county of its extent grows so many or rears or fats so many hogs'. Pork and bacon were widely consumed among the poorer people when they could afford them, for he noted that fewer labourers now kept pigs. The reason for this may have been the enclosing of the commons, though experiments showed that pigs needed to be fenced in or they would devour other crops — and were even found grazing in churchyards when walls and fences were not kept in good repair. The crossing of the Shropshire and Cheshire varieties, Joseph believed, had been beneficial. His final comments on the livestock of the county covered horses, used for ploughing on small farms and for transport, but not bred with sufficient care; rabbits whose warrens were particularly numerous on the Longmynd and Brown Clee Hill; and poultry, with geese reared on commons, and turkeys mainly dispatched to Birmingham. Other fowl were often sold live at markets — which he deplored.

As he turned to consider the rural economy in general, Joseph felt he had to emphasise again the soaring prices of produce over the previous few years: in 1794 the average price of flour was 6/- a bushel (56 lbs.), potatoes 1/6d per bushel, cheese 3½d per lb., beef 3d, mutton 3½d, veal 3½d and bacon 6d – but the prices had at least doubled, and, at their highest in 1801, even quadrupled. The aim therefore had to be to raise productivity on the farms and to improve the rural infrastructure.

He then focused his attention on one of his favourite subjects — roads. Good roads he regarded as of first importance for farmers. In his original survey, John Bishton had judged turnpikes and private roads in Shropshire to be bad. He had insisted that roads should be made properly from the start, and their upkeep overseen by a salaried surveyor appointed by the magistrates. One regular problem was the damage caused to the surface by carts that were overweight. His answer was not to limit the number of horses to four, the existing practice that discouraged horse breeding, but to site weighing machines at tolls. Joseph agreed with these proposals, but cited Mr. Lloyd's view that the turnpike roads had become 'tolerably good' and would benefit from the transfer of many heavy loads to canals. Maintenance was all-important. Too many farmers evaded or largely ignored the existing statutory duty to maintain private roads. Joseph therefore proposed the abolition of personal service on roads, and the annual appointment of a surveyor who, with the support of two magistrates, would have the power to levy a rate. In support he quoted Mr. Tench's opinion that 'the public roads are tolerably good and are in a general state of improvement; the parochial roads are very indifferent and capable of being improved, but are much neglected for want of proper surveyors'. In many of the central and southern parishes, which he knew very well, Joseph asserted that 'there is no tolerable horse road whatever'. He made a series of practical and not over-ambitious suggestions:

1. Make widely available the extracts of surveyors' roles printed by Eddowes of Shrewsbury.
2. Cover road surfaces with small stones or 'skreed gravel' as the best roads were so treated.
3. Cut back hedges and trees where growth obstructs roads and where leaves block drains.
4. Erect more finger-posts with place names on both sides.
5. Paint the names of villages on boards at each end of the settlement.
6. Allow greater flexibility in determining the width of roads.
7. Paint owners' names and details in large letters on some conspicuous part of their wagons.

Throughout his active life Joseph was to take a keen and informed interest in the state of the roads and the journey times taken by both public and private transport, recording precise details in his diaries of his own journeys.

Shropshire was, of course, fortunate to have the River Severn as an alternative means of transport to the roads before the construction of canals in the late 18th century and the coming of the railway in the second quarter of the 19th. Joseph prevailed on his friend Thomas Telford, whom he had known since the building of the new church at Madeley ten years before and with whom he had co-operated on the improvement of turnpike roads, to write the section on river and canal traffic, paying generous tribute to his merit as an engineer and architect and to his personal qualities. The Severn had for centuries been important for trade and had made Shrewsbury 'a sort of metropolis for north Wales'. It had also encouraged mining and manufacture, bringing capital into the county, conveying fuel, and opening up markets for agricultural produce. But no improvements had been made, and in consequence river traffic was still limited by too many shoals, the lack of water in some seasons, and the continued practice of men rather than horses hauling the barges. In 1796 the river flow was sufficiently full for only two months to allow the passage of a boat large enough for the sale of its cargo to cover costs. Flood protection measures, like the building of banks in Montgomeryshire and north Shropshire had only worsened the situation downstream. Telford believed one remedy lay in building locks, which would also facilitate the irrigation of fields and provide power for mills and industry. An alternative would be to collect flood-waters into reservoirs, especially in Montgomeryshire, that would regulate navigation, provide water for canals, and create fisheries. Towpaths for horses, as Mr. Reynolds had provided near Coalport, were also necessary.

Because it had the Severn, Shropshire had been slow to construct canals. It had, however, benefited from the opening of the Staffs. and Worcs. Canal in 1772 that linked the Severn at Stourport with the Trent and Mersey, and the later Severn-Thames Canal that saw iron from Coalbrookdale being unloaded in London in 1791.[4] Canals within Shropshire, Telford maintained, were needed to move heavy goods and to reach areas distant from the river. The hilly nature of much of the county created problems but they were not insuperable. William Reynolds had made a canal to bring iron and coal from Oakengates to his iron works at Ketley, a distance of one and a half miles. In 1788 he had completed an inclined plane with a double iron railway to raise and lower barges 73 feet, a descending full barge drawing up an empty one. He used smaller barges, 20 feet instead of 70 in length. The success of the inclined plane demonstrated the possibility of a canal from Donnington Wood to the Oakengates and Ketley canal. Completed in 1792, it went via the iron-works at Brierley Hill near Coalbrookdale to join the Severn two miles south of Ironbridge, descending 207 feet on an inclined plane and then running parallel with the river to Coalport, a total distance of ten miles. 'Boats pass these inclined planes with considerable expedition', as frequently as six an hour, Telford explained. The water level was maintained from reservoirs and by pumping out mines. It proved that canals could still be profitable when crossing high and rugged ground, for the total cost was only £47,500 and it provided a 6% return on capital — likely to be even higher if the Severn were improved. Coalport, it was argued, could come to rival Stourport as a station for goods coming up river.

It was the rising price of coal at Shrewsbury that led to the formation of the Shrewsbury Canal Company. The construction of this canal which linked the eastern coalfield to the banks of the Severn at Castle Foregate, involved locks, inclined planes and an aqueduct to cross the River Tern at Longden. Telford was consulted about the aqueduct which was manufactured in cast iron by William Reynolds in 1796. At Atcham the 970-yard Berwick Tunnel had to be excavated; a three-foot wide towpath through the tunnel alongside the ten-foot wide canal was made at Reynolds' suggestion. By the time of Joseph's survey disappointment was already being expressed that the price of coal in the county town had not been reduced.[5]

In the north of the county the Ellesmere Canal completed the link between the Severn, the Dee and the Mersey. It crossed the valley at

Llangollen 125 feet above the river level. Branches joined the Montgomery Canal near Llanymynech, and linked Whitchurch with the Severn north of the county town and not far from the end of the Shrewsbury Canal. It greatly benefited agriculture, but also carried coal, lime and slates as well as articles of consumption. Another canal connected Donnington Wood to the Marquis of Stafford's estate at Lilleshall.

Telford's conclusion was: 'Although Shropshire was behind most of the other counties in adopting the plan of forming artificial canals, it has made a rapid progress in the execution of this valuable improvement; and I may venture to say that there has been more ingenuity displayed in the means taken for overcoming the various obstacles which lay in the way of the canals of this county, than has hitherto been shown in those of any other county in England'.[6] Other canals that had been proposed included a link between the Montgomeryshire waterway and Bishops' Castle, a link to the Leominster Canal, an extension of the canal at Lilleshall to the Grand Trunk, and one between Wenlock and Cleobury Mortimer to serve the area between the Severn and Church Stretton and Ludlow. The development that pointed to the future was the laying of iron rails along which horses would draw wagons in tracts of countryside where the terrain was too rugged or the supply of water too limited to make a canal practicable. Horses could draw greater weights when there was a slight downward incline (though lesser weights in the reverse direction). Such railways were very suitable where the goods to be carried were heavy but not bulky. He had seen how William Reynolds' towpath along the Severn had encouraged the development of his works at Coalport and the china and earthenware manufacture there. He favoured high single arch bridges as at Ironbridge and another on his plan at Buildwas after the earlier bridge was washed away by floods in 1795.

Joseph's Survey closed with some sections on commerce and manufacture, which included lists of weekly markets and regular fairs in the county. 'The staple trade of Shrewsbury is in fine flannels and Welsh webs' – the flannels from Montgomeryshire and Shropshire were chiefly sold to London merchants for export; the webs, 200 yards long, from Merionethshire and Denbighshire, were destined for markets in Holland, Germany and America. Many sold at Oswestry were dyed before export and ended up as clothing for slaves in the West Indies and South America. The iron industry in the east of the county, with a great number of blast furnaces near Ketley, employed 6,000; coal production was up to 260,000 tons a year. The production of china had become centred on Coalport and Broseley, not far from Wedgwood's earthenware; quartz and clay were found at Cardington. Smaller enterprises included a mill for dyeing woollen cloth at Leebotwood, and gloves made in Ludlow for the London market. The industrial development naturally stimulated agricultural production, and the demand for workers led to a rising population, especially in the parish of Madeley. The population of Shropshire at the 1801 census was 167,639.

In his conclusion Joseph pointed to shortage of capital and the neglect of their public duties by some large landlords as the principal obstacles to further improvement. He quoted Mr. Harries's three chief recommendations for progress: an Act of Parliament for the effectual drainage of low lands; another Act to establish the sale of grain by weight; and the general adoption of crop rotation on scientific principles.

In a final personal statement he admitted there was some repetition in his Survey: 'Whatever has occurred to myself as a matter of improvement has been incidentally mentioned in the different sections, so I have little to add to the conclusion of this Report, except an apology for not having confined myself strictly to the subject of each section as the plan may seem to require ... I say of every part of the Report for which I am responsible, that I sincerely and earnestly desire it may be regarded as a work of no pretensions on my part, beyond that of having attempted to give such information as may lead to inquiry'.[7] He believed that 'the science of agriculture has been considerably advanced by several of the County Reports and other publications of the Board'. He hoped that his own Report would 'put gentlemen upon thinking of the improvement of the country', for if they extended their thoughts more widely, and applied them more specifically, real benefit would be obtained. Here we hear the authentic voice of one of the figures of what has been called 'the Shropshire Enlightenment'.

11   THE CORBETT INHERITANCE

For the Plymley family at Longnor the early years of the new century were dominated by ill-health. For some time Katherine had been concerned about her brother. In July 1801 a note of alarm appeared in her journal when Joseph arrived home after abandoning his visitation at Stretton on account of prolonged and violent stomach pain. He found relief by drinking warm mint tea and swallowing three grains of Calomel. On some days, she noted, he was better than others, but the pains, which he had suffered for some months, were at their worst after exertion, loud talking or 'earnest discourse'. In consequence, 'he entirely declines company at home or abroad' — by which she meant visiting. She believed he was suffering from the effects of too great exertions of body and mind, probably recalling how their friend Thomas Clarkson had worn himself out in the cause of Abolition some years earlier. Joseph was under particular pressure as he completed the *General View of Agriculture*, 'which leaves scarcely a minute of leisure', and as he insisted on teaching his sons Uvedale and Joseph, now aged eight and seven, as well as serving his churches and discharging his responsibilities as a magistrate. Her advice was to leave the preliminary education of the children to others.

His success as a tutor, however, was evinced by Panton's matriculation at Pembroke College, Oxford, the previous year at the age of fifteen. But perhaps he had pushed him too hard, for Panton had to be treated for a persistently high pulse-rate in the summer of 1801. The friend who came to stay with him in the long vacation, nineteen-year-old Frederic Iremonger, whose rooms in college were opposite Panton's, told them he thought eighteen was young enough to come to Oxford — though he was thinking more of the temptations for the inexperienced to spend too much rather than the academic demands. Panton was well enough to take his friend to see the iron bridge over the Severn, the china factory at Coalport, the inclined plane, and at night to climb Lincoln's Hill 'to see the fires from the works'.

Panton's pulse returned to normal during the family holidays on Anglesey and he was fine for the start of his second year.

Such marked improvement in health did not extend to Panton's sisters. Fifteen year-old Josepha, whose condition had been described as delicate after catching whooping cough the previous year had been left with a persistent, violent cough. She did not leave the house at all during the winter months. Katherine noted that Josepha seemed to be better when they took her off the prescribed opium. When she obviously benefited from the sea air on Anglesey in August, it was decided at the end of the holiday to leave her there at Plas Gwyn with the Pantons; she did not return home till mid-December. In her absence Jane's fragile health seemed to deteriorate. A year younger than her sister, she was gentle by nature and 'loves all the useful works that belong to women'. Like her grandfather she was fascinated by natural history, finding great pleasure in gardening and tending the poultry. Her father welcomed her into the lessons in Latin and Greek he was giving to Uvedale. Strictly religious, she was not attracted to novels and plays with the exception of Shakespeare. What caused the family most concern was her reluctance as a young teenager to have anything to eat before dinner: she maintained that the poor had to go without food and still managed to work. But Jane liked to go for long walks and would come back exhausted. Katherine reported that they urged her and argued with her, but to no avail. She had returned from Plas Gwyn in September quite overdone. They took her to Shrewsbury for electric shock treatment to relieve the numbness that was affecting her left side, cheek and eye. She went three times a week for the first three months of 1802. A new young doctor, du Gard, got her to breathe ether when she had a coughing fit, and came to Longnor to try the effects of raising a blister.

Jane's father was taken ill again, too, with a return of violent, spasmodic stomach pains. Dr. Evans thought it was bile, but Joseph himself was dubious. His skin became rather yellow. He was also suffering from nervous irritability, especially if someone unexpectedly called. At meals the least noise seemed to hurt him. The family advised him to go to Bath to take the waters and at some point in the year he did go, though Katherine did not record it till months later. He also gave up the curacy at Leebotwood and confined himself to morning and evening services at Longnor. He felt relieved when he sent off the final format of his Survey to the Board of Agriculture. On account of his father's illness Panton came home at Easter 1802 instead of visiting a college friend on the Isle of Wight. But his father was well enough to preside at Easter Communion when each poor person was given two or three large loaves. By May, Joseph was able to resume his place on the bench, and even correspond with Sir William Scott, M.P, who was to introduce a Bill into Parliament on the non-residence of clergy. Scott was very grateful for he was anticipating opposition from several quarters — fanatics, the irreligious, opponents of the tithe, and critics of the wealth of higher clergy. Joseph's concern was the same as Scott's: 'to give a fair protection to the clergy and at the same time to ensure a substantial performance of their duty'. Scott asked his permission to publish his letter along with his own speech in the Commons.

Jane, however, had not recovered: indeed, she was so ill that she was taken to her uncle Flint's house in Shrewsbury so that the doctors from the Infirmary were on hand to treat her. Twice she was thought to be dying. Katherine went to stay with her for ten weeks. Sadly, it was during that time that old Mr. Plymley died at Longnor on 29 May 1802. Family life must have been severely disrupted for Katherine's journal was not resumed until November the next year. Joseph's father was in his eighty-sixth year and had become increasingly feeble, but he was a much respected and loved member of the household and the local community. In a codicil added to his will in 1797, he expressed gratitude to 'the dutiful children who do all in their power to make the remainder of his life pass smoothly'. On receiving the sad news Katherine hastened to Longnor. The funeral took place at Leebotwood, where a monument hails 'a long life of usefulness to others and of credit to himself'. Katherine's own recorded view of her father, written months later, was of a faithful man with a high sense of Christian duty but a low opinion of himself. The last words he was heard to utter were: 'I have made my peace with God and am ready whenever He calls me'. When Katherine returned to Jane in Shrewsbury she took Josepha with her, for her grandfather's death had brought back her cough and she had developed convulsive spasms, which sounds similar to her father's complaint.

Josepha was well enough by the end of June to accompany her father and Uvedale to Hereford, where the bishop instituted Joseph as Rector of Holgate; it was the bishop's gift to offset the costs of the archdeaconry. They then went on to London on business, returning via Oxford to collect Panton. Jane returned home after renewed electric shock treatment and shower baths had had little effect. Joseph's wife Matty, who had not been well enough to accompany them, was safely delivered of a daughter on 27 July. At her baptism the newcomer was given the name Harriet. Matty remained ill with fainting fits and delirium. She was still very ill when Katherine, Panton and Josepha set off for Cornwall taking the dangerously sick Jane in the hope that the warmer climate would help to restore her. They chose unwisely to go by boat from Tenby to Penzance — unwisely because the voyage was very slow, they were all sea-sick, and eventually had to be put ashore at St. Ives. Panton went off to Oxford in October, leaving his aunt and Josepha to look after Jane. Dr.

du Gard regularly sent advice by letter, and actually came down when Jane's condition became alarming. They had outings when possible, including a trip to the Scilly Isles, and Katherine found there were 'respectable' people with whom to exchange visits. Panton rejoined them for the Christmas vacation. They did not return home until June 1803. In the same month Panton received his degree at Oxford. The best news was that Josepha's cough had gone, as had all Jane's worst symptoms except a fast pulse-rate.

The family got together again for Christmas 1803. Panton came up from London where he now had lodgings in Lincoln's Hill Fields. Among Joseph's gifts was an elegant silver bread-basket from the Misses Leighton for whom he had obtained £6,000 from a bequest after much legal wrangling. That he was annoyed by the gift suggests he had not fully shaken off the nervous depression from earlier in the year. He presented du Gard, who officially had no private practice, with a telescope he had bought in London and £50 in gratitude for his journey to Penzance to treat Jane. Seventeen years earlier Joseph had sent a painting to Pembroke College as a thank-you gift on completing his degree. He now made a presentation on Panton's behalf: another painting, but this time a portrait of Samuel Johnson, perhaps the college's most famous *alumnus,* a copy of the work of Sir Joshua Reynolds by Frederic Burney, Katherine believed.

When Katherine resumed her main journal in November 1803 some entries were retrospective, including a reference to the publication of Joseph's Survey of Shropshire Agriculture in April, for which the Board paid him a hundred guineas and presented him with twenty copies that he gave to the friends who had helped him. In the new year of 1804 Katherine took Josepha to stay in Shrewsbury for two days, during which Josepha attended her first local ball with the band of the Shrewsbury Volunteers. In the summer, Josepha, just eighteen, and Panton, now nineteen, attended the races at Ludlow and a ball in Ludlow Castle. Letters to Joseph from Wilberforce and Clarkson, noted by Katherine, revived memories of the anti-slave trade campaign: Wilberforce sent personal news of his success in carrying an Abolition Bill through the Commons, though it was thrown out by the Lords; Clarkson reported that he had sold his house on Ullswater and returned to London, where he was again seeking evidence on the slave trade to put before the Lords. In another of his long-standing areas of activity, Joseph succeeded in securing, for the benefit of widows in his archdeaconry, two of the sixteen small houses (and a pension of £40 a year) provided at Lichfield by a new charity. The summer ended with Matty very ill again before the safe delivery of Mildred, her eighth child, on 9 September.

A major change in their lives resulted from the death on 25 October 1804 of Joseph's uncle, Robert Corbett, at Longnor Hall. For some time Katherine had been spending the greater part of every day with him, chatting and reading sermons and prayers. She recorded that in late September he had taken the sacrament 'and the next day following he sent for Mr. Coupland and made a codicil to his will; he was very desirous to do this for he said to my brother, "My will was made under an idea that I should survive my brother [uncle John Flint] and now it is almost certain that he will survive me". After he had made this codicil he said he had settled everything to his satisfaction, and he seemed wholly intent on a better world'. Joseph called to see him occasionally and he asked that Josepha, Jane, and especially Panton, should visit. Joseph read prayers for the sick to him and he was prayed for at the church. Dr. Darwin, who attended him, thought he had a large tumour in the pancreas, although this was not the immediate cause of death; he prescribed opium. Katherine included full details of his last days and his death in her journal.

The will was opened by the solicitor, Mr. Coupland, in the presence of Mrs. Corbett, Joseph and Katherine, but he read out only instructions as to the funeral. Mr. Corbett's wish was to be buried at Leebotwood; he also asked that his first wife's remains should be brought from the vault at Longnor to be buried with him. Eight of his workmen were to attend the funeral and would receive a guinea each. The will, and the drawer and room in which it lay, were then re-sealed. Mr. Corbett was buried on 31 October, with the Rev. Lewis Williams conducting the funeral.

Afterwards, the will was re-opened and read by Mr. Coupland in the presence of the family, including Joseph and Panton, friends and lawyers; Mrs. Corbett, the widow, wished to be there but was advised that would be very unusual. The will, apart from the new codicil, had been made four years before. Katherine summarised it in her journal: 'He has proved his friendship and kindness for his own family. Independent of the settled estates which by the will of Sir Richard Corbett are Mr. Flint's for his life and afterwards come to my brother, Mr. Corbett was possessed of very considerable property; he has made my brother his heir, he has left him all his real and personal estate (one small farm to my uncle Flint excepted), charging them with many legacies, the largest is for £4,000 paid to Mr. Flint, £1,500 to me, £100 to Ann, £100 to Mrs. Corbett', who also received other possessions and a jointure of £500 per annum. The furniture and stock at the Hall went first to Mr. Flint and then to Joseph. £10 was left to the poor of Longnor and £10 to the poor at Leebotwood. Uncle Flint, Joseph and the deceased's wife were named as executors. Mrs. Corbett was very disappointed and angry, telling Katherine she would retire to Bath. She left in a bitter mood only three weeks later.

Katherine added: 'My brother and my uncle Flint (now Corbett, for by a clause in Sir Richard's will whoever possesses the estate must bear that name only) have entered into articles that my brother shall have immediate possession of the estate, he paying my uncle the net annual income for his life, and rent for the Hall and domain, and interest for his life interest in the furniture etc. This is, I think, the best for both parties. My uncle very wisely determined immediately not to come to Longnor, nor to alter his style of living, for he justly thought that at his age [eighty-one] the only use he could wish to make of this accession of fortune was to make better provision for his grandchildren and great-grandchildren [by his daughter]; he is a good and kind man and we all hope he will live to have the comfort of fulfilling his wish — and my brother with a mind so superior, so intelligent and so active will be able to manage the estate in the best manner not only for his own family, but for the comfort of all the tenants settled upon it'.

It was important that Joseph visited London to settle issues arising from the will. Unfortunately, his wife was again ill with inflammation of the lungs and fever, though she was well enough for him to leave in mid-November accompanied by Panton. His mission was to obtain probate of the will, to transfer stock to new owners, and to arrange for his surname to be changed to Corbett. This last was accomplished when it was officially published in the *Gazette* on 24 November. After forty-five years as Joseph Plymley and twelve as Archdeacon, he became overnight Archdeacon Joseph Corbett. His wife and children also changed their surname, but Katherine and her sister Ann remained Plymley.

Joseph was home on 1 December, with the intention of moving into Longnor Hall by Christmas for, although he planned changes at the Hall, Bank House, with its small rooms, was now, with all the comings and goings, 'like a beehive', Katherine claimed. As she recorded these events she reflected on the amazing change in the family's fortunes since her grandfather had gone to seek work in London and her grandmother had been taken on as housekeeper by Sir Richard Corbett. The unborn child her grandmother was then carrying — uncle Robert — had inherited the Hall and the estate when Sir Richard died in 1774 and, on Robert's recent death, his wealth and his estates had passed to his brother but would soon belong to her brother.

Joseph meanwhile was occupied with 'business', as the estates in Shropshire and Montgomeryshire needed attention and he was working on plans for renovations at Longnor Hall. The Hall was still substantially the impressive rectangular building, with two storeys, basement and attics, erected by Sir Richard Corbett in the late 17th century and completed by his son, Sir Uvedale. Then, as today, the principal facades, each of seven bays, face north and south. On the north, or entrance, front the three central bays were carried up to form a gable originally with a semi-circular parapet (as can be seen in the illustration from 1792, twelve years before Joseph moved in). The subsequent re-shaping of the gable in curvilinear form is unlikely to have been carried out by the new owner at this time. Joseph would have been more concerned to ensure that there were enough bedchambers and bathrooms for his large family and visitors. The ground plan of the house remained with its longitudinal division, giving two rows of rooms back to back, one facing the front and one the garden. In the thickness of the dividing wall were three chimneys and two staircases — with the third rising from a room on the south side. The ground floor probably still contained, as a hundred years earlier, a large hall, summer and winter parlours, a drawing room, and a library, with 'Adam' style plaster ceiling and fireplace.[1] Joseph may have re-fashioned the 'smoke room' as a study. Joseph and Matty actually moved in two days before Christmas, taking nine-year-old Helen with them. Katherine, who had gone to London to visit Panton, ended up escorting him home on Christmas Eve ill with scarlet fever. Joseph had never missed Christmas Day at Longnor and as usual celebrated by giving away a 'beef' of 800 lbs. and sending six pairs of warm blankets and a counterpane to the poor at Holgate and warm clothing for the poor on the Corbett Montgomeryshire estate at Leighton.

No doubt the family gathered as usual on Christmas Day itself, but whether it was at the Hall or The Bank is not known. It had been agreed that Katherine and Ann should stay at The Bank, and for the time being the other children stayed with them. It was a significant moment for Joseph's sisters when, a week into the new year of 1805, Josepha and Jane, whom they had brought up from childhood, moved to be with their father at the Hall. Unfortunately, they all caught scarlet fever from Panton, though only Robert was really ill; even Matty went down with it. Jane's illness returned — Dr. du Gard thought it was fundamentally a circulation problem — and her head pains and violent nose-bleeds were treated with five drops of digitalis and five drops of laudanum twice a day. Then came the news that John Partridge, Joseph's coachman, who had gone with Panton as his servant, had died suddenly. After such a difficult start the year 1805 proceeded more smoothly, with all the children, except Uvedale and baby Mildred, moving to the Hall by Easter. In September Mildred, weaning completed, joined the rest of the family. 'All the children have now left us', Katherine wrote, perhaps with relief tinged with sadness, 'except our constant inmate Uvedale'.

Although uncle John received the income from the Corbett estates, Joseph and his family, after their crowded existence at Bank House, enjoyed the benefit of living in the more spacious Longnor Hall. An additional advantage was that they were able to entertain more visitors. In recent years Joseph's nervous exhaustion had meant that only special friends had been welcome to stay, and then for only short periods, but with his Agriculture Report completed, his financial situation improved, and his spirits boosted by the long-awaited move to the Hall, he became more generous with his invitations.

The first to stay was Joseph's old clergy friend, Theophilus Houlbrooke, now their regular correspondent from Scotland; Katherine noted his antipathy to the narrowness and intolerance of the 'sectaries', including Quakers. Then came Paul Panton, Joseph's school friend from Chester days and cousin of Joseph's first wife. It was then the turn of Matty's relations, Major and Mrs. Dansey, who came for a few days. They were followed by Panton's Pembroke friend, the newly-ordained Frederic Iremonger, who preached at Longnor at Joseph's request. Katherine and Ann threw a party at The Bank to celebrate the painting and re-decoration of the house: Joseph, Matty and the children all came, of course, but so did Iremonger, du Gard, their friend and medical adviser from Shrewsbury, and Mr. Corfield, a local clergyman who often took services for Joseph when he was away. Iremonger kindly helped Jane to arrange her collection of shells, minerals and plants more systematically as they were still in her old home.

The really special visitors, however, were Thomas Clarkson and his wife Catherine, he no longer rushing to get away on one of his extended Abolition tours, but willing to stay for several days in July 1805. One day Joseph, accompanied by the family, had to go to Ludlow for his annual visitation as archdeacon, and Katherine was able to entertain the visitors at The Bank. She must have been pleased when Thomas said he preferred her house to the Hall and that he had been particularly happy to conduct his wife round the garden and show her the walk on which he had done some of his best 'thinking'. On another day the new rector of Pontesbury, Mr. Peters, was invited to 'drink tea' with them as he had once had a living on the West Indian island of Dominica, where he had aroused opposition by his sermons criticising slavery. Of course, during the Clarksons' visit there was much talk about the state of the anti-slave trade campaign, and Joseph took Thomas to Llanfyllin in Montgomeryshire to meet two surgeons who had worked on a slave ship and were prospective witnesses before the House of Lords. For the two friends it was quite like old times. Thomas was now much more hopeful that the slave trade would soon be abolished.

But their conversation roamed more widely and touched on more personal issues than on the earlier, hurried occasions. Thomas told them that Quakers had proved so helpful to him in his information gathering on the trade that he had 'formed an intimate friendship with some of them'. Indeed, he was engaged on writing a history of the Quakers, whom he greatly admired without adopting their opinions. Katherine and Ann read the first volume of his History in two days while he was at Longnor. Katherine was still a great admirer of Thomas. She regarded him as a principled and kind-hearted man committed to the abolition of the slave trade, but she was concerned about his faith. He had resigned his Anglican orders because he objected to payment for religious duties, but she doubted if he had become a Unitarian. She was glad when he agreed to accompany Joseph to church on the Sunday for 'my brother when the days are longest catechises the children and gives a lecture afterwards for four Sundays'. When Joseph and Matty returned from Shrewsbury, having gone to see off the Clarksons, 'we all adjourned to our house and took a walk to the Lawley [the elongated hill close to their home] after an early tea'.

Interestingly, their next visitor was Francis Severne, rector of Abberley, a close friend of the poet Robert Southey, whom the Clarksons had got to know in the Lake District. On his return home, Mr. Severne sent Jane a set of Southey's poems. Young Frederic Iremonger was still with them and accompanied Joseph when he made his visitation at Church Stretton. He admired his host's tact when he referred in his charge to the Volunteer Corps exercising on a Sunday. 'He highly esteems my brother, saying he does not know a greater character, discharging the duties of an Archdeacon, a Magistrate, a country Gentleman, a husband and father in the most exemplary manner'.

Early in December came the news of Lord Nelson's death in the very hour of victory at the Battle of Trafalgar. 'Our late great naval victory over the combined fleets of France and Spain off Cape Trafalgar on 21 October', wrote Katherine on 5 December 1805, 'has called forth rejoicings and, what is much better, subscriptions for the widows and orphans of those who fell, almost everywhere. This is the day appointed for a General Thanksgiving; my brother is too unwell to do duty today; I am greatly pleased with his benevolent idea of giving the poor light in their houses instead of an illumination. He distributed today to every poor housekeeper in Longnor, Coreley, Holgate [his other parishes], throughout the manors of Cardington and his manors in Montgomeryshire a pound of Candles. I do not yet know the number, but it must have been very great'.

To mark the end of their first year at Longnor Hall, Joseph and Matty gave several Christmas parties for different groups of friends, including one for his fellow magistrates. He also distributed his customary Christmas gifts to the poor: on this occasion the locals enjoyed gifts of beef after the slaughter of 'a very fine cow'; those in his other parishes and manors received blankets and warm clothing. Matty sent materials for a Christmas pudding to every poor family in Longnor.

❦

Early in the new year — 1806 — Joseph was laid low for a couple of weeks by an attack of lumbago. He recovered from that only to pick up a severe cold after taking a service in February, which led him for a while to lead only evening services. His sister was anxious about his general health and how busy he was; once again she urged him to give up the initial teaching of his children. He was too poorly to attend the Governors' meeting at the Infirmary, which particularly disappointed him as he wished to present a cheque for £123 received from Joseph Reynolds (who addressed him as 'Respected Friend') on behalf of Shropshire Quakers. And when Clarkson wrote to say that Wilberforce would be presenting a Commons motion for Abolition in ten days' time, Joseph was not fit enough to visit local supporters and had to confine himself to writing letters.

The health of the family was a perpetual concern: his sister Ann was almost an invalid, rarely venturing farther than the Hall, which was only just down the road from Bank House; his second daughter, Jane, continued very ill and, like her aunt, required regular medical attention; and the other siblings were naturally a prey to the diseases of childhood. The family made use of new treatments and when the youngest, Mildred, was inoculated against smallpox, once again Joseph met the cost of extending this to fifty-seven other youngsters in the village. Their continued anxieties about health are a reminder of how far the science of medicine has progressed in the last two centuries, of how much today we are protected and able to access the latest treatments and cures.

One of the answers to health problems then, though available only to those who could afford it, was a visit to one of the country's spas to 'take the waters'. That Joseph, with his wife and eldest children should have set out for Bath in April 1806 is therefore not surprising. What does seem perplexing is that they should have chosen to leave two days before the twenty-first birthday of Panton, the eldest son and heir. It can only be assumed that because Joseph frowned on excessive celebration he thought this might be curtailed in their

134

absence. It was not. At nearby Micklewood a sheep was roasted and four guineas subscribed for ale for the populace. There was a bonfire in front of the Hall, and another that Uvedale and his brothers had prepared. Two bonfires blazed on the Lawley and were visible from miles around. The church bells were rung at Longnor, Leebotwood and Welshpool, where the Corbett tenants also roasted a sheep and distributed ale. Katherine and Ann, who were looking after the younger children, invited twenty-two former and present servants to dinner and a bowl of punch. No wonder that Panton, who had returned to his legal studies at Lincoln's Inn, wrote to say how much he was missing his family and friends.

The waters at Bath did little for Joseph, but he and the others still went up to the capital, where he dined with Wilberforce — who ate and worked at a separate table — and accompanied him to the House. Her father took Josepha to visit the Commons, too. They went home in May, the month before Panton was called to the Bar. It must have been as a very proud father that Joseph took his place on the bench at Shrewsbury Quarter Sessions on 2 July where Panton, in wig and gown, took the first step in his legal career. Panton was now unable to keep out of the limelight for when, with some reluctance, he accompanied Matty and Josepha to Ludlow Races he was chosen as Steward for the following year. The next week he was at Worcester to join the Oxford Circuit, before returning to Shrewsbury and then Chester. How much more grown up than his brothers he must have seemed, for when Katherine looked out one day at the end of summer she saw Uvedale (fourteen) and Joseph (twelve), two fit and healthy boys, clearing the hayfield 'in their white shirts, nankeen trousers and straw hats, with gay-looking braces across their shoulders'. They were shortly to go to Abberley to be tutored by Mr. Severne, who found that their father had given them a good grounding in Latin. 'Kind and considerate boys', Katherine found them, recalling how they had scoured the district to find some chicken for Ann when she was disinclined to eat. To her, Joseph was 'lively', and Waties the quietest and most sedentary.

Among the visitors that summer was Dr. Townson, who kindly arranged Ann's minerals, before deciding to leave his own entire collection with them as he was preparing to emigrate to New South Wales. Iremonger came again, his preaching improved since the previous year, Katherine thought. Dr. Smith, the Master of Pembroke College, spent a few days at the Hall, as did the Misses Panton, Paul's sisters from Plas Gwyn.

At the end of October uncle John died in Shrewsbury, a kind-hearted man who had been married for fifty-five years. With his death the older generation disappeared and, of course, Joseph now came into full possession of the Corbett estates, making him a wealthy man.

Their year was not at an end, however, for a general election was called for early November in which Joseph was to play a prominent role in the local campaign. The election was a delayed reaction to the death in January of William Pitt, Prime Minister almost continuously since 1784. Pitt had lived long enough to rejoice at the great triumph at Trafalgar, but Napoleon's crushing victories at Ulm and Austerlitz over the Austrians and Russians meant that Allied victory in Europe was at best a distant prospect. Deprived of his experienced minister, George III had reluctantly accepted a 'Ministry of All the Talents', headed by Lord Grenville but with Charles James Fox the leading figure. In spite of Fox's death in September, the new government faced the imminent election with some confidence.

There were then county and borough seats. Joseph, as a landed gentleman, qualified as an elector in the county. Since 1774 one of the two seats for the county had been controlled and filled by a member of the Hill family, whose two branches lived at Hawkstone and Attingham. It was the retirement of Sir Richard Hill, the first prominent Evangelical to sit in the Commons and who had supported the anti-slave trade campaign in co-operation with Joseph, that opened the prospect of a contest in the county. The other sitting member, Kynaston Powell, had shared the representation for Shropshire with Sir Richard since 1784; both were Pittite Tories. Sir Richard had hoped to be succeeded by his nephew, Colonel John Hill, but was persuaded to support John Cotes of Woodcote. Joseph had a good opinion of Cotes, but when Sir Corbet Corbet came forward as a candidate he felt obliged to back his distant relative. Cotes, however, had such support that Joseph was asked to persuade Sir Corbet to withdraw, which he did at the last moment 'to preserve the peace of the county'.[2] Kynaston Powell and John Cotes were elected unopposed.

It was very different in the borough, where Joseph was also qualified to vote through his property in Shrewsbury. 'The political character of the borough's M.P.s [had come] to depend on rival interpretations of the qualifications for the franchise'.[3] This was determined by the party in power in the Commons, with the result that from 1723 to 1774 it had been limited to the Corporation — which was under Whig control. This was so entrenched that the party leaders had agreed that the county would return two Tories and the borough two Whigs. But the suicide of the famous Robert Clive of India, one of the town's M.P.s, during the 1774 election campaign, and a court ruling three years earlier that had extended the franchise to all burgesses assessed to the local rates, blew this agreement apart. The upshot was the election of William Pulteney, later to become a Pittite, who served as an M.P. for thirty years until his death in 1805. His fellow M.P. for the borough until 1796 was John Hill, brother to the county member Sir Richard. In that year an Attingham Hill, William, successfully contested the seat with a Hawkstone Hill. Like many other boroughs, Shrewsbury had a reputation at election times for corruption and bribery.

Since the last contested election in 1796, Joseph had become a much more considerable figure in the borough as well as the county. When the candidates presented themselves in November 1806, William Hill, now supported by both branches of the family, was nominated by the long-serving county M.P., Kynaston Powell, and seconded by Joseph. Hill was certain of success, but the other seat was vigorously contested by two very different candidates — the Hon. Henry Grey Bennett, grandson of the Earl of Tankerville, but a radical Whig, member of 'the Mountain'[4] and would-be humanitarian reformer; and Thomas Jones, a Tory who came forward under the banner of 'Jones and Independence', claiming to be the true successor of Pulteney, who had ended the Corporation's long control over elections in the borough. Jones had earlier sat as M.P. for Weymouth. Katherine considered Jones's sponsors to be 'of low extraction', men whom she respected for their industry in making money but who had not cultivated themselves for society!

Joseph, who spoke on the hustings, was attacked by Jones for alleg-edly evicting a tenant. He defended himself with so excellent a speech (wrote Katherine) that some of his hearers were won over, and Kynaston Powell, an experienced M.P., told his wife when he went home 'that he would give a thousand pounds that he was capable of making such a speech'. Joseph had seconded the candidature of William Hill, but he was also drawn to Bennett as a strong opponent of the slave trade; Jones, on the other hand, had earlier voted against Abolition. Half way through the twelve-day poll, Joseph duly cast his ballot for Hill and Bennett. Katherine described how Jones's carriage was followed by a mob, and Bennett had to hire a rival mob for his own protection. As it was, Bennett's neck was cut by a stone thrown by an oppo-nent, while Kynaston Powell and Joseph were hissed on entering the town. Jones, who had lived in the constituency for only six months, continued to make inflammatory speeches. He was even overheard in his harangue to cry 'Down with the Archdeacon!' In his final, spirited speech, Jones denounced 'a most monstrous coalition of candidates' and 'a most unexampled combi-nation of the surrounding nobility, gentry and clergy', besides 'altered assessments, sham succession, false inhabitants, swapped voters, resurrec-tion men, paper-eaters, and a monopoly of agents'. Katherine noted that he had so influenced the minds of 'the lower ranks' that servants had become insolent. For her, the election was to decide whether order and democracy should prevail. In the event, Hill and Bennett were elected, but with the latter only nineteen votes ahead of Jones. The joint victory procession was hissed, abused, and pelted with dirt. Jones's own procession was more impressive, with trumpeters on horseback At the Hall Joseph gave a dinner party for Hill and Bennett, together with thirty other gentlemen and the most respectable tradesmen. Jones, however, had the last word, with a petition challenging the result. The *Shrewsbury Chronicle's* laconic, and only, comment on the election read: 'The contest for this Town is one of the most spirited ever remembered'![5]

☙

While the agitation in Shrewsbury rumbled on for some months, a long-overdue measure was brought before Parliament. Clarkson had written in November to say that the government was pledged to support the abolition of the foreign slave trade, and that Wilberforce would then introduce a Bill for total abolition. This was part of a clever stratagem devised by James Stephen, Wilberforce's brother-in-law and an M.P. who was to play an increasingly important role in the anti-slavery movement. He had realised that allowing the trade in slaves and other cargo carried in neutral vessels to West Indian islands held by Britain's opponents in the war, France and Spain, was bene-fiting our enemies. With the connivance of Wilberforce, and the strong support of the Prime Minister, Lord Grenville, the Slave Importation Bill was intro-duced to stop the slave trade to foreign states in the interests of Britain's war effort. Such action would, of course, involve stopping and searching ships flying the flag of a neutral country, vessels that were in fact often British ships carrying slaves but unable to hoist the Union Jack because they were trading with the colonies of countries with which Britain was at war. With Wilberforce keeping quiet, and acting as if the Bill had nothing to do with the cause of Abolition, this measure had been passed by both Houses in May 1806 and given the royal assent, without the opponents of Abolition realising its true significance — for the effect of the Act (and of the 1805 ban on trade with Dutch Guiana) would be to reduce the British slave trade by more than half. In place of Wilberforce's annual Abolition Bill, Fox, capitalising on the changed mood in Parliament, had had the glory to carry by a good majority the following motion: 'That this House conceiving the African slave trade to be contrary to the principles of justice, humanity and sound policy will, with all practical expedition, take effectual measures for abolishing the said trade, in such manner, and such period, as may be deemed most desirable'. Support for Abolition had been demanded of many candidates in the recent election, and one Abolitionist had even been elected for Liverpool! The coming triumph, however, could not conceal the tragedy that since 1792, when Dundas's advocacy of gradual abolition had won the day, well over half a million Africans had been torn from their homes and families and transported, in British ships alone, to the New World.

The Abolition of the Slave Trade Bill was proposed in the House of Lords by Lord Grenville himself, in January 1807, the very month that a similar measure (unfortunately without adequate machinery for enforcement) was placed before the United States Congress. In spite of the continued opposition of several royal dukes, the Bill was approved by 100 votes to 34. With Panton sitting in the gallery, as his father had done in 1792, the Bill was finally passed by the Commons on 23 February 1807, by 283 votes to 16. Panton's first act was to write to the family with details of that historic moment. The Solicitor-General, Sir Samuel Romilly, had elegantly 'contrasted Bonaparte spreading misery over Europe and Mr. Wilberforce diffusing light over Africa',[6] at which the whole House rose to give unprecedented applause. Wilberforce burst into tears. The Bill received the royal assent on 25 March. One old campaigner, John Newton, who was to die in December, had lived just long enough to hear the glad news.

At Longnor Hall the family rejoicing over the progress of the Abolition Bill was muted by Jane's critical state of health. After years of debilitating illness she finally died on 9 March 1807 at the age of nineteen. The little girl who had been thrilled when Thomas Clarkson put his arm round her neck on his first visit to the Plymleys, and who had at once volunteered to give up the use of sugar, had, like Newton, lived just long enough to know that the British slave trade was at an end. The family's distress was acute for she was the first child to die, apart from the infant boy taken from them back in 1784. Joseph had lost his beloved daughter, Katherine the girl she had brought up since her mother died when she was a fortnight old, but the most distressed was Josepha, Jane's sister and almost constant companion for the whole of her life. Panton postponed his return to the legal circuit to spend longer with Josepha. Katherine found solace in the words of an Isaac Watts' hymn, 'There is a land of pure delight'.

∗

The petition against the election of H.G. Bennett in November was upheld on a technicality, 'for he had neglected to qualify himself before the poll'. Before a by-election could be held, however, the ministry had resigned, in face of the king's implacable opposition to their proposed measures to ease the restrictions on Roman Catholic regiments and officers in the British Army imposed, along with other restrictions on holding public office, in the 17th century. The king's new chief minister, the Duke of Portland, called another general election only six months after the last. As always, local issues and rivalries were everywhere important, although when the dust settled the new government was found to have strengthened its position on account of backing for the king's hostile stance on the subject of Roman Catholic Relief.

In Shropshire the county seats were not contested, with Kynaston Powell, nominated by Joseph, and John Cotes returned unopposed. In the borough the candidates were the same as the previous year — William Hill, certain to be chosen, H. G. Bennett and Thomas Jones — but the result proved to be different. 'The admission of the votes of non-resident assessed burgesses had decided the 1806 election; their rejection was to decide that of 1807, when both Bennett and Jones claimed the support of the town tradesmen'.[7] It was a bitterly fought campaign, characterised by bribery, malicious publications, scandal-mongering and violence. As Jones had been attacked in the previous election for his opposition to Abolition, Bennett was now under fire for his support of Roman Catholic Relief. Joseph was shocked by the level to which the debate descended. He set out his own views in a speech to a meeting of Bennett supporters that Katherine reproduced at length, and that shows clearly why he was in demand as a spokesman on such occasions.

He began by claiming that there are times when silence or forbearance become injudicious at least, if not criminal. He went on:

> I make this observation with reference to a series of publications that have been circulated in the town, tending to mislead the best feelings of the mind, tending to destroy the charities of social life, tending to tear asunder the links and bonds of mutual assistance and mutual good-will, which the necessities of human nature so essentially require.

The real interests of the town had been misrepresented:

> It is for you gentlemen to say how far it has now become a duty that we owe to truth, a duty to the peace and welfare of the town ... to publish some contradiction of these errors, and endeavour to give some juster view of what our conduct has really been and the principles on which it has been founded.

He spoke, he continued, not out of friendship to Hill and Bennett:

The interest I feel to be attacked, the interest I feel to be endangered, is no less than the free and unbiased use of our elective franchise. Are we to be told, gentlemen, that we may give a vote to Mr. Hill if we do not interfere in the appointment of his colleague? Is it manly, is it decent, is it constitutional, that we should barter away half of that right that the law gives us? Gentlemen, I never interfered in the politics of this town; it is not likely that I should ever interfere in them ... I can safely say that I never attempted any influence among you beyond that of a temperate opinion, temperately expressed. I never sought any power among you beyond that which ought to belong to everyone who has the honour to be a burgess of this town, the power or the liberty ... to vote for those persons whom I in my conscience think best qualified to serve the interests of this town, and the interests of the country at large. Gentlemen, I beg leave to declare, and I trust that those who know me will give me credit for the declaration, that I say nothing out of enmity to Mr. Jones, or out of enmity to any of those by whom he is supported. I would not rob Mr. Jones of any fair ground on which he may rest his pretensions, but I am anxious that the high and constitutional ground on which Mr. Bennett stands may not be misunderstood. Mr. Bennett did not seek to disturb the peace of this town; Mr. Bennett was invited here. I had no concern in the invitation, but I look upon his election as most honourable to himself, most honourable to the party by which he was brought forward, and most honourable to the electors by whom he was returned to Parliament. Since that period, however, another cry has been raised against Mr. Bennett, as if the gratings of political discord were not sufficient scourge for the sins of the town, an attempt has been made to introduce the deeper horrors of religious dissension.

He then read part of a letter from Mr. Bennett saying he supported further Catholic Relief 'upon the sole conviction that the safety of the Empire, endangered by the discontent of its most vulnerable part, might be strengthened and secured by the proposed relaxation of the existing law' — opinions that had been held by Mr. Pitt and many ministers. Bennett, he assured them, was a strong Anglican and would support such a measure in future only if the king, Parliament and country were united upon it.

Dr. du Gard, who was present, told Katherine that her brother's speech was interrupted by repeated applause. Bennett's supporters were glad to have such an independent and authoritative figure on their side, a man of integrity who could claim the moral high ground, a leading Anglican who favoured some reform of the laws that made Roman Catholics second-class citizens.

The meeting carried five resolutions: that they viewed with concern the 'calumny and delusion' by which Mr. Jones's cause had been supported;

that Mr. Bennett was just as much identified with freedom of election in the borough as Mr. Jones; that Mr. Bennett was invited and supported by a number of respectable burgesses engaged in or connected with the trade of Shrewsbury; that they viewed with disdain 'any attempt to interfere with individual discretion as to what tradesmen should be employed or what tenant selected'; and that thanks be given to Mr. Bennett, Mr. Corbet of Sandon (chair) and the Archdeacon.

But the outcome of the poll was in the hands of those who determined which burgesses had the right to vote. Katherine lamented in her journal that the Mayor and the assessor, Sergeant Pennington, had disbarred many country gentlemen, although, after much dispute, Joseph's own franchise was confirmed. 'The town, I am told, is a most disgraceful scene of riot and confusion'. She recorded that many men without the vote, women and children, too, were shouting 'Jones for ever', even in their village. After twelve days the poll closed and it was announced that Jones, who received 138 'plumpers',[8] had beaten Bennett by 24 votes. Even after the declaration, feelings continued to run high. On the night the poll closed the 'Talbot', where Bennett and his friends were dining, was besieged by a mob of 300 and many of its windows broken. Mr. Hill declined to be 'chaired' — carried through the streets in a victory procession — which offended Jones who was chaired alone. Hill tried to smooth things over by giving one dinner for those who had voted for himself and Jones, and another for those who had voted for him and Bennett. There were charges and counter-charges for assault, but Bennett, who was said to have spent £20,000-30,000, eventually withdrew his petition against the election result. Four years later, on the death of Sir Thomas Jones, Bennett was chosen unopposed to replace him.

The election over, the family still had to learn to live without Jane. Although Panton was Steward that year, they could not face going as a party to Ludlow Races in July. Uvedale, however, jumped at the chance to accompany his brother and enjoyed dancing at the ball and the public breakfast. The ladies were the ones most affected by Jane's loss — Josepha went to stay at Plas Gwyn for three months, and Katherine had a slight seizure. Mrs. Corbett was well enough in September to take the older children to Shrewsbury Races and to see *Hamlet*, but suffered a miscarriage two months later. During the winter Joseph suffered another long bout of lumbago.

Their grief and continuing spells of ill-health did not prevent entertaining visitors at the Hall. After the death of old Professor Mainwaring, long-standing rector of Church Stretton, his successor Thomas Coleman came to dine. When Coleman dispensed with Richard Wilding as his curate, since he intended to serve Stretton himself, Joseph invited his friend to act as his curate at Longnor, which enabled him to take some services at his other parishes of Coreley and Holgate, and to have cover when he was away or ill. Each Sunday Wilding dined with them, which Katherine, herself always a guest on Sundays, approved: 'As he is a sensible man and has considerable information his society is agreeable'. Mrs. Corbett of Bath, uncle Robert's widow stayed with them and many of her acquaintances were invited to meals to meet her. Mr. Bennett, the defeated candidate dined with them on several occasions, Joseph demonstrating that his guest's radical ideas did not debar him, for they saw eye to eye on Catholic Emancipation as well as some local issues. On another occasion Lord Clive, Lord Powis and Mr. Jenkinson of Pitchford, brother of the future Prime Minister Lord Liverpool, were the guests. Another welcome visitor was Paul Panton who played his violin to Josepha's piano accompaniment; they also played at The Bank, with Josepha using Katherine's pianoforte. Katherine herself played every night for Ann to relieve the fainting fits to which she was prone.

Several friends died in these years, including M. Pelletier, aged 50, the older children's French teacher; Mr. Vinicombe, Panton's former tutor and Pembroke College's 'brightest ornament'; and then Dr. Smith, Master of the college, who had become a regular visitor. But the old friend most missed was Lewis Williams, rector of Woolstaston since 1780, whom Joseph had served as curate over twenty years earlier. Katherine spent some time sorting out his belongings and, with the help of the blacksmith, distributing clothes and household goods among the needy of Woolstaston; the books she kept. They erected a memorial tablet in the village church.

As the years passed the children grew up and developed their individual gifts. Uvedale and Joseph were eventually joined at the school at Abberley by Robert and Waties, who had assumed the role of hay harvesters as their older brothers took up different pursuits. Helen was at school in Ludlow; Joseph jnr. loved music and learned to play both flute and violin. Katherine had entertained them all to Christmas dinner in 1807; she, Joseph, Matty and M. Pelletier made up a four for whist, while Ann sat down to 'Commerce' with ten nephews and nieces, Harriet and Mildred on the laps of the most senior. At New Year 1809 the five boys and the five girls, even Mildred at only four, danced at The Bank, to the delight of Ann lying on the sofa; Josepha danced for the first time since Jane's death two tears before. A few days later at the Hall, Katherine and Matty joined in as Panton had brought two friends. The next month Joseph took Uvedale to enter him at

Pembroke College, while Panton put his brother's name down at Lincoln's Inn.

With Panton now elected to the Corporation at Shrewsbury and Uvedale a student at Oxford, perhaps Joseph felt that the recurrence of his lumbago betokened his advancing years. Certainly his sister worried about him, noting that he no longer talked with his old animation. 'We are very anxious about him', she wrote, adding that 'few lives can be more valuable'. Around the time of his fiftieth birthday, he took Matty and Josepha on two visits to Cheltenham to take the waters. But his usefulness was far from finished. In 1808 he had the honour of serving as Treasurer to the Salop Infirmary, a post usually filled by members of the aristocracy.[9] His archdeacon's charge at the visitations that year, that once more touched on the subject of clerical non-residence, won praise from the Bishop of St. David's. He was still active in encouraging improvements in the village, supervising the labourers who gave a proper course and level to the Cound Brook and built a bridge over it. He continued to take a keen interest in wider issues, although he told Wilberforce that while the slave trade campaign had gripped him, general politics passed him by. He also corresponded with Wilberforce about British involvement in the Peninsular War in Spain. Clarkson tried to enlist his support for a new campaign to end the death penalty for many crimes. Another Clarkson letter expressed deep concern at Joseph's state of health, and while asking for details of the Lancastrian School in Shrewsbury, as well as sentences given at the local assizes, urged him to get someone else to find out these things. If Joseph was low in spirits, he would have been lifted by the receipt of a copy of Clarkson's two-volume *History of the Abolition of the Slave Trade*, which he had inscribed:

> To the Rev. Joseph Plymley Corbett, Archdeacon of Salop, a most zealous and indefatigable fellow labourer in the Great Cause of the Abolition of the Slave Trade, and to whose active exertions that sacred Cause is peculiarly indebted, this work is most gratefully and affectionately presented by the Author.

And, had he known of it, he would have prized the tribute his sister recorded in her journal in November 1809:

> Through life we have been much obliged to my brother, our happiness has been in a great measure derived from him and his family; we should have been insulated beings without him, now we are cheered by our nephews and nieces.

12   THE INHERITANCE DISPUTED

On 28 April 1809, shortly before his fiftieth birthday, Joseph received a letter from a friend in London enclosing a printed sheet that he had picked up at a dinner party. This had been issued by Miss Corbett, daughter of the late Sir Charles Corbett, Bart., who had inherited the title on the death of Sir Richard Corbett in 1774. The paper, addressed to the Nobility and Gentry, claimed that her father should have inherited the Corbett estates as well as the title, but had been deprived by the actions of the late Mr. Corbett, Joseph's uncle Robert. The paper went on to solicit subscriptions to fund a court action, claiming that a number of bankers had already contributed. Joseph asked his lawyer son, Panton, to consult a solicitor and to seek the opinion of two barristers.

The solicitor, Mr. Rosser, and one of the two barristers, Mr. Richards, had acted on behalf of the family back in 1791 when Richard Corbett, son of Sir Charles, had made a legal challenge to Sir Richard's will. In her journal for October 1809, Katherine quotes at length from 'a very accurate statement' drawn up by her brother when Richard Corbett filed a bill in Chancery in 1791. At question was the validity of the codicils added by Sir Richard in his last years. Joseph had written:

> Sir Richard Corbett, Bart., upon the decease of his brother, Mr. Edward Corbett, who died 30 July 1764, writes to Mr. Elisha [solicitor] to consult with him about alterations in the disposition of his affairs, and in the latter end of the same year, executes a will devising his estates to Charles Corbett of London for life, with remainder to his first, second etc. sons, and in default to Mr. Flint of Micklewood (now Mr. Corbett of Longnor) with the same proviso, and so on to Mr. Richard Flint, Mr. John Flint, Mrs. Plymley (sister of the said Mr. Flints), her son then born [Joseph], his first, second etc. sons, to any other sons Mrs. Plymley might have, remainder to right heirs. Note — the Mr. Flints were sons of a Miss Corbett and the nearest relations Sir Richard Corbett had, he and they being equally descended in the fourth degree from Sir Edward Corbett making them third cousins, whereas Charles

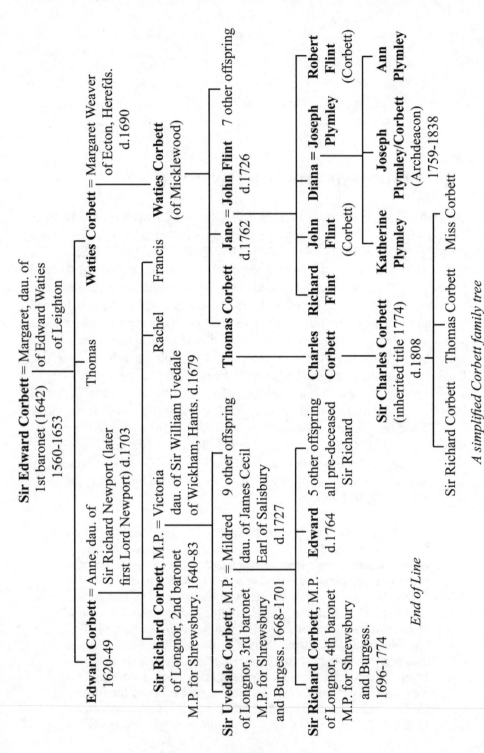

A simplified Corbett family tree

Corbett was a third cousin once removed, and Sir Richard Corbett knew little of the latter, but had always been much connected with the former — In the latter end of the year 1770 Charles Corbett, whose conduct before was not unimpeachable, absconds, having committed one fraud in his capacity of a lottery office keeper to the amount of £990 — In 1771 we find Sir Richard Corbett writing to his lawyers, Mr. Elisha and Mr. Ashby, that he had some time been dissatisfied with the disposition of his property, and was determined that Charles Corbett and his issue should never inherit his estates, he orders either a new will, or codicil to the old will, as may be deemed most secure, to be drawn, for the purpose of taking Charles Corbett and his issue out of the entail of his estates and to confirm all the remainders as they then stood; and this desire and intention he most fully expressed by instructions in his own handwriting by a variety of letters corroborative of the same. And he gives effect to these intentions by a codicil executed 9 June 1771, and confirms such codicil in another 31 August 1771, added for the purpose of leaving £200 to a church, and in appointing an executor in the room of one deceased 1 July 1773, again ratifies and confirms the codicil of June 1771. — In September 1774 Sir Richard Corbett departs this life and Mr. Corbett inherits under the said codicil of 1771 for near seventeen years.

It was on 11 June 1791, Joseph's account continued, that Richard Corbett, eldest son of Sir Charles, and who had been tried for the capital offence of burning down his master's house in 1784 but subsequently acquitted, filed his Bill in Chancery praying to have the will of 1764 established only and the later codicils set aside. Uncle Robert's lawyers prepared their case thoroughly:

The evidence for the answer consists of letters from 1764 to 1773, showing the intention of Sir Richard Corbett in the disposition of his estates, the manner of his transacting other business previous thereto, the similarity of all his proceedings in ordering, directing and executing the codicils in question with others, his usual modes of doing business before and after that time. — Parole evidence of his executing the will and codicils from some witnesses still living, proof of the handwriting of witnesses deceased, proof of all the handwriting requisite; of his transacting other business to June 1771, and also of his having acted since that time as a county Magistrate, and appeared in his corporate capacity as Alderman, at house meetings in Shrewsbury.[1]

The family had wanted the case to be heard as soon as possible, but the plaintiff's lawyers used delaying tactics — for which, as Dickens knew well, the Court of Chancery was to become famous — and it was not until

147

October 1794 that the commission was directed to sit at Shrewsbury to take evidence. According to the minutes of the Chancery Commission, the plaintiff had asked for a postponement as his clerks had failed to inform him of the date for the commission to start work. The plaintiff, Richard Corbett, was told that the examination of the defendants' witnesses would be conducted first, giving him two or three days to prepare his witnesses.

As Joseph further stated, those examined on behalf of the defendants were able to verify that Sir Richard Corbett was of sound mind when he had the codicils added to his will:

> The only two surviving witnesses proved the execution of one of the later codicils, and the handwriting of all the subscribing witnesses was verified. A letter from Sir Richard Corbett to one of the subscribing witnesses now deceased, asking him to attend this execution of the most material codicil was found by the said witness's nephew during the time of these examinations and verified, together with two letters from Sir Richard Corbett to Mr. Hill of Tern, father of the late Lord Berwick, on other business and written in years subsequent to that in which he executed the codicil in question. The appearance of Sir Richard Corbett at a Corporation meeting in Shrewsbury soon after executing the said codicil was proved by the books, and part of the conversation there spoken to by one of the surviving Aldermen. An interview with him on business much about the same time was deposed by Mr. Luther, a gentleman of some estate in the neighbourhood and in the Commission of the Peace for the County, and his presumed general capacity for business at all times sworn to by three respectable inhabitants of the Parish of Longnor who had known him from their childhood, one of whom proved the execution of a bond for money borrowed from his brother not long before Sir Richard Corbett's decease, and the execution of two leases, one in each of the two last years of his life, was proved by his valet or head manservant, who spoke also of his continued capacity for business. The testimony of this last witness was not intended to be offered as he was a legatee under one of the later codicils, but the defendants' solicitor chose to call for him, deeming that no objection as the legacy was in money and had been paid to him. He lived with Sir Richard Corbett many years previous to and until his death.[2]

After the evidence taken at this commission was published, the plaintiff pursued his cause no further, and his own counsel moved to dismiss the Bill. The court agreed and the case was dismissed.

To understand why, fifteen years later, the authenticity of the will and codicils was again challenged it is necessary first to register that Sir Charles Corbett had died in 1808. Thirty years earlier, as soon as he had inherited the title, he had come to Shrewsbury and issued 'ejectments' to the family's tenants as though he had also inherited the estates. He had then sold his annuity to commence legal proceedings. But these were soon abandoned, and from that time he had been content to receive an allowance of half-a-guinea a week from Robert Corbett. In 1791 he had disclaimed all knowledge of and participation in the Chancery suit brought by his son. When he suffered the further indignity of his house being stripped of all its contents by his wife, Robert Corbett again offered him financial help. After his uncle Robert's death in 1804, Joseph had raised the weekly payment to Sir Charles to one guinea, paid every Monday morning by a Mr. Hammond. But when Sir Charles died in March 1808 his son Thomas immediately sent a 'rude and insolent letter', maintaining that his father had suffered unmerited misfortune and applying for help for his family. In an extraordinary twist to the story, Thomas died of a burst blood vessel on the very day appointed for his father's funeral. When the undertaker refused to conduct a joint funeral because he saw no prospect of payment, Panton was approached and through him Joseph agreed to meet the costs. Joseph also went to visit the widow, whom he offered to set up in business, and Sir Charles' daughter, who was offered a £20 a year allowance. She chose to live with her brother Richard, who now had the title and who accepted an annuity of £100. To Katherine's mind, they had been very well looked after; no doubt it looked different from their side.

It was this daughter, egged on by some very dubious characters, who saw the possibility of at least making money out of this situation and had the flyer printed, which, as we have seen, was received by Joseph from a friend on 28 April 1809. Three weeks later, Dr. du Gard at Shrewsbury advised Katherine that he, too, had picked up a copy of Miss Corbett's paper — which he thought, recalling the scurrilous publications when the poll was held two years before, was 'an electoral squib' from Mr. (now Sir Thomas) Jones. It was agreed to keep quiet about it in Shrewsbury. Shortly afterwards, however, an item appeared in both local newspapers soliciting subscriptions for the family of 'the late Sir Charles Corbett' to assist the son in making his claims. It was thought that they raised about £100 in these ways, including a contribution from the Bishop of Durham! The topic was much discussed in Shrewsbury, where there were still people bearing grudges from the elections who were glad to embarrass the archdeacon. Joseph even had one of Miss Corbett's papers thrust into his own hand as he left a Board meeting at the Infirmary. He considered taking legal action, which Panton supported, but decided not to proceed. Then an article about Sir Charles and the Corbett estates was published in *The Gentleman's Magazine*.[3] It referred back to his obituary that had appeared the previous year. That account of his life included the claim that it was 'an unfortunate accident' with a lottery ticket — that came up with a prize of £20,000! — which had led to the change in Sir Richard Corbett's will that deprived Sir Charles of the estates. It had reported that his latter days 'were clouded with absolute penury'. The paper published in *The Gentleman's Magazine* of June 1809 first painted a picture of the Corbetts as an illustrious family, listing their significant roles over the centuries and the noble families they had been linked with by marriage. When it turned to Sir Richard's will of 1764 and the later codicils, it asserted that: 'He lived to a great age, and in his last years became quite childish', and that 'an interested relative influenced him'. It even claimed that: 'The whole County, on the death of Sir Richard, rang with the report of the transaction, as Sir Richard's incompetency [*sic*] to make any bequest was fully and generally known'. 'The present Sir Richard', it continued, 'unhappily does not possess the means of recovering his right', and his sister 'is resolved to prosecute the legal claims of their birth', but was suffering from depression and unmerited poverty. It appealed, therefore, for subscriptions from the Nobility, and especially 'the Female Nobility', to make possible the prosecution of their claims in a Court of Equity. Lawyers, it was alleged, considered the late Sir Richard to have spent his last years 'in a state of mental imbecillity [*sic*] and that his absolute incompetency' meant he was open to manipulation by a close member of his family. The article concluded with a named lawyer's opinion that the signature on the key codicil was written more clearly than the signature on the original will and was unlike Sir Richard's customary handwriting.

On 30 October, two days before Joseph returned from taking the waters at Cheltenham, a man called at the Hall and thrust a missive for the archdeacon into the hands of the cook. It turned out to be a Chancery writ summoning Joseph to appear on the first day of term, 6 November, at the suit of the now Sir Richard Corbett. Joseph at once contacted his Shrewsbury solicitor who asked their London colleague, Mr. Rosser, to represent him. The copy of the bill filed by Sir Richard that Rosser sent on to them covered the same ground as in 1791, and as set out again in *The Gentleman's Magazine*: the unfitness of his namesake in the early 1770s to change his will because of his age and imbecility of mind, and the influence that uncle Robert had over him.

Although Rosser, and indeed Panton, considered it unnecessary on account of the strength of their case, Joseph sought counsel's advice on how to keep proceedings short. This was obviously a wise move when it was found that the other side had retained Sir Samuel Romilly, 'an eloquent Chancery pleader' and former Solicitor-General. Under these circumstances Sir Richard properly refused his annuity, but his sister continued to press for her payment even though it was thought she might be married to the man, said to be a Methodist preacher, who was hawking her paper round the bankers and other prospective subscribers.

In the Court of Chancery things moved very slowly, retarded further by the plaintiffs' need for money and their recognition that when the issue was resolved they would lose their justification for begging aid. Meanwhile, they were actively seeking information from local people, asking in particular if Sir Richard in his last year had appeared at the 'cockings' (cockfights) at Longnor, perhaps an indication of his state of health. The letters of inquiry came via the landlord of the 'Blue Boar' at Ludlow and were apparently sent by a Miss Beddoes, an eccentric lady at Longville who had once dined at Longnor Hall. One letter was sent to a doubtful character called Griffiths — known locally as 'Jack the Jumper' — who showed it around as he was illiterate and as it offered half-a-crown a day for his inquiries. Joseph's friend and curate, Richard Wilding, 'who is never given to judge hastily or to take anything upon slight grounds', informed him that about ten years earlier Miss Beddoes had taken a fancy to a sea captain and made a voyage with him to America, that she was now over thirty, and that having been taught French by a refugee monk she had become a Roman Catholic and attended mass at Acton Burnell. The vicar of Wistanstow, Robert Johnson, whose congregation included her parents, passed on the information that she was causing them so much uneasiness that her father had her letters delivered first to him. Mr. Johnson convinced them that their daughter was writing the letters in question but signing them 'Willet'. Joseph's fellow magistrate, Thomas Stackhouse, contrived to procure a letter from Miss Beddoes which confirmed that the Willet letters were in her handwriting.

A certain Richard Williams, once a servant of uncle Robert and remembered as sulky and violent-tempered, but not averse to asking Joseph or Panton for financial assistance, now took Miss Corbett and her 'husband' as lodgers at his house in London. Soon after Joseph succeeded to the estate, Williams had called at Panton's chambers to assert that his father was not the rightful heir. He now claimed to be the principal witness in the case, though he had not been more than fourteen when old Sir Richard died. He

151

told Panton's clerk that they had had a letter from Ludlow offering assistance; this correspondent was most likely the eccentric Miss Beddoes, whose intervention, nonetheless, may have encouraged them to file the bill in Chancery. When Williams called again on Panton to request payment of a bill for his child's schooling, which Panton had agreed to settle, he told him, in front of a witness, that Bond — for this was the name of Miss Corbett's lover — was 'a great rascal'. He divulged, too, that Bond regularly received letters from a Longnor local calling himself 'Thomas Forrest', who kept him informed of what was going on in the village and what he had learned from elderly folk in the neighbourhood like 'old Marston the carrier'. He also reported that Bond had had agreements drawn up by lawyers to divide Miss Corbett's share of the property between her and himself. Panton learned that Williams had had letters printed outlining their claims that he was sending to all Members of Parliament.

It seems clear that while the alteration in Sir Richard's will had understandably shocked and distressed Charles Corbett and his family, who had expected to inherit the estate as well as the title, they had allied themselves with a very shady character in Bond. Whether or not he was ever married to her, he certainly exercised a great and malign influence over Sir Charles's daughter. Bond was clever, manipulative, and a seductive speaker. Even Thomas Clarkson later warned Joseph that Bond told a plausible story. And it would have sounded plausible to people ignorant of the details of the case. So when Bond and his agents paid visits to Longnor and its neighbourhood to try to find persons willing to testify that Sir Richard had become senile — and that 'uncle Robert', his steward and principal beneficiary, had exercised improper influence over him — ordinary folk were confused. Could the allegations be true? They did not want to lose their landlord who, as their parson, too, was generally loved and admired, but could it happen that the court would find against him? Such people did not know what to think or do as years passed and the case did not come to court. Individual reactions no doubt varied according to the credence given to rumours and the opinions held of those locals who sided with Bond.

Richard Corbett himself, or Sir Richard if he used his title when at work, was employed in the East India docks, earning 14/- to 18/- a week. An informant 'rather high in East India House' advised Panton that the Directors were asked for donations by Corbett and Bond 'early in the business'. They had inquired into it but did nothing more. Corbett was soon complaining that he was receiving nothing from the subscriptions, the money having all gone to his sister and Bond. She was now close to her confinement with what was assumed to be Bond's child; some years before she had had a child by another man. Corbett now had the effrontery (in Katherine's eyes) to petition the court to allow him to sue *in forma pauperis*, which would be less costly. At Joseph's request, his lawyer, Robert Pemberton, went to London to consult with counsel. They agreed with Panton that Richard Williams should not be asked to swear an affidavit of his disclosures in Panton's office as 'he is a bad man and our only reason for believing what he has told Panton is the probability of it'. But they did agree to move in the Court that Corbett should not be allowed to plead as a pauper. The Chancellor rejected this, but his disapproval of the measures used by that side made Joseph's counsel confident of victory when the cause came up. One of the lawyers told Pemberton that in the City Bond's 'character was most notoriously bad, and that they would so advise Corbett's lawyers'.

Bond lived up to his reputation by placing garbled accounts of what the Chancellor had said in several newspapers, again soliciting subscriptions. He sent an advertisement for the *Shrewsbury Chronicle* to Mr. Hipkiss, then a preacher at the Methodist Chapel in St. John's Hill, who took it to the editor. At his request, Mr. Sandford, the bookseller, agreed to receive any contributions that were forthcoming. Sandford also had handbills printed in Shrewsbury to the same effect and distributed them all about the town on 17 March 1810, which was a Fair Day. Copies were the next day 'strewed along the turnpike road between Dorrington and Leebotwood, particularly near Longnor, by a man on horseback; this man called at the door of the public house in Leebotwood with his face covered with a handkerchief, and threw a handful of these handbills in; he afterwards did the same at the blacksmith's there'.

Panton, in London, sent his father a copy from *The Globe* of a statement giving a false picture of what had happened in the Court of Chancery; *The Packet* and *The Statesman*, the most violent of what Katherine termed 'these Jacobinical papers', carried similar accounts. Panton had now come round to Joseph's view that they should insert in some newspapers extracts from the court stenographer's notes to refute the prejudicial accounts that were being printed. They debated whether to use *The Globe* and *The Courier* or the more respectable *Morning Post* or *Morning Chronicle*. What they had feared then occurred — a copy of *The Globe's* one-sided account appeared in the *Shrewsbury Chronicle*. The following week it reproduced the court stenographer's short-hand notes, and a week later Eddowes' *Salopian Journal*[4] printed these at greater length. With so much publicity the family at Longnor felt under increasing pressure, which intensified when they rose one morning to find that more than forty young trees planted in the lawn in front of the Hall had been cut off below ground level and then stuck up close to where they had been planted. 'I cannot help supposing', Katherine wrote, 'that it is connected with the present machinations against us, for my brother does so much good to all around him'. Gradually, however, with no further news emerging from the Court of Chancery, the issue must have lost its novelty and the normal pattern of country life resumed.

⤙⤙

While the family at Longnor coped with the stress caused by the challenge to Joseph's inheritance, they were more than usually beset by illness. But good news, particularly of the lives of her nephews and nieces, predominates in Katherine's journal. On 18 June 1810 Matty was 'put to bed and has a nice, fat little girl', who was baptised and given the name Emma by her father that same evening. Katherine, Panton and uncle Robert's widow stood as godparents. Emma was Matty's ninth child, and Joseph's thirteenth. Her oldest half-brother was now twenty-five and established as a barrister, whilst her full brother Uvedale, at seventeen, was at Oxford, where Joseph jnr. had just been elected to a scholarship at Pembroke College. The scholarship was welcomed for its financial assistance and would afford him practice of reading in chapel 'as he is intended for the Church'. A lot of thought was being given to the future of Robert, only fourteen but keen to go into business. He was the subject of a discussion Panton had in London with Thomas Clarkson, who favoured a banking house for Robert but believed he should wait for two years and improve his general education, before spending two or three years in a counting house prior to setting up in business himself. Clarkson, who had written to Joseph lamenting evasions of the ban on the slave trade, expressed his intention of visiting them in the near future.

They had a variety of other visitors. Dr. Luxmore, Bishop of Hereford, came to stay overnight after conducting his visitation at Stretton and before going on to Pontesbury for a confirmation service for seven hundred! Dr. and Mrs. Adams admired the alterations Joseph had made at the Hall, particularly 'the prospect from the back of the house now the kitchen garden is removed'. They were pleased to see 'the air of much comfort in the houses and gardens of the village', where Joseph had also made improvements. Dr. Adams was thrilled at the sight of Caer Caradoc by moonlight and asked if they could climb the Lawley. The next morning, they went first to the 'Court House', a building with glass doors that Joseph had had erected at the foot of the hill,

154

and where they were able to drink tea round a large oak table. They took frequent rests on the way up, but when they reached the ridge and walked along, Dr. Adams was somewhat panicked by the heights. Young Frederic Iremonger came again and enjoyed singing with Harriet (aged eight) accompanied by Josepha. While with them he read family prayers and preached at Longnor. A quite different guest was Mr. Bennett, the defeated candidate in the 1807 election, but shortly to be elected on the death of Sir Thomas Jones. On a visit to Madeira and Tenerife his ship had captured two slave ships off the African coast and escorted them back to England. Mr. Pennant, invited as a specialist in natural history, admired the drawings made by the late Mr. Plymley, Katherine and Joseph.

At this time Joseph was encouraging a young local man to become a schoolmaster. Samuel Lee was the son of a carpenter and joiner at Longnor. He had attended the local school between the ages of three and twelve, and was then apprenticed to his half-brother John, a builder in Shrewsbury. It was while they were building a new chapel at Acton Burnell that he had picked up a Roman Catholic missal and been fascinated by the Latin language. At the age of seventeen he had purchased a copy of *Ruddiman's Grammar* from a second-hand stall and taught himself Latin. With no teacher to guide him, not even a friend to discuss his studies with, he had gone on to teach himself the Biblical languages of Greek and Hebrew. Fond of music, he had learned to play the flute and horn, and had joined the Shropshire Ringing Society. Through these years, he told Joseph that he never sat up later than 10.00 pm and never earned more than 22/- a week. Joseph had met him at his sister's house for she still lived in the village. He found him to be naturally quiet and without affectation. Samuel was now twenty-six and had been married for a year to a dressmaker from Newark. He confided that he had written Latin verses, a dialogue in Greek in favour of Christianity, and a composition in Hebrew. He always carried a Greek New Testament in his pocket. His latest ambition was to learn Arabic with the help of a grammar. Joseph immediately recognised Samuel's extraordinary talent and regretted he had not known him earlier when he could have found him a place at Pembroke College. He now suggested to his young friend that he could help him, if he wished, to become master of a charity school in Shrewsbury, though he warned him that 'he had to consider whether his temper could bear the irritation and trials he would meet with from idle and stupid boys, this being as necessary a qualification for being a teacher as learning'! In spite of this warning, Samuel decided to take up the proposed position at Bowdler's Foundation School[5] where Joseph encouraged him to take on private pupils to supplement his income. Writing to Robert, Joseph told his son of Samuel's remarkable story and ended: 'The most valuable inference to be drawn from this account is to show what may be learnt by those who apply with all their mind'. But Joseph knew that it was not just by his industry that Samuel had made himself a master of several languages: he had a rare gift. Notwithstanding his new educational responsibilities, Samuel was soon reporting that he was making good progress not just with Arabic but with Persian also. Joseph helped him purchase a good bed so that he could supplement his income by taking a boarder. The tutors at Pembroke were impressed by Samuel's writings that Joseph had sent them, and regretted that as a married man he was barred from membership of the college. Joseph's greatest contribution was to introduce Samuel to Dr. Jonathan Scott who had been Persian secretary to Warren Hastings and Oriental Professor at the East India College in England. Scott feared that Samuel Lee would work himself to death, but in fact he was managing very well and expressed delight with a Persian dictionary that Joseph had bought him for twelve guineas.

Joseph must have wished that he still had the stamina that Samuel possessed because he continued to carry many responsibilities and was constantly concerned about his family — the boys' careers and, sadly far too often, the health of the women and girls. With Panton a practising barrister, and Uvedale in his pupillage with a Special Pleader — for which his father paid £100 a year — Joseph's attention was concentrated on his younger sons. Joseph jnr., who needed extra tuition in his first year at Oxford, was destined for the Church, while Waties, at fourteen and still at Abberley with Mr. Severne his tutor, would also take holy orders. It was Robert, not sixteen till January 1812, who was foremost in his father's mind. Heeding Clarkson's advice, Joseph favoured a bank as safer for Robert's moral character as 'there are so many temptations to act not strictly legally in mercantile concerns'. He was placed in a banking house in the City with a Mr. Forster, known to a family friend, and began as a junior clerk with a salary of £70 a year; he shared Uvedale's chambers at Lincoln's Inn. Katherine, who was very fond of him, was anxious that for one who loved country life and pursuits he would not be happy working long hours in a bank, but she was pleased when he asked to receive the sacrament 'before going out into the world'. When he could not get home for his first Christmas, he asked them to send him a goose pie and some Longnor ale; Katherine added some mince pies.

Robert's absence meant that for the first time the whole family was not together for Christmas. And 1811 had been a difficult year, putting a great strain on Joseph. The anxiety over the legal dispute and illness was compounded by

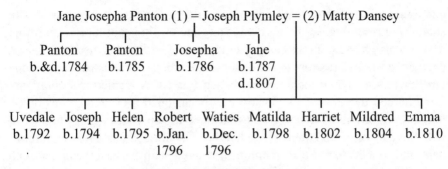

Jane Josepha Panton (1) = Joseph Plymley = (2) Matty Dansey

Panton	Panton	Josepha	Jane
b.&d.1784	b.1785	b.1786	b.1787
			d.1807

Uvedale	Joseph	Helen	Robert	Waties	Matilda	Harriet	Mildred	Emma
b.1792	b.1794	b.1795	b.Jan.	b.Dec.	b.1798	b.1802	b.1804	b.1810
			1796	1796				

Joseph's family

freak weather. A great storm on 27 May had caused the Cound Brook to rise so high that temporarily the Hall was cut off from the church. It was worse in other parts of the county: a cloudburst over the Stiperstones produced a flood that moved 'like a monstrous serpent' and swept away several cottages. Three were drowned in Minsterley and four in Pontesford. There was flood damage in Shrewsbury, Meole bridge and Wyfold bridge were carried away and Walkmills inundated. Joseph and Matty, with Helen and Matilda, were away taking the waters at Leamington Spa and Cheltenham, but Dr. du Gard who visited the stricken areas described the damage to them and launched a fund for the victims.

Helen, their eldest daughter, had accompanied her parents in a quest for better health as she had been suffering from stupor and then violent convulsions. She had been given electric shock treatment when her jaws clamped tight, making it almost impossible to take food or medicine. Dr. du Gard had stayed overnight to attend her. Matilda's ulcerated throat developed into a quinsy. Joseph's sister Ann remained an invalid, up for only a few hours a day, though she still prepared medicines for those at the Hall and the local poor. She even managed to respond with alacrity when Joseph's waggoner, Richard Burgess, fell from the cross-shaft and was run over by his own cart. Ann was able to take down the details of the will dictated by the dying man. Helen and Matilda made good recoveries while away from home and were fit enough to attend a Commemoration Ball at Oxford with Uvedale and Joseph jnr. and to enjoy a party on the river.

Late in the year illness struck again. Josepha, who had stayed at Plas Gwyn on Anglesey in the summer, suffered terrible headaches and Dr. Evans applied leeches to her temples. Joseph wanted du Gard to see her, but there had been such ill-feeling at the Infirmary over his election as a physician that he and Evans were not on speaking terms. Joseph determined to reconcile them, telling Evans that 'we never could want a motive as Christians to subdue our resentments'. Evans denied any such feeling, but Joseph knew that Mrs. Evans had sent an unpleasant letter to du Gard on his election. Joseph persuaded the two doctors to see Josepha together. 'I doubt whether anyone but my brother could have accomplished this', was Katherine's comment. They agreed that Josepha's malady was occasioned by a 'dangerous determination of blood to the brain' and continued to apply leeches. Katherine sat with her daily and read the Bible to her, but Josepha felt that death was imminent and looked forward to reunion in heaven with her sister Jane. Joseph was extremely distressed, telling Katherine that 'he did not know that he had ever felt greater weight upon his mind'. Panton came to see her, and a slow improvement began. But then typhus fever struck Joseph's dairymaid, Molly, and a servant boy, William, and there were fears for Ann who had had a long visit from a poor young woman asking for medicines for her family who were down with the fever. Du Gard sent Harriet, who had been staying at The Bank, back to the Hall and forbade any movement between the two homes. The servants recovered, but Ann remained in a 'gentle delirium'. Yet after Christmas she too began to improve, though she did not come downstairs.

They must have prayed for better fortune in the new year of 1812. But it was not to be. Joseph's wife had become ill with pain and fever on 29 December. Du Gard came and bled her and said there was no cause for alarm. Yet she became worse and Katherine admitted she would have been very worried had she not seen Matty recover from such illness many times. By 4 January, however, she was delirious and breathless. A blister was applied, but her condition deteriorated and she died on the afternoon of Sunday, 5 January, as the bells were ringing for the evening service. She was forty years of age and had been married to Joseph for twenty-one years. Joseph again had to suffer the loss of his beloved wife. Katherine wrote: 'I do not think I ever saw her look prettier than in the last year of her life'. She described Matty as plump and rather short, having a fair complexion and dark brown hair. Besides caring for her husband and nine children, 'she had spent a great deal of her separate income in buying clothing for the poor, principally for children; she paid for the making of many and she made many herself, it was her principal needlework, and she gave to a great extent for many miles round — the bundles that now lie ready to be given, some made, others put together for making, speak as it were from the dead of the alms deeds that she did'.

Katherine, remembering how devastated her brother had been by the death of his first wife, Jane Josepha, twenty-four years before, must have feared for him. But Joseph was now a more mature man, experienced in life's ups and downs, more assured in his faith and, above all, aware that his first priority was to comfort the children. Katherine wrote: 'It is impossible for me to do justice to the holy calmness and pious resignation in his behaviour', when she saw him immediately after the death. 'His behaviour indeed was beautiful and a pattern to all — he took every meal with his family, and was at all times ready to converse with them and to console them'. In the evenings before the funeral he read aloud to the family. The burial service at Leebotwood was conducted by Mr. Wilding. As Joseph had determined that when his time came he would have no lead coffin, there was none for Matty. After the boys had returned to their work and studies, Uvedale wrote to his father that all was well with Joseph and Robert, and thanked him for his letter with its 'excellent and comfortable advice'. In time a plaque was erected in Matty's memory:

> Disinterested and unaffected in every situation, she was exemplary as a faithful wife, an affectionate mother and a liberal benefactor to the poor. She had passed through many years of bodily pain, which as it had not diminished the patience of her mind, so neither had it injured the beauty of her person, when by a short illness she was lost to this world January 5th 1812, aged 40 years.

Joseph received many letters of condolence. Mr. Severne, tutor to the boys, wrote: 'You who have arrived to a higher degree of excellence than most of us can ever attain to, can convert such trials into blessings'. And Lord Muncaster, who had also lost a wife and a daughter, expressed his faith that 'those who have left us are not only safe from the miseries of this life, but they are gone to an abiding City — and we have the confident hope that God is with them'. Emotionally Joseph seemed to hold firm, but the heart palpitations and fever that du Gard treated arose, his physician believed, from his distress of mind. Panton took over the evening readings to the rest of the family and, Katherine observed, stayed at home 'to dedicate his time to the comfort of his father'. Lord Muncaster came to stay in March and gratified Katherine by getting Joseph talking freely again. Only at the end of March — recalling what had happened after his first wife's death — did Joseph resume his normal clerical duties. A fortnight later he preached at St. Chad's in Shrewsbury on behalf of the newly-formed Auxiliary of the British and Foreign Bible Society. He took as his text 'Thy kingdom come', speaking for forty minutes, rarely looking at his notes. Katherine thought she had never heard him more impressive. Yet she noted, 'Though not yet fifty-three he looks so good and venerable', and the next month, after a cold, 'he looks pale and rather shrunk, he has for the last few years drunk very little fermented liquor, he now wholly abstains from it'. Of course he continued to be anxious about Josepha's health and Robert's slow progress in the bank, but was heartened by young Joseph's examination success at Oxford and by a splendid letter from fifteen year-old Waties then being tutored by Frederic Iremonger at Winchester. He was deeply concerned, too, for the young girls who had lost their mother — on her death Matilda was thirteen, Harriet nine, Mildred seven and Emma not yet two. Once again Katherine assumed the role of substitute mother visiting the Hall daily. The boys were older and better able to cope: Uvedale felt he could take Joseph and Waties to hear an oratorio at Covent Garden.

Through all these family vicissitudes Joseph was never able to escape from the dark shadow of the impending legal challenge. The other side had published their evidence, which Katherine had described as a 'strange mass of false-hood' and 'a farrago of absurdity as well as wickedness'. News came early in 1812 that Bond had put down the case for hearing before the Master of the Rolls, which at least was likely to be quicker than the Court of Chancery. Panton then reported that Bond's witnesses were being questioned, not before a Commission as he had said, but by the Public Examiners in London. Sandford, the Shrewsbury bookseller, had visited Longnor to try to meet two old inhabitants, but when he inquired at Hammond's shop, he was told by Hammond that he had been a servant of Sir Richard and that his master had been perfectly sensible in the last fortnight of his life. Nonetheless, by late February three locals had appeared before the Examiners: Richard Williams, Rebecca Roberts and John Hodges. Hodges was a Coldstream Guardsman, son of a butcher in Longnor, and regarded as a man of bad character who had deserted his wife and family to join the army. Joseph himself, little more than a month after Matty's death, had gone up to London, where he consulted with his lawyers and met his eldest son regularly. They decided not to cross-examine, keeping their own case secret. Two other witnesses had come forward for the plaintiff: Edward Jones, who had not lived locally till long after Sir Richard's death, and uncle Robert's former huntsman (but only after the old baronet's death). Katherine thought that their opponents' strategy was most likely to try to get her brother to compromise. On Joseph's return, though he talked cheerfully, he looked ill and did not go out for two weeks. Then came a letter from uncle Robert's widow, who was staying in Oxford, recounting that Bond had even approached her for a subscription;

she had heard that he had raised over seventy guineas in Oxford alone. Bond, meanwhile, had had £50 damages awarded against him for assaulting an old man he lived with, but still 'had the effrontery to go begging about with his evidence in his hand'. The man assaulted wrote to Joseph to tell him that Bond was a villain and so was Richard Williams, who was prepared to give perjured evidence against Joseph while asking him to help him get promotion in the Customs House.

At last the case came before the Master of the Rolls, who directed that it should be heard at the next Spring Assizes in Shrewsbury. Joseph was unhappy with the delay because he wanted it over and as it offered Bond more time to beg. Clarkson had also encountered Bond and advised Joseph that he told a plausible story, with great emphasis on the codicil, 'made while the testator was insane and under the influence solely of those to whom he left his estate'. Clarkson put so many questions — Katherine thought it was the legacy of his slave trade interrogations — that Joseph wrote him a full account of the whole business. Clarkson replied: 'He half frightened me. I feel very miserable on your account. Can I be of use in this affair?' He mentioned that Bond was said to have raised £300-£400. Joseph's response was that Bond was a mendicant preacher 'who thought it would be a good story to beg upon. He is an indefatigable man, and in spite of rebuffs and contempt, he has continued to get from the unwary money to some amount'.

While Bond and his associates welcomed the delay and continued to fund themselves through others' subscriptions, Joseph and his family had to go on living under a cloud while discharging their various responsibilities. Joseph told Clarkson: 'I am much flattered by any concern my friends express upon this subject, but I really feel none myself'. Behind this calm was his deep Christian faith: 'We know that He suffered most who deserved the greatest honour, and therefore His servants who do not merit honour should not repine if they are the subjects of false accusations'. He carried on with his church duties, his guest preaching and his visitations. He was conscious in 1812 that there was less cordiality than usual at these meetings with the clergy, but put it down to differences of opinion on the Bible Society — which was opposed by the High Church party, including their friend Frederic Iremonger (see Chapter 15). But his 'charges' were still extolled. The Bishop of Hereford described them as 'rational and pious, and sure, I think, to make very good practical impressions on the younger clergy, and refresh them in the elder'.

Within the family it was Robert who was still causing him the greatest concern. Although he had now become head of the junior clerks, Robert was fired by the celebrations of Wellington's victory over the French at Salamanca, and told Panton he wanted to join the army. His father wrote him a long letter opposing such a step on religious and personal grounds. 'The Gospel of Jesus Christ and one great object of His mission was to put a stop to warfare. All His principles go to inculcate peace'. If Robert were a soldier he could be involved in an unjust war and would be under orders to go out and kill. He would know nothing of the comforts of a home, would be poorly paid and could sustain wounds or be taken prisoner. He urged him to pursue his banking career. When Robert came home their discussions continued, with the eager young man unable to answer his father's arguments but still attracted to the army. He accepted, however, that he was young — only sixteen — to make such a big decision, and agreed he would not sign up without his father's consent.

It was from Lord Muncaster that Joseph learned of the assassination of the Prime Minister, Spencer Perceval, in the lobby of the House of Commons in May 1812 by a deranged intruder. He is the only British Prime Minister to be assassinated. With the king's renewed mental incapacity seeming permanent, the Prince of Wales, now Prince Regent, accepted the succession of Lord Liverpool as head of the continuing Tory ministry; he was to remain Prime Minister for the next fifteen years. His hold on power was strengthened by the election of October 1812. In Shropshire, Kynaston Powell and John Cotes were returned unopposed for the county seats. In Shrewsbury, too, there was in the end no contest as Benjamin Benyon, a local manufacturer, withdrew before the poll was completed and the sitting M.P., William Hill, had retired before the election. His fellow M.P., H.G. Bennett, came top of the poll, which prompted him to write to the radical peer, Lord Brougham, 'Who would have thought that the Mountain could have lifted so high its head?' The other successful candidate was General Sir Rowland Hill who was with the army in Spain and who in fact never took his seat as he was ennobled in 1814. 'The speeches on the hustings suggest the growth of an opposition to interference by the gentry in the choice of one M.P.', thought Katherine, though she sensed no repetition of the rancour of 1807. Joseph was asked by Sir John Hill to propose his son. He did so, he said, not because of his merits as a military commander, but for 'his Christian graces of mildness and humility', for his valour, and for his strict attention to human suffering. Joseph no longer had a vote in the borough as he lost his lodgings when uncle John's widow gave up her house in Dogpole. Panton and Uvedale worked for the Hill party and welcomed other members of the family when they came to see the town members chaired. 'It was much the finest sight of the kind I have seen', wrote Katherine.

At the end of November uncle John's widow, 'our good old friend Mrs. Corbett', died in Shrewsbury at the age of eighty-four. Joseph was not well enough to attend the funeral, although, at du Gard's insistence, 'he has left off flannel next to him' and wore a strong, warm calico shirt instead of a linen one. All the family gathered in Longnor for Christmas 1812. Robert had left the bank and embarked on a course of academic study. Panton and Uvedale went off to parties and took part in an amateur production of *'Puss in Boots'*. Helen, young Joseph and Robert were taken to the Christmas Sessions Ball at the Lion Inn in Shrewsbury. During the winter Joseph developed 'his usual complaints and the irregularity of his pulse is very great', sometimes stopping every other beat. He was, of course, suffering from stress as Panton warned him early in the new year that the case was likely to come on soon. Joseph's lawyers successfully opposed the plaintiff's plea to the Chancellor to read out the evidence taken at the Examiners' Office of persons who might not be living at the time of the trial or sick or not able to attend — thought to be a ruse to avoid cross-examination. It was arranged for a legal official to bring the original will and codicils to Shrewsbury. By March Joseph was busy preparing for the trial, including interviewing witnesses who lived at a distance. One day he was accompanied by Helen and Harriet to Powis Castle; on another he took Helen and Mildred 'out for an airing'. His lawyer, Robert Pemberton, went with him to Ludlow and Stafford. Meanwhile, Katherine learned that Bond was encouraging 'some person or persons in the neighbourhood who are determined to give my brother all the expense and, if they could, uneasiness in their power. It is extraordinary that such a man should have enemies, but superior ability, such as he has, does in some minds create envy'.

Katherine was probably right that some of the antagonism to her brother arose out of envy. But, as a prominent public figure, he had inevitably caused offence to some by the stands he had made on various issues; there were supporters of Sir Thomas Jones who were still bitter about the archdeacon's backing for the rival candidate, Mr. Bennett, in the elections of 1806 and 1807; and there may even have been some families still harbouring grievances against the Corbetts on account of the clearing of cottages to provide building land for Longnor Hall nearly one hundred and fifty years earlier. Yet the almost universal rejoicing after the court case was finally decided in Joseph's favour shows that those hostile to him were very few in number. And we know from Katherine's observation before the court hearing that her brother remained serene 'through all the trouble and thought which of necessity falls upon him'.

Panton had been concerned about the selection of twelve jurors from the list supplied by the Sheriff of Shropshire but, on 6 March 1813, Katherine quoted from his letter, 'The jury is struck and is come down'. Ten days later Bond, Richard Williams and two associates appeared in Longnor and tried to gain admittance to several old persons' houses. They were generally ill-received, but Bernard Hodges and Farmer Williams — who 'ought to have known better' as his father had signed the codicil — sided with them on promise of reward. Thomas Everall, eighty-seven years old, had his house invaded three times but dismissed them angrily. They were staying at the public house in Leebotwood where Bond 'preached with great vehemence of voice and gesture ... abusing my brother for keeping the rightful owner out of his estates'. Panton, riding by, could hear him! They picked up two infamous women — Mrs. Haynes of Dorrington and Elizabeth Hanford once of Longnor, 'whose illegitimate children the parish had had to maintain'. Once before they had approached her to swear that 'Sir Richard was become child-like and no better than an idiot', and she had refused saying she would not die in her bed in peace if she uttered such a falsehood. But as their offers of reward increased she gave way. Bond and his friends gave great alarm to local people and Joseph's tenants, who had never encountered persons like these before and, while loyal to the archdeacon, did not know how to respond. Fortunately, however, increasing numbers of respectable people and some simpler folk offered to testify on Joseph's behalf so that by the time the trial began he had fifty witnesses. Katherine was honest enough in her journal to admit: 'Though certain of the justice and strength of our cause, yet as the time drew near the proverbial uncertainty of law very often occurred to me'. She drew strength, like her brother, from her faith: 'I resigned all into His hands who knew the whole of our existence and what was really best for us'.

Joseph went to Shrewsbury with Katherine the day before the hearing began. Lawyer Pemberton had already interviewed the witnesses at the 'Talbot'. Even their old cook, Matty Brown, who had served uncle Robert and then Joseph for over forty years, had volunteered her services. Panton, Uvedale and Dr. du Gard accompanied Joseph to court on the morning of Saturday, 20 March. The courtroom was crowded and the atmosphere tense. A young man, who had climbed to an elevated position and was asked to move, fell and impaled himself on a guard's pike; he was taken to the Infirmary but died. After a delay, the case of Corbett v. Corbett was heard before Mr. Justice Bayley and the special jury. Mr. Daunsey, representing the defendant, Archdeacon Corbett, took the lead under the direction of the court. He opened the case in support of the codicils in 'one of the most eloquent and luminous addresses we ever witnessed, of above two hours' continuance', reported the *Salopian Journal*.[6] He took them through all the details of Sir Richard's will of 1764, which had made the late Mr. Corbett (uncle Robert) one of his trustees and executors. He explained that after the heir, Charles Corbett, became insolvent at the end of 1770 — Joseph had decided that no reference should be made to his embezzlement of lottery funds — Sir Richard made a codicil the following June which 'took the said Charles Corbett and his issue out of the limitation', leaving the estates in the first instance to the late Mr. Corbett, 'with remainders over, as in his will, directing the persons who should be in possession of his estates to take the name of Corbett'. This was confirmed in further codicils of August 1771 and July 1773. Mr. Daunsey 'then proceeded to bring forth his proofs, consisting of depositions taken in a former suit [1791] instituted by the present plaintiff, and dismissed of his own motion when set down for hearing by the defendant; full instructions from Sir Richard Corbett to Mr. Ashby. in writing, respecting the codicil in question; various letters from him on the subject, expressing his anxiety to have it completed, and his satisfaction at the disposition he had made, both before and subsequent to its execution; also letters to other persons, at and after this period, on different matters of business in which Sir Richard was concerned, some of them as trustee jointly with the late Thomas Hill, Esq., for the Condover estate, and proofs of his writing in the capacity of a magistrate; and the whole establishing beyond all doubt, the fact of his competency to business, and also proving the handwriting of the testator to the three latter codicils, and of the subscribing witnesses thereto'.

It sounded, and was, overwhelming. Bond's counsel, behind whom he was sitting, were overheard urging him to give up long before he did. As the *Salopian Journal* related: 'When about half of the written documents had been gone through, and before any of the respectable witnesses, who were ready on the part of the defendant, had been examined, Mr. Jervis, for the plaintiff, shortly addressed the jury, stating that his client was totally ignorant of the written evidence, which he [Jervis] considered as so convincing and conclusive, in proof of the authenticity of the codicil in question, that he would not attempt to produce evidence which could contradict it. The learned judge then observed that he should have stopped the case sooner if it had not been a pauper cause, and addressed the jury shortly, saying that no case was ever more clearly established, and that the defendant was undoubtedly entitled to the verdict which they immediately gave for him'.

While the court was in session, poor Katherine was waiting anxiously at a friend's house nearby. Dr du Gard, called from the hearing to a patient, assured her that the written evidence was so strong that 'it was impossible to entertain a doubt of our success'; the court, he added, was 'never known to be so crowded'. But it was not until Panton arrived 'with the happy intelligence that a verdict was given for my brother' that she could at last relax and offer up her thanks to God. At the court itself, 'the shout when the verdict was given was in a manner universal, and was no sooner heard than returned by the crowds who were assembled by the County Hall, and now the bells in all the churches began to ring'. Hastening to meet Joseph, she 'found him, as before, serene'. The local paper reported that the crowd outside the hall 'proclaimed the joy and pleasure with which this verdict was received, confirming the possession of the estate to a family, than which, we may safely assert, one more generally and highly respected and beloved, is not among us'.

Uvedale was the first to get to Longnor with the news. Within minutes crowds had gathered in the hope that the archdeacon would return that evening, 'intending to take the horses off and draw him home'. But he stayed overnight in Shrewsbury. His carriage, containing only two maidservants, was cheered wherever it passed on the way back to Longnor. Unfortunately, the parish clerk had the church keys with him in Shrewsbury, but they broke open a door and set the bells ringing — though Leebotwood claimed that theirs rang first! Seventeen bonfires, several on the Lawley, were visible that night from the Hall. The people of the village paraded with music, the public houses at Dorrington were illuminated, and crowds of people flocked to the Hall to dance on the lawns. The celebrations went on for days. On the Monday a sheep was roasted at Leebotwood, and the next day another at Longnor, with beef, potatoes and beer given to the poor. So many gifts rolled in that it was decided to give 10/- to the poor every Sunday until it was all gone. An effigy of Richard Williams on a pole was carried through the village, shot at and then buried. Katherine walked about with her nephews and nieces and 'of course we were loudly cheered'. A large procession with a band went to the Hall to 'chair' Joseph; finding that he was having tea with Katherine they crossed the road to The Bank and played 'See where the conquering hero comes'. Joseph went out to thank them for their kindness and said he was glad that they had showed their liberality to the poor. 'The applause was unbounded'. Parties and dances continued, with the young Corbetts having the time of their lives. At Cardington a hundred old women and others were regaled with tea and other refreshments. A week after the trial a procession from the Longnor paper mill made its way to the Hall carrying a banner emblazoned with Joseph's name. He stood them all beer, and he and the family mingled with them to shake their hands. A band played, a small cannon was occasionally discharged, a sheep roasted, and dancing went on to a late hour. They could see the glow in the sky from a huge bonfire at the Leebotwood limeworks. On Monday, 29 March, a procession headed by a band went up the Lawley and along the ridge, with a great pole drawn by twelve horses. As the pole was raised, firearms were discharged, and Mr. Shuker christened it 'The Pole of the Lord of the Manor of Lydley and Cardington'. Panton expressed thanks on behalf of his father. The band then played the National Anthem, more shots echoed round the hills, and there was dancing on the level stretches. The pole flew a flag with the Corbett crest and boasted a weather vane with the four cardinal points in large letters. Since that time a new pole has always been erected to mark the coming of age of the heir to the lordship of the manor. It is the seventh or eighth such pole that graces the Lawley today. They then descended to the Court House where there was dinner for a large number and a concourse of hundreds. 'All wore the appearance of rural festivity and harmony', an exuberant Katherine recorded. 'I was delighted to see the country fellows dancing in their smock frocks and the young lasses whose dress bespoke them farmers' servants ... They danced with all their heart and full of spirits'. When Katherine realised she had upset some people by leaving early, she organised another dance a few days later with music from Richard Evans, the gardener, on his violin and Richard Everall, the gamekeeper, on the tambourine. After supper the entertainment went on till 1.00 am.

Samuel Lee had come over to Longnor after his pupils were dismissed, and was also present at a celebratory dinner given by Joseph's friends in Shrewsbury at the 'Raven and Bell'. 'After the usual routine of toasts, Mr. Harley, the President, rose and after a most appropriate eulogium on the character of the Archdeacon as a Divine, a Magistrate, a Patriot and a Gentleman, concluded by proposing his health, which was drunk with enthusiasm and with three times three'.

Those in the Longnor area who had sided with Bond were for some time almost afraid to leave their houses, but Katherine rejoiced at the generally kindly feelings which 'make the rich and the poor see their want of each other'. Judge Bayley, in a letter to Panton, had written: 'I sincerely congratulate you on the decision of yesterday, because the matter must now rest for ever, and every mind completely satisfied. I never saw a Cause in which the disposition was so completely made out to proceed wholly from the testator, and nothing could be more reasonable than that the testator should prefer that party who was nearest to him in blood. I hope your father's mind has not been made very uneasy by the contest, and that it will soon recover its composure'.[7] He need not have worried. The nasty activities of Bond over a period of months and the preparation for the trial, coming so soon after Matty's death, had taken their toll of the archdeacon, but his faith had not wavered. The Sunday after the hearing his counsel came to breakfast and accompanied the family to church. Joseph preached on: 'In the world ye shall have tribulation, but be of good cheer, I have overcome the world'. To Katherine's mind she had 'never heard him more impressive and when, after having spoken of the power of Christianity to overcome those troubles that arose from the world, he proceeded to show likewise its consolation in mitigating those severer trials occasioned by the temporary separation by death from those we have best loved, he became so much affected as to proceed with difficulty, everyone felt for him and many were greatly affected'. It was because he was so human, so compassionate, so loving a pastor that he was so widely admired and so greatly loved.

As for Bond, nothing more was heard of him for a year. He then wrote to Joseph asking for an increased annuity for Sir Richard and for the payment of arrears. Joseph agreed to pay the arrears, but did so through a third party in the hope — probably forlorn — that Bond would not get his hands on the money. When, after another year, the news was received that Sir Richard had died, Joseph made arrangements to pay an annual sum to his widow.

13   THE ARCHDEACON AS MAGISTRATE

It was in the spring of 1798 that Joseph agreed to serve as a Justice of the Peace for the hundred of Condover, where he lived, as Sir Thomas Edwards had died and Joseph's uncle, Mr. Robert Corbett, was elderly. It was not an easy time to be appointed. The government was struggling to raise finance for the war against France, and there was widespread poverty and unrest. All this meant increasing demands on the magistracy, for the justices were then not just the arm of the law but also the agents of local administration. One person at least had no doubt of Joseph's ability to cope, for Katherine wrote: 'No gentleman in the county is equally qualified to discharge the duties it now imposes'.

Like other magistrates he was immediately involved in endeavouring to introduce the increased assessed taxes. When the war with France had first broken out in 1793, Joseph had been unwilling to respond to government appeals for voluntary donations to aid the war effort (see Chapter 9) as he did not consider the war was just or necessary, but rather was a reaction against the French Revolution, with whose proclamation of *Liberté, Egalité et Fraternité* Joseph at that time had much sympathy. But the meteoric rise of Napoleon Bonaparte (though he was not First Consul until 1799) did threaten this country, and Joseph consequently believed the increased taxes to be justified. His sister noted he was always at Pitchford (where Petty Sessions were held) as the business for the hundred had fallen almost entirely on him. He had a stream of visitors asking his help in explaining and calculating their taxes. These visits continued when he was made a commissioner for the new land tax and then, as Pitt finally turned to income tax to ensure the government's ability to prosecute the war, a commissioner for that too.

Close to Joseph's heart was the poverty of the people all around him. The disruption of trade by the war, increasing demand as a result of the growing population, as well as some bad harvests and the deliberate holding back of grain supplies by farmers and dealers, led to rocketing prices of basic foodstuffs. As a landowner Joseph's 'peculiar care' was his own labourers, to whom in the severe year of 1801 he gave away rice and broth thickened with vegetables. As the local priest and archdeacon he had a deep concern for his parishioners in Longnor and Leebotwood, Coreley and Holgate where he saw the suffering for himself.

But it was as a magistrate that he was able to take the most effective action. Under the great Elizabethan Poor Law the Justices of the Peace were to appoint overseers of the poor in every parish. They were to work with the churchwardens, and the parish was entitled to levy a poor rate, confirmed by the justices, to provide the necessary support. By the late 18th century the basic duties of the overseers were to relieve the sick and old, and to apprentice poor children. As Joseph responded to Wilberforce's plea for enlightenment as to the true state of affairs in the countryside and what Parliament could do, he maintained that the poor did not need further legislative help but administrative action. 'The poor', he wrote, 'only suffer great distress from want of the laws in their favour being enforced, not from want of such laws'. He believed that it was the responsibility of the justices to make the law known to the overseers of the poor and to the more affluent inhabitants so that prompt relief could be given. 'There is no bound to the extent of relief to be given to the poor by the laws of England'. The problem, he went on, was 'the supineness with which laws are generally administered'. It was the duty of the magistrate to make it clear to the overseers, and through them to the parish vestries, that of two evils they had to choose one. 'That as the price of provisions was too high for the price of labour, they must either reduce the price of the former or raise the price of the latter'. Magistrates, he argued, could raise the price of labour by the day, by the year, or in task work, and from time to time, or they could ensure that provisions were sold at prices appropriate to the pay of labour. Overseers could collect a rate by the week; if there were not enough people to pay it, magistrates had the power to levy a rate on another parish or on any persons within the hundred — or even the county. He concluded that new regulations were unnecessary: what was needed was that the detailed provisions of the Elizabethan Poor Law Act of 1601 should be made really familiar. By no means all of his fellow magistrates would have shared his opinions as many were struggling to maintain their own standard of living and were unhappy at the increased demands made upon Justices of the Peace. Although Katherine's journal made no reference to it, Joseph must have encountered great reluctance to support, and probably some outright opposition to, his intention to relieve poverty by making full use of existing laws. After all, it was only five years since he and his family had come under fire from some of their fellow landowners for their pro-reform stance in the heady days immediately after the outbreak of war.

In spite of Joseph's efforts, poverty persisted and was to become even more acute in the years of depression after the Napoleonic Wars ended. References in Katherine's journal and, from 1814, in his own diary entries, show how frequently he had meetings with poor law overseers in local parishes — Pitchford, Stapleton, Condover, Stretton, Frodesley, All Stretton, Smethcott, Cardington, Rushbury, Pulverbatch and Preen are all mentioned, some several times over. Generally they would have been routine meetings, but on other occasions there had been complaints from the paupers of inadequate provision. His sister's praise for his liberality in his orders to parishes for poor relief is evidence that Joseph was inclined to take the side of the poor.

As a magistrate it fell to Joseph to examine newcomers who claimed poor relief as to whether this was justified under the Laws of Settlement. These had been passed by Parliament in the 17th century to provide clearer definition to what had always been recognised in a somewhat general way that a parish need only relieve its own poor. The Settlement Acts laid down that a person obtained a settlement by birth, by serving an apprenticeship within its boundaries, by being hired for a year (which had led to shorter contracts), by paying rates, and, in the case of a female, by marriage. Joseph examined Thomas Higley as to settlement in 1816, and in September of the same year he recorded that he had examined Richard Parker of Longnor who had lived in Birmingham for twenty years and now sought parish relief. Economic depression after the long wars meant widespread hardship: Joseph noted in June 1817 that he had never known so many applicants for poor relief. His diary records his examination of Sarah Small for a settlement in 1818; ten years later he noted his examination of Robert Cadwallader, a poor boy, and his mother, as to whether he could claim settlement at Comley. In none of these cases did he record his final judgement. As a humane man, Joseph would have been reluctant to use the law to get rid of paupers, and he was anxious about the attitudes in local communities towards those who might become a charge on a parish. In 1832 he recorded the story of a young woman whose husband had a settlement in Longnor by apprenticeship. Her husband deserted her and she was sent to Longnor by magistrates in Manchester. Three weeks later she was walking in the road with her child when she collapsed and died, probably of 'a rupture in the heart', Joseph thought. He wrote in his diary: 'May she have been prepared for this awful call, and may it have been a warning to the parishioners for increased preparation'. Yet it was the long-established practice everywhere to forward vagrants from place to place to avoid their becoming a charge on a parish. The conveying of vagrants had, indeed, been the major charge on the county rate earlier in the 18th century. On a more positive aspect of the Poor Laws, he would have used his influence as archdeacon to persuade local farmers and craftsmen to take on poor children as apprentices.

Joseph would have had a triple concern for mothers of illegitimate children — as a Christian pastor, as the upholder of morality, and as a magistrate who could come under pressure from local people to remove a pregnant unmarried woman before her baby was born and became a charge on the parish. If a woman with a bastard infant was committed to gaol, it was not the duty of the gaol authorities but of the parish to pay for its maintenance.[1] What to do about illegitimate infants and their mothers was a problem that magistrates had to face frequently. If we take the references to the issue recorded in the archdeacon's diary in just one year, 1818, we find Sarah Pritchard, Harriet Heighway of Smethcott, and Mr. and Mrs. Sheppard's maidservant examined by him. A Sarah Goodman was committed to gaol by the magistrates meeting at Craven Arms accused of concealing or destroying a birth. Putative fathers were sometimes questioned by him and may have been pushed into matrimony: two men named in that same year of 1818 were John Evans and Robert Heighway.

The Commission for the Peace was headed, in Shropshire as in other counties, by the Lord Lieutenant. The Justices of the Peace, who discharged the responsibilities, met every three months in Quarter Sessions and monthly in the local Petty Sessions. They had become less socially exclusive during the reign of George III, but they were still principally drawn from the landed gentry, lawyers, doctors and, increasingly, clergy. Archdeacon Corbett figured prominently among the clerical magistrates, on the bench infrequently at Quarter Sessions, but very active in their committees, and most assiduous in his attendance at Petty Sessions in his local area.

The Shropshire Court of Quarter Sessions' first permanent chairman was Edward Pemberton, who held the position from 1785 to 1797. He was succeeded, in the year that Joseph became a magistrate, by Sir Corbet Corbet, who served as chairman till 1822. Joseph was then invited to take the chair but, at the age of sixty-three, declined. As the justices at Petty Sessions referred the more serious criminal cases to the fuller bench at Quarter Sessions, so the justices there committed the most serious offenders to trial before the itinerant judges at the Assizes. Quarter Sessions met at the Guildhall in Shrewsbury until the new Shire Hall was completed in 1786. Its sessions began on a Tuesday and continued for two or three days. On one occasion in 1817, Joseph noted, his lawyer son Uvedale was at the Sessions three days running till 11.00 pm, but added, 'I suppose this is an unprecedented session'. The justices in Quarter Sessions had oversight of Dissenters' meeting-houses, lunatic asylums, theatres, Friendly Societies, printing presses and savings banks. From 1792, to deal with an increasing volume of business, it set up Committees of Visitors to licensed houses. The first permanent standing committees, Gaol Visitors and Auditing Justices, also date from the 1790s; by 1801 a committee of twelve magistrates (three for each quarter) was established to oversee the County Treasurer's and Gaol accounts. As the *Victoria County History* comments: 'Named to that committee, as was natural, were some of the court's leading members like Sir Corbet Corbet, Archdeacon Plymley [it was 1801], Rowland Hunt and the Rev. Edmund Dana' — and Joseph had been a magistrate for only three years! The new body came to act as a General Purposes Committee.

County Treasurers were appointed under the terms of the County Rates Act of 1738. John Flint, Joseph's uncle, was Treasurer from 1764 till his death in 1806; he was also the postmaster of Shrewsbury. He was succeeded as Treasurer by his son-in-law. For years the county rate was fixed at £278-13-0, normally levied twice a year, but by the turn of the century it averaged no less than £5,769 per annum as a result of inflation and 'the court's more ambitious interpretation of its functions in response to the contemporary administrative revolution'.[2] His diaries make clear that Joseph was frequently called upon to act as one of the auditors of the county's accounts.

He was even more closely associated with the gaol. Shrewsbury's prison, which had been built in 1705, was visited by the reformer John Howard several times between 1774 and 1776. His recommendation led to the appointment of an apothecary and a surgeon to serve there from 1780. A strong letter was sent to the Secretary of State in 1785 complaining that there were thirty-one convicts in the gaol who had been awaiting transportation for up to two years, incurring the cost of maintenance and the risk of gaol fever.[3] The letter seems to have had one desired effect, for the inadequacy of the original building was recognised and work began on a new gaol on Castle Hill in the same year. It was completed, with a House of Correction alongside, in 1793. The new gaol was the work of commissioners appointed under a local Act of Parliament. Prominent among them were the Rev. Edmund Dana (by whose name the present prison is sometimes known as it is alongside the street called The Dana), William Smith and Rowland Hunt. The cost of £30,000 was levied on county and borough rates. The prison was built by Thomas Telford, to a design by J.H. Haycock, who had been influenced by Howard. It contained an infirmary and a chapel, with separate accommodation for different categories of prisoners, including debtors. With the new building came new, more enlightened regulations tempering retribution with efforts at reformation. Prisoners could now work and earn small amounts, and good conduct was rewarded from funds privately subscribed to the prison charities founded in 1797.[4]

The formal custody of the gaol had always been in the hands of the Sheriff, but it was run by a gaoler under the supervision of the Justices of the Peace. The Gaols Act of 1791 stipulated the quarterly appointment of visiting county justices, mainly those living in or near Shrewsbury, who could inspect the gaol weekly. They had an important say in the appointment of the gaoler. Running costs, of course, rose under the new regime. From 1796 they were well over £1,000 per annum, from 1806 they were over £2,000, and from 1816 £3,000 — 'much the greatest item of county expenditure'.[5] The gaoler was paid £300 a year from 1806, reduced to £200; in 1823 the chaplain received £150. Joseph was an early appointment to the Committee of Quarter Sessions whose role was to audit accounts and to inspect the prison regularly. His diaries reveal that he carried out these duties with his customary commitment and attention to detail, spending four hours there on one occasion, not arriving home till 6.00 pm and late for dinner. He was sometimes consulted about the discharge of a prisoner, the gaoler once actually coming to his house. In 1817 he noted on an examination of the gaol that there were two hundred prisoners, including forty-five in custody for debt. He also recorded that he had written to the Home Secretary, Lord Sidmouth, in 1821, reporting on the gaol and listing the convicts held; two years later he wrote to his young successor Robert Peel (later Sir). He was involved with appointments to the prison, interviewing candidates for the post of officer there in 1823.

An order of the Court of Quarter Sessions to visiting magistrates in 1822 reveals a problem in a mixed gaol. Joseph and his colleagues were 'to adopt such temporary measures as may appear to them desirable to guard against that immorality with reference to the Female Prisoners which there appears to the Court too much reason to believe has hitherto prevailed, and also requesting their particular attention to the locking up of the Female Prisoners'. There was also to be frequent inspection of the bread supplied and the correct weight of the loaves. In 1828 they were alerted to the problem of intoxicated prisoners brought in by intoxicated constables! Not until 1839 was a regular police force set up in Shropshire.[6] Joseph did not divorce his role as a priest and archdeacon from his activities as a magistrate, regularly meeting and corresponding with the prison chaplain. On a visit to Chester in 1833 he preached at a service in the chapel of the City Gaol. By then, over seventy years old, he had less contact with the Shrewsbury gaol, his son Waties, himself a magistrate, increasingly standing in for him.

The improvement of the road system and the construction of bridges constituted another area of responsibility for the justices. Shropshire owed its network of turnpike trusts to the magisterial class acting as a pressure group in Parliament to secure the passing of local Acts. In his survey of agri- culture in the county, as we have already seen in Chapter 10, Joseph had described the value of turnpike trusts and he was frequently at meetings about them or inspecting their upkeep and improvement. He was also aware of the importance of good local roads to villages and farms. He once noted going to Leebotwood to view 'a road under indictment'; years later there was another such at Acton Burnell. Whenever he travelled he kept detailed records of the state of the roads, the mileage covered and the time taken, calculating the average speed of public transport, including stops, at around seven miles per hour. In July 1818 he made a note that Robert on the Irish Mail did the journey from Shrewsbury to London in 21 hours 40 minutes. Since he trav- elled a great deal to discharge his responsibilities, and later to visit members of his family, Joseph must have spent hundreds if not thousands of hours in his carriage or a coach. In his later years his son Waties more and more often took his place at turnpike meetings.

Improvements in roads had to be accompanied by the building of bridges. The construction of what were known as 'county bridges', as at Atcham, consumed as great a portion of the county rates as conveying vagrants and running the gaol put together in the early years of George III. Costs increased when Thomas Telford was appointed as the county's first surveyor in 1787. He held this post until 1834 when there were over eighty 'county bridges'. As the *Victoria County History* says: 'His ideas were taken up and publi- cised by leading members of the Court [of Quarter Sessions] like Archdeacon Plymley, with whose family Telford was on friendly terms by 1793'.[7] Most of the forty-two bridges built under Telford's direction were county bridges like Montford and Buildwas, but modest bridges over little streams, like the one by Longnor Hall advocated by Joseph could also be very important.

Joseph's membership of several committees of Quarter Sessions involved time-consuming activities, but his commitment to Petty Sessions in the hundred of Condover meant court sessions every month as well as the necessary preparatory and administrative work. In January 1821 the pressure led him to bemoan in his diary that he had never had to deal with so many complaints, warrants and summons — as well as appeals. There were also special meetings three times a year — in January to receive the report of the previous year's highway surveyors and to appoint new ones; at Easter to receive reports from the overseers of the poor; and at Michaelmas to hold licensing sessions for innkeepers and ale-house keepers. This last was far from automatic: a licence was refused for a public house at Picklescott, the 'Seven Stars' at Pontesbury was thoroughly examined, and after consulting the Supervisor of Excise a summons was granted in 1818 against some innkeepers for brewing with wormwood and gentian instead of hops. There was also an annual appeal at the Sessions for volunteers for the militia; where this failed to meet the stipulated complement a ballot was held among those eligible. A midsummer meeting saw the divisional magistrates sitting as tax commissioners. In addition, there were annual appointments of parish constables, not a popular role but necessary before the regular police force was created. The monthly Petty Sessions were held at Stretton in the south of the hundred and at Pitchford or Dorrington further north. His fellow magistrates had proposed in 1806 that some Sessions should be held at Dorrington for the archdeacon's convenience. He had reciprocated by inviting them to dine with him on such occasions rather than at the public house.

With such demands made on their time, justices expected support from higher courts. When Joseph and his fellow magistrates received a *mandamus* (command) from the Court of King's Bench in 1820 that seemed to change the accepted interpretation of a law, he exploded in his diary that if this was not rescinded 'I shall not choose to act as a magistrate in future'.

The number of justices on the bench at the Sessions fluctuated. As the years passed, Joseph was frequently not well enough in winter, sometimes for weeks, even to leave the house, but there were occasions when he was the only magistrate present, as in June 1817 when he was besieged by claimants for poor relief. At that time he was the only magistrate in Condover hundred except for Mr. Jenkinson, the Prime Minister's brother, who was often away. It was more usual for two or three justices to be present. Over the years the names of other magistrates mentioned include Sir John Edwards, Mr. Thursby, Mr. W. Smith, Mr. Joseph Loxdale, the Rev. Richard Wilding, Mr. Clive, Mr. Bather, Mr. George Benson, and Mr. Thomas Stackhouse. There was a time in 1820 when Stackhouse was out of the country and Wilding ill, leaving Joseph as the sole functioning magistrate in both the Condover and Munslow hundreds. It is therefore not surprising that Joseph introduced his son Panton as a magistrate when he had served some years as a barrister and lived at Leighton Hall. From 1824 his younger clerical son Waties joined him on the bench and gradually assumed his place.

Richard Wilding deserves more than a passing mention. He had supported Joseph in the anti-slave trade campaign, and served for years as a fellow justice and member of the Quarter Sessions General Purposes Committee. He was rector of Easthope for forty years, supplementing his stipend with a succession of curacies, serving Longnor and Leebotwood in this capacity for some years until the archdeacon's son Joseph was qualified to take over. Unfortunately he over-spent on extending his property at All Stretton and, as Katherine rather tartly observed in 1817, had managed his estate so ill that he had been in debt all round the county for some years. He was repeatedly arrested for debt but bailed by his friends to keep him out of prison. His plight was made worse by his unambitious sons who were content to farm or work in a counting house. He was also inclined to drink excessively. When he tragically lost his favourite daughter, Joseph had to guarantee payment of the funeral costs. At length he was persuaded to sell his estates, which were bought by Mr. Benson of Lutwyche, who left Wilding his house at All Stretton rent free. Yet Katherine noted that when he met or dined with them he never talked about his affairs. In 1818 he was finally apprehended and committed to Shrewsbury Gaol, where he lived in a comfortable apartment in the gaoler's house, 'surrounded by books, very happy, and comparing his life to that he had at college forty years ago', according to Katherine. Apparently he even continued to act as a magistrate in the prison. In consequence, Joseph at that time was often on the bench alone, and had only his son Joseph, ordained as a deacon, to help serve his churches. Wilding was released, but his health deteriorated and he died in June 1820 while Joseph was away in London — but he returned to conduct the funeral. In his diary appreciation of an old friend, Joseph made only a passing reference to Wilding's improvidence: 'He was a man of learning, of great taste for literature, fond of gardening and one of the greatest planters, if not the greatest, in the kingdom in proportion to his property. He was a man of great plainness in dress and manners, spoke concisely, but his words were generally weighty. He was almost constantly at home and very accessible as a magistrate, and spent his income, and more than his income, in employing labourers for the improvement of his property'.

When Joseph noted 'Petty Sessions' in his diary he included no details of cases or proceedings or verdicts. But it is possible from other brief entries of summonses, examinations and warrants to form some picture of the sort of offences he was dealing with and sometimes passing on to higher courts. Unsurprisingly, in a period of depression and dire poverty, there were many instances of theft. A warrant was issued for Samuel Hanford for stealing coals and, in the middle of another winter, warrants for two men accused of stealing wood and another for removing a hedge. In a country area there were frequent thefts of livestock — Richard Smith was suspected of stealing ducks, John Halbeday and George Howells of stealing sheep, and Richard Pinches of the theft of a horse. One of Joseph's own carriage horses was taken from the fields but quickly recovered. Sir Edward Smythe's gamekeeper apprehended a poacher with four hares and seventeen gin-traps on him; he must surely have been more severely dealt with than Robert Burgoyne who was gaoled for three months for shooting a hare on a Sunday. There were also instances of burglary, George Darby and Richard Littlehales named as suspects on different occasions.

It is easy to think of the above as lesser crimes, but in the early 19th century over two hundred offences were punishable by death. These capital crimes included burglary, robbery, forgery, horse-stealing, and shoplifting of goods worth as little as five shillings (worth perhaps £20 today), as well as the more serious murder, wounding and sexual crimes. As a magistrate Joseph was involved in the early hearings of these more serious offences, issuing a summons, examining the accused, and issuing warrants for arrest. Very often he refers to the committal of persons accused of felonies without specifying the precise offence, for example Richard, Sarah and George Blakemore in May 1817. Cases of assault were common, often within families. John Harding was arrested for assaulting his mother; Edward Shuker after a complaint by his father; and, probably within the same family, Mrs. Shuker made allegations of disturbing the peace against her husband. A 'riot' in Dorrington in September 1818 led to Thomas, Elizabeth and Martha Fox being taken into custody as no-one would provide sureties, but they were released the next month.

Joseph was the magistrate who initially dealt with a number of major crimes. He heard the evidence of William Owen who accused Richard Kite of wounding Elizabeth Cund, whom he visited and questioned in the Infirmary. He issued a summons against Edward Laws for assaulting John Bridgman, a tanner of Little Stretton. It fell to him to issue a warrant for the arrest of John Matthews of All Stretton for attempting to violate Maria Pardoe, a

St. Mary Magdalene's church, Little Hereford,
where Joseph married Matty Dansey, 29 December 1790

*The Archdeacon's illustrations of St. James' church, Cardington,
in the Wenlock Deanery volume of his visitation in 1793*

*The Archdeacon's illustrations of Holy Trinity church, Hol(d)gate,
in the Wenlock Deanery volume of his visitation in 1793*

GENERAL VIEW

OF THE

AGRICULTURE

OF

SHROPSHIRE:

WITH OBSERVATIONS.

DRAWN UP FOR THE CONSIDERATION OF

THE BOARD OF AGRICULTURE,

AND INTERNAL IMPROVEMENT.

BY JOSEPH PLYMLEY, M.A.

ARCHDEACON OF SALOP, IN THE DIOCESE OF HEREFORD,
AND HONORARY MEMBER OF THE BOARD.

"Hate not laborious work, neither husbandry, which the Most High
"hath ordained."

ECCLUS. C. Vii. V. 15.

LONDON:

PRINTED BY B. McMILLAN, BOW-STREET, COVENT-GARDEN,
PRINTER TO HIS ROYAL HIGHNESS THE PRINCE OF WALES;
FOR G. AND W. NICOL, PALL-MALL, BOOKSELLERS TO HIS
MAJESTY, AND THE BOARD OF AGRICULTURE; AND SOLD
BY G. AND J. ROBINSON, PATERNOSTER-ROW;
J. ASPERNE, CORNHILL; CADELL AND DAVIES,
STRAND; W. CREECH, EDINBURGH; AND

Title page of A General View of the Agriculture of Shropshire

Left: Corbett coat of arms in the east window of the chancel of St. Laurence's church, Church Stretton

St. Mary's church, Leebotwood (above and top right). The external memorials to members of the Corbett family lie to the north side of the church

Shrewsbury Prison. This main gate is all that remains of the gaol opened in 1793, shortly before the Archdeacon became a visiting magistrate. The figure above the gate is the prison reformer John Howard

Holy Trinity church, Hol(d)gate, where Joseph became incumbent in 1802 and was succeeded by his son in 1819

*Archdeacon Joseph Corbett. The portrait was painted in early 1819,
shortly before his 60th birthday*

Interior of Longnor Hall in 1964.
The library is on the left, and staircase on the right

Longnor Hall today

girl aged under ten from Little Stretton. He had to take action in the one case of murder that features in his diaries when he issued a warrant for the arrest of Samuel Franks for allegedly killing his father in February 1816. He summoned witnesses whose evidence, it may be presumed, led to the exhumation of Richard Franks, buried three weeks before, and the examination of the body by a doctor in the presence of the coroner. The next morning, Joseph noted, the coroner came to breakfast with him. At the Assizes the team of prosecutors in this case included Joseph's second son, Uvedale, making his court debut. His brothers, Panton and Robert, were there to hear him; Joseph himself could not be present, but had attended years earlier on Panton's first appearance at the Assizes.

The case in which Joseph became most closely involved was the stabbing of Thomas Williams at Church Stretton. Joseph went there to take depositions that led to the charging of Thomas Farmer, J. Watkins and Richard Edwards with maliciously wounding Williams on 15 December 1821 after arguments in three public houses in the town. At the Lent Assizes of 1822 in Shrewsbury the cases against Watkins and Edwards were dismissed, but Thomas Farmer was sentenced to death. Joseph wrote to the judge, Baron Garrow, to intercede for Farmer's life. Whether or not he was successful is unknown, but the judge had warned Farmer that there was little chance of avoiding execution. That was not always the case, because in many instances those convicted were reprieved and the sentence commuted to transportation. In his introduction to his analysis of the legal reforms carried out by Robert Peel as Home Secretary in the 1820s, Professor Norman Gash wrote: 'In theory England had one of the severest penal systems in Europe; in practice it was lenient, defective and haphazard'.[8] Thomas Clarkson had also taken up the cause of penal reform and wrote to Joseph asking if he could find someone (Clarkson knew he was not well) to note the sentences meted out at the Shrewsbury Assizes in the spring of 1809. Three of those found guilty at that court were sentenced to death, but before the judges left the town two had been reprieved — perhaps an example of what the reformer Sir Samuel Romilly described as a 'lottery of justice'.

Petty Sessions received frequent complaints from persons aggrieved on some issue. Joseph had to follow up many of these — complaints from maidservants about ill-treatment, from an apprentice who alleged his master kicked him, and regular complaints about non-payment of wages. Joseph the magistrate did not forget that he was also archdeacon and priest. He made pastoral visits arising from cases, as when he went to see the wife of the convict Robert Pinches. He wrote to the overseers at Rushbury about Martha

Miles who was described as 'a dangerous lunatic', and had a man who had been released from the hulks (prison ships) admitted to the Infirmary.

-℮℮

In her journal of January 1806 Katherine referred to the Christmas party that her brother had thrown for his fellow magistrates. She went on to describe how the previous day they had dined together at the Hall for the first time since Joseph had extended this invitation on days when the justices had agreed to meet at Dorrington for the archdeacon's convenience. She singled out for mention Mr. G. Thursby who was also a keen naturalist. Katherine relished the opportunity to join her brother's professional colleagues, as she always welcomed his invitation to be present when the Justices of the Assize and the accompanying bevy of barristers came to dinner. This custom had been introduced by Joseph's uncle Robert in his years at Longnor Hall, though it is possible it originated with Sir Richard Corbett who had also been a magistrate. She recollected the time when Mr. Dean, a young barrister, had commented: 'Here we all appear on the most sociable and friendly terms in familiar inter-course; one of us [it is likely that he was referring to the archdeacon], by his talents and character arrived at the first rank in his profession, laying all distinction aside, and conversing on the most perfect equality; others, as years and experience entitle them, taking the lead in conversation, one or another, as chance and subjects lead them; and the youngest of us freely giving our sentiments upon any subject that occurs'. It is an attractive picture of the sort of occasion that Joseph most enjoyed, with open conversation among a group of educated professionals. Katherine later recalled one such dinner when a discussion on poetry arose and Helen, Joseph's daughter, felt able to express her opinion.

On these occasions Joseph, as a Christian clergyman and archdeacon, was perhaps able to convey to his guests a sense of their grave responsibility at the forthcoming trials. One year, at the request of Baron Richards, the senior judge present, Joseph agreed to arrange a special Holy Communion service — to which villagers were hurriedly alerted — so that the sacrament could be administered to a judge consumed by anxiety about his responsibility to make life or death decisions on offenders. In time, first Panton and then Uvedale, Joseph's two oldest sons, became barristers and were sometimes present at the dinner with the visiting judges.

-℮℮

One senses that the archdeacon as a magistrate on the bench was committed to the upholding of the law, but always humanely. It is fortunate that at the end of his *A General View of Agriculture in Shropshire* he set out his view of the wider role of the magistrate in society:

> The office of a Justice of the Peace is somewhat expensive and very laborious, more especially as the same persons are, in general, the acting commissioners of taxes. Still many country gentlemen do great service to the public, by submitting to what I may call this disagreeable necessity; for I know not whether it is not essential to the proper strength and harmony of our constitution, that persons of independent fortune should continue freely to execute the laws committed to their trust; that they should as magistrates oversee and direct the police of the country; and as commissioners of taxes judge between the executive power and the people, and that without fee or reward; because the notoriety of their having no other interest in the trouble they take than what is common to all subjects of the realm, ensures a more ready acquiescence in their decisions, and must add to the weight of beneficial influence.
>
> Still in the execution of most laws there must be some extent of cooperation. Few persons like to be informers, few like to be complainants, unless their passions are warmed, or their interests distinctly injured. From the former circumstance many trivial accusations are brought forward; from the latter thieves are apprehended and prosecuted. But that cattle are straying in the roads; that nuisances are left on the highway; that work is not provided for the poor; that servants are enticed to the ale-house – upon these and other occasions, individuals are rarely sufficiently injured to give their time and trouble in praying justice, though there are laws which, if inquired after, would redress most of the evils complained of. A watchful magistrate may do much, but he cannot do everything. Persons of large fortune should consider the burthen of this office as a kind of tax arising out of the interest they have in the welfare of the country; and though it is far from being the case that there is no feeling of this kind, yet it were to be wished that this feeling stood higher, and that persons of property, instead of wishing to educate all their sons for situations by which they may advance the honours or opulence of their families, would consider how the heirs to large estates could be best formed to that highly important, but oftentimes mistaken character, a *country gentleman.* Nothing low, or idle, or flippant, or profligate, belongs to this character. Like every other post in human life it is a post of duty. Independent of the assistance required from him in administering the justice of the country, he should be the adviser and peacemaker of his district; he should cooperate in

the improvement of rural arts; he should be the pattern of improved husbandry; he should set an example of scrupulous obedience to the laws in his own person, and endeavour to sustain the tone of Christian morality throughout his neighbourhood.[9]

These are the principles by which Archdeacon Joseph Corbett sought to regulate his own life. Yet over the more than three decades as a magistrate that remained to him when he penned these sentiments in 1801, he must have been frequently disappointed that too few 'country gentlemen' felt a vocation to the magistracy and that not all of those who were his fellow justices shared his high ideals.

14 LIFE FOR THE LONGNOR FAMILY AFTER THE NAPOLEONIC WARS

More than two years elapsed between the court decision in March 1813 in favour of the archdeacon's right to the Corbett inheritance and Napoleon's final defeat at the Battle of Waterloo, but the Emperor's ultimate overthrow seemed inevitable after the disastrous retreat from Russia in 1812. A Sixth Coalition against the French was formed and Napoleon was forced to fall back on France after the so-called Battle of the Nations at Leipzig in October 1813. Threatened with the invasion of France, Napoleon abdicated in April 1814. The Great Powers at once signed the Treaty of Fontainebleau, which exiled the ex-Emperor to the isle of Elba and restored the Bourbon monarchy in the person of Louis XVIII. Within days the news reached England. Everywhere there were demonstrations of national rejoicing. Joseph's son Uvedale was in Bath from where he wrote to describe the celebrations and illuminations: 'The good people of Bath are almost distracted at the good news, and every person, animal and place, from the finest lady to the chimney sweep, the coach horse to the lap dog, the abbey to the boats upon the canal, are dressed with laurel and white ribbon'. Wealthy people began to talk of going abroad again. July 7 was declared National Thanksgiving Day, marked in Longnor by a crowded service at which Joseph preached. But he discouraged costly illuminations; instead he spent £20 on candles for all householders who would accept them in any of his parishes.

There was great excitement in Shrewsbury when it welcomed Lord Hill, one of Wellington's successful generals in the Peninsular War. As Sir Rowland Hill he had been elected an M.P. for Shrewsbury in 1812, when his candidature had been proposed by Joseph. On account of the war the general had never been able to take his seat in the Commons, and when he was raised to the peerage a by-election had to be held in May 1814. There was considerable support for Joseph's son Panton to stand, but he and his father disapproved of the improper expenses that would be incurred. In the event Richard Lyster was elected to serve alongside H.G. Bennett. But when Lord Hill came to the town in June 1814 it was not as an ex-member of Parliament but as a war hero. It was estimated that a crowd of 30,000, including the whole family from Longnor Hall, gathered to greet the general riding at the head of fourteen troops of yeomanry cavalry. He addressed the multitude from the balcony of the Lion Hotel, where in the evening there was a magnificent dinner and ball. Katherine was delighted to be introduced to Lord Hill, who pleased her still more by praising her brother's character and expressing gratitude for Joseph's generous speech on his behalf at the election of 1812. The next day Joseph went with the Mayor and Corporation to present the general with the freedom of the borough in an elegant gold box. Joseph was asked to deliver an impromptu address proposing that the freedom of the borough be conferred also on Lord Hill's five brothers, four of them distinguished soldiers and one a diplomat. Joseph's own health was drunk with the toast of 'Archdeacon Corbett and success to the Abolition of the Slave Trade'. Lord Hill was to gain further honours as the commander of the right wing of the Duke of Wellington's army at the Battle of Waterloo. His statue, still one of Shrewsbury's landmarks, was erected in the year after the battle. The words of the tribute at the foot of the column are similar to Joseph's eulogy in 1812 and may have been written by him.

As negotiations for a general peace settlement got underway, Thomas Clarkson contacted Joseph about what could be done to ensure that the abolition of the slave trade by other nations should be included in the final treaty. But by the time they met in London in July, the Peace of Paris had already allowed the French to revive the slave trade for five years. Together they went to a meeting of the committee formed to challenge this concession. When the call was made for another petition campaign, Joseph feared that his physical powers could no longer sustain the efforts he had made in 1792, but he wrote to leading gentlemen in Shropshire on the issue, and responded to a personal plea from Wilberforce. At Joseph's request the Sheriff of Shropshire agreed to call a county meeting to propose an address on the matter to the Prince Regent. It was drawn up and moved by Joseph, seconded by Kynaston Powell, one of the county M.P.s. Mr. Eyton, the rich and influential banker from Wellington, could not be persuaded to sign the petition, though he at length agreed not to oppose. The four or five who did oppose were described by Katherine, in the privacy of her journal, as 'violent High Church people'. Sir John Hill, who was moved to tears by Joseph's compliment to his military sons, reciprocated by insisting that the archdeacon was 'the only person to bring the question of the slave trade forward, the only person who can manage anything'. As he had been so prominent in the county meeting, Joseph did not intend to attend the town meeting, where doctors Darwin and du Gard were to support a petition, but at the last minute Robert Pemberton sent a carriage to rush the archdeacon to the meeting where he surpassed himself with a speech following those of the proposer and seconder. The proposal was carried *nem. con.* when John Wingfield, an opponent at the county meeting, told Joseph he had removed all his doubts. Pemberton rejoiced that he had sent for him, and Dr. Darwin touched him on the shoulder after his speech and thanked him for recalling his old feelings. On hearing the news Clarkson sent his congratulations: 'You have done indeed great things for us in consequence of having obtained the county'. Joseph's speech at Welshpool that won the unanimous backing of the meeting for a petition to both Houses of Parliament in favour of the Abolition proposals for the Peace Treaty, elicited an immediate and succinct response from Wilberforce: '*Veni, vidi, vici,* you may say'. Katherine also recorded her reflections: 'My brother put his hand to the business early in life, he has watched over it ever since, and he feels happy and comfortable in his mind that he has left nothing undone'.[1]

The responsibility for achieving the British aim of ending slave trading by France, Spain and Portugal now lay with the Foreign Secretary, Lord Castlereagh, who led the team of negotiators at the Peace Congress. He succeeded in getting the Powers to agree to concert their efforts for the entire and definite abolition of a trade 'so odious and so strongly condemned by laws of religion and nature', but it was much harder to ensure that this was put into practice. Help came from an unexpected quarter. In March 1815 Napoleon, who had escaped from Elba and made a triumphal return to Paris, announced an immediate end to the French slave trade. Although he was defeated at Waterloo on 18 June and Louis XVIII restored again, Napoleon's abolition of the slave trade was not reversed. Unfortunately, as Joseph's diary for 1815 has not survived, and as Katherine, returning to her journal in December 1815 after a long break, looked back only as far as July, there is no record of their personal reactions to the news of the great victory at Waterloo or of the local celebrations. The implementation of the pledge by the Great Powers to work to end the slave trade, embodied in the final settlement at Vienna, now rested with governments and the British navy, though the latter's interception of foreign ships suspected of carrying slaves caused international protests. Clarkson kept Joseph informed of his efforts to win the personal support of Alexander I, the Russian Emperor. Alexander had visited England, been taken to a Quaker service, and confirmed his opposition to the slave trade, declaring his wish 'to wipe away such a pestilence from the face of the earth'. Clarkson kept up the pressure and advised Joseph in 1818 that he was off to the Congress of the Powers at Aix-la-Chapelle, where he believed Spain and Portugal would pledge to end the trade in 1820.

The end of the long war with France and the general peace settlement at the Congress of Vienna were greeted with relief at Longnor and throughout the country. But peace brought its own problems. 'The post-war years were scarred by distress and discontent. Prices and wages fell in all sectors, while discharged soldiers and sailors added to unemployment'.[2] Shropshire was spared the agitation experienced in the main industrial areas, although the great iron works in the east of the county 'no longer throbbed to meet the previously insatiable demand for armaments',[3] and the demand for coal inevitably diminished. Nor did Shropshire witness the mass protests of suffering workers, the marches of the unemployed, or Luddite attacks on machinery. Its people only heard or read about the 1816 Spa Fields Riot in London and the Peterloo Massacre in Manchester in 1819.

But everywhere felt the effects of the trade depression with its concomitant unemployment, falling wages and poverty. And Shropshire did not escape the appalling weather of 1816 with little sunshine and abundant rain. The harvest was stunted and prices of staple foods rose sharply. The suffering of the labouring classes was intensified by the 1815 Corn Law, passed by a Parliament where the landed interest was over-represented. The new law laid down that wheat could not be imported until the price at home reached 80/- per quarter, which kept prices artificially high. Even when, as in the freak year of 1816, the price of grain reached 100/- a quarter, thus triggering the release of foreign corn, the effect was to cause prices to tumble just as the home harvest came on the market, so damaging the agricultural interest.

In that same year Katherine observed the contradictory effects on the wealthy of the arrival of peace: 'The rage of tours to the continent is now epidemic', she wrote, with the result that much money was leaving the country at a time of distress, yet two named gentlemen had had to go abroad because they could not afford the upkeep of their 'princely mansions'. It was at this point that Katherine contrasted two recent deaths, reminiscent of Dives and Lazarus. The first was of their old labourer, Edward Edwards, who met his end 'resigned and tranquil'. The second was of the wealthy Mr. Eyton, Receiver-General for the county, who lived in great style and was held in so much awe by servants and even friends that he was known as 'King' in the Wellington neighbourhood. He had been a partner with his brother-in-law in a Shrewsbury bank. When the word got round that he had defaulted on his payments to the government, alarm spread, and there was a run on the three other Shrewsbury banks. One failed and the others were bailed out just in time with money from London. Eyton had in fact embezzled the money and gone on living in pomp and arrogance. When his crime was exposed, Eyton committed suicide, firing a pistol down his throat. The whole story, wrote Katherine, 'forcibly teaches us how little the pomp and elegancies of life are connected with happiness'. All landowners were under pressure from rising poor rates, poor harvests and low prices that meant farmers could not afford to pay their rents. On 12 August 1819 Joseph wrote in his diary: 'The worst rent day I ever had'. By the end of 1822 he lamented the impact on him of the general failure of income 'which I have endeavoured to meet by abiding at home'. He also lost heavily when the trading company his son Robert had joined, and on whose business he had travelled to St. Petersburg, went bankrupt, for he had invested £2,000 on his son's behalf. Meanwhile, Panton was grappling with the consequences of the financial collapse of the bank at Welshpool.

It was, of course, the poor who suffered most. It has already been noted that as a magistrate Joseph found himself besieged in 1817 by claimants for poor relief, and that he was pressed by Wilberforce to keep him informed of how bad the situation was and to suggest ways of relieving distress. Katherine's view in April 1817 was that 'the times were never known so unfavourable to Commerce, to Agriculture, and consequently to any person'. One day Joseph 'saw a shoemaker from Wistanstow for whom I signed a certificate prior to his embarking for America'. Increasing numbers saw that as their best hope for the future. As Robert went to London to look for a new opening, Katherine wrote of the ruinous state of commerce, the impact on the gentry of widespread defaulting on the payment of rent, the poor almost starving, and the increased number of beggars as more were thrown out of work. In such hard times the cost of poor relief soared, parishes struggled to meet the increased charges, and farmers, behind with their rent, employed as few labourers as possible.

The severe economic dislocation of these years found expression in political as well as economic protest. But whereas in the 1790s Joseph and Katherine had sympathised with calls for reform and recorded some details of what happened locally, twenty-five years later there is almost no such reference in diary or journal. The great protests go unrecorded, William Cobbett's very influential *Political Register* gets no mention, and the government's repressive Six Acts passed in 1819 raise no protest. But what rates as significant when one is thirty may no longer do so when one is past the mid-fifties. Joseph's busy life continued, and he was now more concerned about the family than general political affairs. His sister's journals, too, increasingly feature the activities of her nephews and nieces. On her fifty-seventh birthday in 1815, Katherine expressed her thanks to God for her health, her brother and sister 'and the family growing up around us'.

There is abundant information about the family at this time from which to select. The month after the successful conclusion to the Corbett inheritance case, Joseph had set off for London, accompanied by Uvedale, Helen (aged eighteen) and Matilda (fifteen), with Katherine as escort for the girls. Ann looked after the younger children at Bank House. After over two weeks in the capital, Joseph returned to Longnor much better in spirits and health. A protracted tour in the summer brought further improvement.

It was during that summer that Panton's friendship with a young lady from Lichfield blossomed. Lucy Favoretta Jones, twenty-two years old, was the daughter of a physician who had been at Edinburgh University with Paul Panton — so the families knew each other. By November Joseph was communicating with Dr. Jones about a marriage settlement. With bequests from a grandmother and an uncle Lucy was quite well off, and Joseph gave the Leighton estate to Panton, reserving an annuity for himself, and would settle £800 per annum on Lucy. On discovering that the settlement ran to 109 folios he realised it had to be shortened! The marriage was celebrated at Lichfield in April 1814. Joseph and several of his children took themselves off to Cheltenham — and the others went to Katherine — so that the couple could stay at Longnor Hall as their new home was not yet ready. After the wedding, their carriage was drawn the last mile to the hall by a party of tenants preceded by a band. 'The village', Katherine wrote, 'was a scene of gaiety, bells ringing, music playing, guns firing, young folks dancing, and bonfires blazing'. Katherine found Lucy 'perfectly free from affectation'. Dr. Jones was disappointed at Joseph's absence, but perhaps it was all too near for him to his own wife's death. Dr. du Gard, who was in the congregation crowded into Longnor church on the Sunday to see the bride, praised Lucy's 'everyday good qualities' and her 'modest, unaffected dignity'. Panton and Lucy's first child was born the next year. At her baptism, conducted by her grandfather, baby Favoretta was carried on the 'bearing cloth' that had been used for Lady Mildred Corbett's children in the 17th century and at the christenings of Joseph and Panton — and which is still used by the family today. When the restoration was completed, the family took up residence at Leighton Hall, near the Welsh border.

Joseph's second son, Uvedale, having graduated from Pembroke College, Oxford, and completed his terms at Lincoln's Inn, went on a continental tour for some months with friends, visiting France, Italy and Switzerland. He returned home laden with gifts for all the family. He was called to the bar in 1815. The first time he appeared alone as prosecutor was at Shrewsbury Assizes where he won his case and earned praise from the judge. Meanwhile, Joseph jnr. had graduated from Pembroke in 1814. He followed his father into the Church and was ordained in 1817. 'May the profession he is undertaking be a source of usefulness and comfort to himself and to the people among whom he may administer the offices of the Church', was the prayer Joseph expressed in his diary for his son. Waties, the next son, was admitted as a Pensioner at Trinity College, Cambridge, at the age of seventeen in 1814. One may wonder why not Oxford and Pembroke; probably it was his own choice. Among his friends at Cambridge was Thomas Clarkson's son Tom, with whom he went to stay when the college was closed by typhus fever at Easter 1815. In time he too would be ordained and, like his brother, succeed his father in one of his local parishes. Of his sons, therefore, Joseph had only Robert without a settled career. And Robert was still a problem. He had entered a bank in London as a junior clerk at the age of fifteen, had failed to win his father's approval when he had yearned to join the army the next year, and had returned home to pursue a further course of study. After twelve months he returned to London to join the firm of Oswell, Selby & Co. who traded with Russia. He kept the underwriter's ledger, visited Lloyds when goods were being shipped and corresponded with their agent in St. Petersburg. But he still wanted to join the army. In spite of his father's prayer that trade associates would not lead him into immoral speculation, he dabbled in dubious financial investments and lost money. His father bailed him out, but he insisted on repaying him later. He was highly enough regarded to accompany Mr. Selby to St. Petersburg in June 1816, but four months later his company was another victim of the trade recession. Robert came home, but his job was gone and so was the £2,000 Joseph had invested to cover his son's training. Robert returned to London and set up in business with a friend, renting a first-floor room to serve as their counting-house. In less then a year it was wound up. Robert certainly lacked Midas's touch, but Katherine thought he had a heart of gold, relating (as his father did in his diary, too) that on a journey to Shrewsbury he had organised a lift to the Infirmary for an intoxicated waggoner who had been run over. He was also a young man of integrity: 'To say he has an honourable mind is nothing in your family, all of them have', a lawyer observed to Katherine.

With his daughters, Joseph's concern was not to find careers but to keep them in good health. The eldest, Josepha, aged twenty-nine in 1815, had never fully recovered from the shock of her sister Jane's death eight years earlier. She often went to stay with the Pantons at Plas Gwyn or at Parkgate on the Dee estuary where she could swim or go sailing, but her headaches persisted. She was well enough, however, to begin a Sunday school in Longnor for fifty youngsters, some from neighbouring parishes. 'She goes every Sunday morning', wrote her proud aunt, 'to hear the children read. The good effect is already perceived in the village, all is quiet instead of children playing and quarrelling. She goes again after evening service to hear their catechism'. Waties assisted when at home. As the Sunday school met in the village school, the master also attended, and Joseph who, since moving to the Hall had paid him to educate the poor in the village, gave him an addition for the work on Sunday. Joseph was delighted to see the church 'enlivened by the straw bonnets that Josepha gave to her Sunday school scholars at Christmas'; the boys received neckerchiefs. Josepha also assumed her late stepmother's practice of producing clothes for the poor. She made and gave away clothing and baby linen to sixty-seven persons in 1815.

Helen was Joseph's eldest daughter by his second wife, Matty. She did not face the major health problems that had beset her half-sisters, but there were occasional crises. At the age of twenty-one she suffered a repeat of the convulsions that had afflicted five years before. She then developed an eye problem and was twice taken to London by her father to be examined by a leading oculist. Her younger sister, Matilda, seems to have enjoyed better health for the only references to her in these years were to her first ball at Christmas 1814 at Condover, when she was sixteen, and to her taking violin lessons from a visiting teacher. It was the family custom for the youngest girls to go to their aunt Ann at Bank House on Sundays, when Katherine always dined at the Hall. Ann loved to tell them Bible stories. Harriet, aged fourteen, and Mildred, twelve, were confirmed by the bishop at Stretton in 1814. Then illness struck. Within months, both of them were suffering spasms that in Harriet's case were so severe that she had to be held down. Joseph feared she was close to death and the doctor stayed several nights at the Hall. It was months before they were well enough to go out. Joseph then took them out in the carriage for 'an airing', once to view the ruins of Wenlock Abbey.

Emma, the baby of the family, was only five in 1815, but already able to read a chapter from the gospels each day to Josepha. One wonders whether there was some genetic defect that accounted for the family's poor health since Joseph had suffered spasms after his first wife's premature death, but medicine was relatively undeveloped and early deaths not uncommon. It is noticeable, however, that the boys enjoyed better health: did the girls get enough exercise, purposeful activity and companionship of their own age outside the family?

⚜

Joseph's own state of health worried his sister. In 1814 she wrote: 'Except for the little journeys he takes he has no recreation', and two years later that he was 'more of an invalid than usual'. In his own diaries, of which the first to survive begins in 1814, he kept a record of when he was not well enough to take the services on a Sunday or could not attend some other function. He clearly suffered from the cold and was therefore at his worst in the winter when he was sometimes unable to venture out for weeks. In February 1814 he noted it was his first visit to Shrewsbury for four months. He lived very simply. When asked what the archdeacon liked to eat, Katherine answered: 'Nothing was easier, for my brother never eats but of one thing and drank only water', but his meat had to be thoroughly done. In December 1814 he was confined to his chair with lumbago, had to walk with a stick, and had not been able to shave before breakfast. Although a stove had been put in the church at Longnor that same month (at Leebotwood in 1822), he was not well enough to take the Christmas services. The weather was so bad in 1816 that on 20 June he had breakfast for the first time without a fire — and they were lit again in July, when he reckoned that it had rained every day for two months. In February 1817 he clearly felt a little guilty about how many times he had not taken the services: 'It is always hard to decide between the duty of taking care of our health, and taking care we do not neglect other duties unnecessarily on that account. May I be influenced to the proper determination'. On his fifty-ninth birthday he summed up how he felt: 'I suffer no absolute decrepitude or bad pain, though my health is not vigorous'. He would have been very surprised had he known that he had another twenty years to live.

There were, however, two benefits of his indifferent health and long periods at home — firstly it reduced his expenditure and secondly it gave him more time to read. It is only through the occasional references in his diaries that

191

we get an insight into the range of Joseph's reading. Religious works naturally feature prominently — *Elements of Christian Theology*, the Bampton Lectures on the Holy Ghost, Bishop Watson's *Apology for Christianity*, and Paley's Sermons and Tracts. In 1814 he read through six volumes of Orton's Bible Commentary, one volume every two months. His studies were not narrowly Anglican: he enjoyed a biography of Richard Baxter, especially 'the history of his own mind'; he praised the Christian spirit of some Roman Catholic nuns; he admired the faith of a young dissenting minister from Liverpool; and he was particularly struck by the *Life of Richard Davies*, the first Quaker in Welshpool who had been protected by Thomas Corbett, 'brother of our direct ancestor'. He enjoyed *The Life of Bishop Porteus*, whom he had met early in the Abolition campaign, commenting that 'he steered clear of enthusiasm'. Mrs. Carter's Letters were similarly approved as 'truly pious, but nothing fanciful or enthusiastic'. Archdeacon Corbett, his reading and comments suggest, was a broad Churchman, responsive to true faith in people of any denomination but believing religious zeal had to be tempered by reason.

Joseph especially enjoyed reading biographies, particularly of recent great figures. Lives of Robert Clive, John Howard (prison reformer), Thomas Day (educationist, anti-slavery campaigner and member of the Lunar Club), Frederick the Great, King James II, the Duke of Marlborough and John Wesley are mentioned in his diary. He was pleased by the Life of his old college friend Thomas Beddoes written by another Pembroke man, Thomas Stock, but thought it needed more anecdote. He was a great admirer of Charles James Fox, reading his biography and six volumes of his speeches: 'a monument to his vast intellectual reach and debating powers'. Collections of letters similarly fascinated him: two volumes of letters of famous people from originals in the Bodleian Library, while those of Benjamin Franklin provided a very good account of the War of American Independence. He was a great admirer of Dr. Johnson, sometimes critical of *The Rambler*, but revelling in his *Tour of Scotland* and *Lives of the Poets*, and always dipping into Boswell's Life of the great man. Travel books were another genre to Joseph's liking; his comments range over Persia, Tonga, Albania, 'the civilised people of western Korea', and the letters of the British Consul in Tripoli at the end of the 18th century.

Sometimes Joseph would read poetry to his daughters in the evening — he refers to Byron's *The Corsair*, which he thought not as fine as *Childe Harold* but better than *Lara* that he found obscure. He read to Helen the first volume of Milton's *Paradise Lost*, praising the learning and the poetry, but regarding the imagery, descriptions and speeches of the bad spirits 'unnecessarily dreadful'. On reading Congreve's plays he decided they were too immoral to be in his library, whereas a novel called *Self Control* rose 'to the character of true Christian morality'.

When it came to novels, Joseph seems to have read them with a guilty conscience. After finishing Fanny Burney's *The Wanderer* he wrote in his diary: 'I do not like reading novels. They create an interest you are eager to satisfy and therefore interfere with your time'. He thought they were best for people who are ill! — and it was at times when he was not quite well enough for business that he tended to turn to novels. When he got to the end of Maria Edgeworth's *Patronage* he commented: 'Many novels give admirable directions for the conduct of life, yet I doubt how far they are improving: the reader is too much interested in the story to attend sufficiently to its moral'. There is truth in what he says, but for the modern reader his views may appear rather narrow. It is therefore reassuring to hear his opinion after reading Jane Austen's *Northanger Abbey* and *Persuasion* to his older daughters: 'They represent very exact copies of human nature among persons of good and moderate fortunes, and with much quiet humour draw portraits from which most domestic circles of the same rank in life may draw very useful conclusions'. So when he encountered real quality he felt no guilt. It is a pity we do not have his daughters' reactions. Another novel that won Joseph's commendation was Scott's *Waverley*.

If Joseph's bouts of ill-health gave him greater opportunity to read, they made it more difficult for him to discharge all his responsibilities. The effect on his church attendance has already been noted, and he was relieved when his son Joseph was ordained deacon in 1817 and at once took the Good Friday and Easter Sunday services at Longnor and Leebotwood — with a very pleasing voice and manner in Katherine's opinion. After his ordination as priest the next year, young Joseph took over responsibility for the church at Leebotwood. The archdeacon's role as incumbent at Longnor of course involved much more than conducting the services on Sundays, one with a sermon, and Holy Communion four times a year. There were occasional baptisms, marriages and funerals, and each summer he catechised and taught about fifty children. They were then presented with a Bible, New Testament or Prayer Book according to their wants. One Christmas, the Sunday school boys and girls were presented with shoes or cloaks. Then there were pastoral duties. He visited Mary Clouds in April 1816 four times in the week before she died, taking her the sacrament one afternoon. Among others he called on were a collier injured in a pit accident at Ketley who had moved to Longnor; a young woman from Enchmarsh under the delusion that she had sinned against the Holy Ghost; a sick soldier, William Everall, in Longnor who received Holy Communion; William Watson, his oldest tenant 'living under the Lawley', who had had a seizure; Mrs. Morris, a poor ill woman, and Elizabeth Hodges, who both received the sacrament. One day he took 'sick Communion' to six persons. He talked and prayed with James Lee who came to see him 'under strong delusion of mind'. Katherine was pleased to record an increase in 1815 in the size of congregations which had necessitated the enlargement of the gallery. From September 1822 there was one service each on Sundays for Longnor and Leebotwood, alternately morning and evening.

As archdeacon his duties were more wide-ranging. Every year he had to conduct his visitation in May at Ludlow and Church Stretton, delivering his charge to the gathered clergy, swearing in churchwardens, and entertaining the clergy, and sometimes wardens too, to dinner at a local inn. Several times he commented on the number of wills he had to prove, that is to grant probate. Then there were new or repaired churches or parsonage houses he had to inspect — Woolstaston church and the parsonages at Clun and Knighton in July 1815, the new gallery in Chetton church in May 1817, the new church at Churchstoke the next summer, and Hopton Wafers in August 1820 to consider the proposed enlargement by the bounty of the patron. Clergy sometimes came to see him about problems — Mr. Johnson of Wistanstow had breakfast with him one day — but more generally minor issues were dealt with by correspondence. At times, however, there were difficult personal problems: in August 1816 he had to investigate the complaint of the churchwarden at Cardington against the vicar after two Sundays had passed without a service; in May 1818 he was 'trying to maintain peace' between Mr. Layton of Acton and the Rev. Frederick Holmes; in 1820 he saw Mr. Heighway of Woolstaston who was complaining of the curate there. In May 1819 he received a letter about Richard Bowen, the vicar of Myndtown, who was a prisoner in The Fleet in London, but he died soon afterwards, and the archdeacon was then trying to sort out his debts. On another occasion he received a tricky letter from the apparently deluded Rev. John Turner asking the archdeacon to dismiss him as unfit to continue as curate at Edgton. Trickier still was the visit of a Mrs. Hall and her daughter Harriet who swore that she was with child by the Rev. Edward Powis, jnr., the curate of Stapleton.

Joseph would have been much happier dealing with the needs at Stretton. His friend and lawyer, Robert Pemberton, who had moved from

Longnor to Condover Hall two years earlier, had died suddenly in 1816 at the age of fifty-two. Katherine thought it the greatest loss to her brother outside the family for he had been 'his confidential attorney and a wise and liberal-minded friend with whom he could freely converse upon any subject'. A man of 'universal benevolence', he had left a large sum to secure a good living for his son, Norgrave, 'a pious young man' who had wished to take orders. When Thomas Coleman, the rector of Stretton died young in 1818, Joseph, one of Robert's executors, negotiated the purchase of the advowson (the right to present) there on Norgrave's behalf for £11,000. Norgrave himself filled the vacancy. He guided the new young rector as he tried to reorder the interior of the church after presenting the lovely stained-glass east window to mark his arrival. The Corbett coat-of-arms may still be seen at the head of the window, together with those of the rector, the bishop and the king.

Because Bishop Huntingford was also Warden of the college at Winchester (which Katherine thought was 'hardly compatible with the Bishopric of Hereford') and was away for many months each year, Joseph frequently instituted new clergy on the bishop's behalf — Mr. Cadwallader at Abdon, Mr. Stephens at Willey, Mr. Pallett at Monkhopton all appear in his diary. As archdeacon Joseph seized opportunities, through clergy absence or illness, to preach in other churches, among them Pulverbatch, Stapleton, Wistanstow, Cardington, St. Chad's in Shrewsbury, Tenbury, Stretton, Smethcott, Woolstaston and, for the Bible Society, Welshpool and Newport.

His duties as a magistrate were reviewed in the last chapter, and his role as President of the Shropshire Auxiliary Bible Society will be considered in the next, but Joseph had other varied responsibilities. He still ran the charity for Clergy Widows and Orphans that he had taken over from his predecessor as archdeacon in 1791. This involved writing reports and regular meetings at the 'Crown' in Stretton to audit accounts and to determine the distribution of charity funds. In 1821 he noticed that it was the thirtieth anniversary of his administration of the charity. He was still on the management committee of the Infirmary, which meant more meetings — at one he proposed the appointment of a new surgeon. At a special service in St. Mary's, Shrewsbury, on behalf of the Infirmary, Katherine noted how Panton's young wife, Lucy, with a plate at the door, curtsied every time a donation was made; perhaps it helped to raise the large sum of £278. Joseph often recorded recommending patients for admission to the hospital. There were further meetings as a trustee of Shrewsbury School and also of Stretton School, where he gave strong support to young Norgrave Pemberton and preached on behalf of the Sunday school. He recruited influential and wealthy men for the Stretton trustees from among his fellow magistrates — Wilding, Stackhouse and Jenkinson, who had all known the young rector's father. As a member of Shrewsbury Corporation, Joseph seems to have recorded his presence only at meetings when the Mayor was to be elected. In 1817 he was offered the position of Alderman, but declined on account of his health and the pressure of business and so that in the future he would not be proposed for Mayor himself. 'The resolution of the house was that I should be fined £50 for not accepting the office of Alderman, and that £49-19-6 of the money should be returned' — in consideration, Katherine added in her account, 'of the services he had always been ready to render to the town and of the respect entertained for his character'.

Joseph, of course, also had his extensive estates to manage. His diaries contain occasional references to his activities as a landowner. One day he rode out 'to direct repairs and planting'; at other times he recorded the planting of 109 trees at Bentley Ford, the planting of 630 trees (400 oaks) in the enclosure by the new bridge at the end of the Lawley, and 'the planting of 500 trees, including 360 oaks, in the part of the plantation nearest Samuel Burgess's'. There are records of sales and land transactions: the sale of timber from the Leighton estate in 1814 for £1,195, the joint purchase with Mr. Loxdale of Clatterwood Mill, the sale to Mr. Fewtrell of Green Farm with 150 acres, and the purchase of Thomas Williams' estate at The Forge which he then made over to Panton. Katherine lamented the decay of Lydley Hayes, the nearby house where Mr. Russell had cheerfully welcomed her as a child, but thought Joseph was right to have it pulled down. It had been neglected after her uncle Robert had let it out to tenants, including the Rev. John Witts, another contemporary of Joseph's at Pembroke and, Katherine thought 'the last of the good old sort of neighbour'. Joseph himself took good care of his tenants' houses. When Katherine accompanied Norgrave Pemberton on a tour of Longnor homes 'in search of bits of carved oak belonging to old beds etc.' for his proposed reredos in St. Laurence's at Stretton, he was 'full of admiration at the neatness and excellent repair in which my brother keeps the houses in the village'. As late as 1823 Joseph was still climbing up to the top of Hoar Edge with three men to point out to them the work he wanted done in planting, building stone walls for enclosures and so on. He was one of the promoters of the enclosure of waste lands in Cardington in 1814, poring over the draft Bill with his lawyer and neighbour, Robert Pemberton, and going up to Parliament to hear the Bill committed — when he was delighted to find the committee's chairman was an old acquaintance from Oxford days whom he had known as Mr. Ashley but who was now Lord Shaftesbury, father of the famous factory reformer.

Although Joseph was often confined to his dwelling for weeks in the winter, he seized opportunities for travel in the better weather. The summer of 1813 saw him spending three weeks in Scarborough with some of the children, and then going on to Scotland where he stayed with Archibald Alison in Edinburgh and visited Glasgow and Loch Lomond. On the way home he called on Lord Muncaster in the Lake District before he visited a relative in Clitheroe and preached in the church there. In all he was away for six weeks. The next year he spent a few days in Cheltenham to take the waters, drinking a pint and a half of the spa water before breakfast each day. From there he went on to Oxford and attended Evening Prayer in Pembroke Chapel, where he must have gazed with pride and pleasure at the altar painting he had presented on his graduation twenty-seven years before. A visit to see the Severn Boar [*sic*] proved a disappointment, but he enjoyed the journey home through east Wales. On a second visit to Oxford that year they saw the Emperor of Russia and the King of Prussia in procession, and Joseph was in the Sheldonian to see them awarded honorary degrees. Going on to London he attended a meeting of the Committee for the Abolition of Slavery (no longer just the slave trade), with Clarkson in the chair. He spent time with Uvedale and Robert, both then living in the capital, as well as meeting Wilberforce and Samuel Lee. He still found time to visit Parliament and two art galleries. Katherine went with the older children to see the great Edmund Kean as Iago at Drury Lane. In October he was in London again, journeying on to Maidstone to collect his son Waties, who was with a tutor there. He travelled with him to Cambridge where Waties took up his place at Trinity College. 'May God grant him health and the inclination to pursue his studies' was his father's prayer. While in the city, which he thought much improved since he had taken his M.A. twenty-two years earlier, he met Clarkson, whose son, Tom, was another Trinity freshman, but failed to locate Samuel Lee.

In the capital again in 1816 to consult about Helen's eye problems, he managed to meet Wilberforce as well as family members. As the years passed such visits became more rare, but in 1819 he at last gave in to pressure from the family and agreed to have his portrait painted a few months before his sixtieth birthday. The London artist, Mr. Phillips, began work in February, but Joseph had to return in March for further sittings. He doubted whether it was worth the time and the £100 fee, but it is the only picture we have of him. Robert maintained it was inaccurate because Joseph was holding a letter in his hand, which would assuredly have been answered before he seated himself. But Robert added that it was 'a valuable resemblance of one who must always be most dear to us all', while Panton considered it would be valued as a good portrait of a person 'whose public character in the County of Salop, and indeed out of it, stands so high, and whose private excellence can only be properly appreciated and known by his own family'.

Visits to Plas Gwyn and Parkgate continued for the sake of the girls' health — he was able to leave them there with Josepha when business demanded his return. Increasingly his travels were linked with visits to his children — Panton at Leighton Hall, Uvedale and Robert in London, and later Panton in London, Uvedale at Tettenhall, and Helen in Oxford. While calling on Panton's in-laws in Lichfield he was able to meet up with old associates like Thomas Gisborne and Mrs. Falconer 'whom I had not seen for forty years'. On his way to a few days at the seaside on the Dee estuary, he met Thomas Telford in Ellesmere. While in Cheltenham he stayed some days with his old friend, Mr. Howell, whom he found unhappy, depressed and drinking heavily, although some were surprised that Joseph should consort with such a dissolute character.

Friends, of course, came to visit him, and sometimes breakfast as well as dinner became a social occasion. He was less averse to casual company than he had been and occasionally dined out, but he steered well clear of the regular social circuit. In April 1818 he gave vent to his feelings in his diary: 'The whole system of dinners is contrary to reason. You meet, it is said, for conversation, and you are to talk and eat at the same time: two engagements incompatible with decency and comfort. But the solacing effect of more meat and drink than is good for health is, for a time, to beget more complacence of mind, and thus those tempers and dispositions mingle at dinnertime, that could have no pleasure in meeting at other times, will then pass current'. Yet dinners at the Hall were very important to him, for he even recorded what was eaten. But as the years passed, contact with many old friends was maintained only through correspondence — Archibald Alison sent him a volume of his sermons, Theophilus Houlbrooke wrote to say that at over seventy, and thirty years a widower, he had married again. Letters passed more regularly between him and Wilberforce and Clarkson, both of whom he endeavoured to meet when he was in London. He heard occasionally from Robert Townson, still in Australia and still aggrieved at the treatment he had received. At the end of each diary page he noted how many letters he had received and written. When he totted them up at the end of each year, it appeared that on average he wrote twelve to fourteen letters every week.

Death was depriving him of some close friends: Frederic Iremonger at an early age, John Witts of Lydley Hayes, Robert Pemberton, and Thomas Coleman at Stretton. Joseph also regularly recorded local deaths, especially of the very old. Thomas Everard, 'weaver and cockfighter of the village' at the age of eighty-four; Bernard Hodges, blind for many years, aged eighty-two; Elizabeth Kyte suddenly in middle age; Mr. Heighway, a young farmer at Leebotwood; William Brown, a pauper but once miller in Longnor, about eighty; Mr. Brazier, 'an old and respectable tenant' was followed to the grave by his wife two days later; Richard Brown, 'shopkeeper of this village and constant in his attendance at church', died suddenly aged fifty-two; and Andrew Skitt of Longnor died of consumption, aged twenty-four. After recording the death of Thomas Taylor, who rented a small tenement at the stone quarry and whose wife was ill and his son mentally deficient, Joseph added: 'What misery there is in the world and how frequently should we contemplate those whose situations are worse than our own?' He allowed the married daughter to keep the property so that she could care for her mother and brother. He kept some record of the movements of servants: Matty Brown, their old cook left the Hall after fifty years of faithful service, Elizabeth Burgess after forty-eight years, but John Bright after only one year — 'the only servant I have found desirous of leaving me' — but he presented him with a Bible. On the marriage of Nancy Carter ('our upper servant for eight years') to William Cund, Joseph met the cost of the wedding dinner for them and their friends. When Matty Brown was in her final illness, Josepha, Waties, Harriet and Mildred all went to see her. Rowland Hodges, who had been with him for thirty-three years as successively postilion, footman and butler, 'a decent, industrious and respectable man, and an excellent husband and father', died aged sixty. Richard Evans, his gardener for fourteen years, died aged only thirty-three, while William Samuel, an infirm man of sixty-nine who also worked in the garden, was found dead at the gate.

Of the younger local friends who visited frequently, Dr. du Gard was the family's medical attendant and often stayed overnight if one of the children was seriously ill. Katherine, who was clearly fond of him, recorded some details of his life. When his mother died, he had been sent alone across the Atlantic at age thirteen to live with an uncle 100 miles from New York. Only £1,000 of his father's estate remained for him, and Joseph helped to get him his position at the Infirmary. In 1820 he married the daughter of the organist at Hereford Cathedral.

But it was Samuel Lee whose career they followed most closely, delighted to learn that as he was born on 14 May 1783 his was almost certainly the first baptism that Joseph conducted. Joseph encountered him again when he was twenty-six and pursuing his language studies while still working as a carpenter. The loss of his expensive tool chest in a fire led him to think of

becoming a teacher, an ambition that Joseph encouraged. 'It is to his goodness that I am indebted for the situation I at present fill', Samuel wrote, 'and
for several other very valuable benefits which he thought proper generously
to confer'. But after a few years Samuel began to tire of his schoolmaster
role and longed to extend his language skills. The Baptists offered him ordination if he would go to India as a missionary, but he was more drawn to
the Church of England. Dr. Jonathan Scott, to whom Joseph had introduced
Samuel, regarded him as 'possessed of talents in the acquisition of languages
beyond any man I ever knew'. At dinner at Longnor Hall, Scott remarked
that Samuel reminded him of the poet Shenstone's little mouse: 'A river or a
sea / was to him a dish of tea / and a kingdom bread and butter'. Scott tried
in vain to interest the East India Company in his young friend. Wilberforce,
however, was all in favour of his being used to instruct intending missionaries. Samuel himself was keen to go to India, even though it would mean
leaving his wife and family, but Scott believed he should first go to university
because 'with his amazing facility for acquiring languages he possesses taste
for elegant composition, and has no slight poetical talent'. James Anderson,
a famous orientalist, was equally impressed. The Church Missionary Society
(C.M.S.) came up with an offer that resolved the situation: £50 for one year to
place him at a college and then employ him to instruct missionaries. Queens'
College, Cambridge, accepted him, Scott raised more funds, Joseph assured
Wilberforce of Samuel's abilities, Dr. du Gard got permission from Colonel
Hill for Samuel to use the library at Hawkstone, and Scott, who now saw the
destruction of Samuel's tool chest as providential, made his house in Bath
available to him. In return for his instructing their students in the long vacation, the Missionary Committee offered to pay for accommodation for Samuel
and his family and to meet his travel expenses.

There was some anxiety about how Samuel's wife would cope with the
sudden change in his life, but Katherine found her, when paying a visit before
she moved to London, 'a pretty, modest looking woman with much civility of
manner'. Dr. Buchanan of Queens' College was so impressed with Lee, and
so convinced that he should take his degree, that he offered support of £150
a year. Samuel and his wife dined at Longnor Hall on 10 April 1814 prior
to their departure for Missionary House. The link with the Corbett family
continued, for Samuel often took tea with Joseph's son, Waties, at Trinity.
In addition to his degree course studies, Samuel was engaged in completing
the translation of the New Testament into Syriac for the Bible Society, using
three ancient manuscripts, one a thousand years old. He was also working on
a Persian translation of the Old Testament as well as learning the Ethiopic
and Coptic languages. Katherine wrote that she never passed the house in

Longnor where Samuel was born without marvelling at his achievements. 'He is a distinguished honour to our village'. Samuel graduated in 1817 and continued his translation work in an astonishing range of languages — the Malay New Testament, the Syriac Old Testament, and the Prayer Book and Genesis in Hindustani. He received complimentary letters from the Bishop of St. David's and the Oxford Professor of Arabic, though others were jealous of his progress and, Scott claimed, tried to hold him back. Samuel simply carried on, obliging the C.M.S. by writing a brief history of the Syriac Church in India. He lost his youngest child, but Mrs. Lee gave birth to a girl late in 1817. When he called to see Joseph the next April he told him of his ordination by the Bishop of London. He preached so powerfully at St. Chad's in Shrewsbury for the Bible Society that Scott wept for joy when he got home. Samuel took on a curacy near Cambridge while he saw his Ethiopic Bible through the printers. And then, in March 1819, the wonderful news reached Joseph that, less than eighteen months after his graduation and at only thirty-five years of age, Samuel had been elected Professor of Arabic at Cambridge by a large majority, including ten heads of college. The university's M.A.s overwhelmingly supported the early grant of his M.A. to enable him to take up his chair. He had received a testimonial from the Syrian Archbishop of Jerusalem who was amazed at his fluency in Syriac and Arabic and at the clarity of his intellect. Scott published in the *Salopian Journal* copies of testimonials sent to the Vice-Chancellor of Cambridge supporting Samuel's election as a professor. Yet when he visited Longnor in May 1820 to see his sister and old neighbours, Katherine wrote that 'he retains all the simplicity of manner he ever had, with the polish of good society'. He preached in Longnor church morning and evening to what must have been incredulous congregations. In the 1820s, with the help of two visiting Maori chiefs, he compiled a grammar and vocabulary of the New Zealand language. The final items of news that Katherine recorded of him were the death of his wife, a royal grant to supplement his income, his election to a Fellowship at Queens', his re-marriage to a pious lady who had been a family friend for years, and another visit to Longnor where his presence 'drew my brother out to converse more than he now often does'. Joseph's own evaluation of his friend and protégé was that he was 'the most remarkable linguist perhaps that has been'. He had 'proved himself *sapiens abnormis*'.[4]

‹‹

A few weeks after Samuel Lee took up his chair at Cambridge, the death occurred of Richard Lyster, M.P. for Shrewsbury since 1814. Panton was immediately approached to be a candidate, with the strong support of the

Corporation and the trading interest. When he consulted his father about standing, Joseph went to Hawkstone and Sundorne to sound out the Hills and Corbets. The landed interest decided, however, to back the notorious John Mytton, twenty-two-year-old son-in-law of the former M.P., Sir Thomas Jones. Joseph considered a contested election undesirable, but Uvedale, Robert and young Joseph urged their brother to stand and his candidacy met with strong support in some quarters. Panton asserted, 'I will not purchase the vote of any elector', and that if chosen he would enter Parliament with no party attachment. Katherine, who was present at his nomination, said the burst of applause 'electrified me from head to foot'. Joseph himself made a speech following the two candidates. Polling began on 17 May — Joseph's sixtieth birthday — and lasted for eight days. Katherine daily noted the fluctuations in the voting. As soon as a hired mob shouting for Mytton appeared on the scene, Panton began to lose ground. His opponents accused him of being 'too poor' to bribe; his supporters retorted that he was 'too pure'. The popular view was that it was 'the Foxhunters against the Bible Society'. The moment his opponents brought in a hundred colliers violence erupted: Panton's 'chair' was upset and he was dragged to safety in the 'Talbot'. Panton discouraged his people from even approaching the polling station. 'I believe', wrote Katherine, 'the pride of aristocracy in this instance has united with the lowest of the people to keep out any candidate who is supported by the trading interest'. At the close of the poll, Panton had 287 votes and Mytton 384. Nevertheless, Panton's backers celebrated his campaign in great style at the 'Talbot' and the 'Raven and Bell' — and in Welshpool, Longnor and Dorrington. It all added to his costs that were estimated at £2,000 — and that without bribery and treating.

Panton's efforts were not without reward. As the *Victoria County History* says of Mytton: 'He quit the Commons even more swiftly than Westminster and Harrow Schools, for in 1820, the year before he fled from his creditors, he did not stand'[5] at the election called following the death of George III. Panton and his father had sent a 'thank you' of game or half a guinea to all the burgesses who had given their support in 1819, and Joseph had advised his son to be ready to stand again as it would be 'an honour and a duty to serve'. At the request of the Mayor, Joseph moved an address of condolence to the new king on the death of his father at a meeting of the Corporation in February, and a few days later Panton began his canvass. Mytton, who had been in the House only once — to take his seat — retired, and as no-one else came forward there was no contest. On election day, Panton and his brothers, surrounded by gentlemen, tenants and neighbours from Welshpool and Leighton, wearing purple and orange colours, rode into Shrewsbury. Katherine was there, but

Joseph stayed quietly at home, though he went to hear the speeches. The chairing procession lasted two and a half hours. 'I never saw him look better, indeed he looked very handsome', was his admiring aunt's verdict on the boy she had brought up. Bennett, the sitting M.P., proceeded to the 'Lion', and Panton to Mr. Craig's new house in the Market Square. As Panton addressed the crowd from the balcony, his little son asked, 'Papa, what are you talking about?' Panton would have liked a joint dinner with the re-elected H.G. Bennett, 'but the violent party people on both sides made it impossible'. In the event, Panton's dinner was held at the 'Talbot', and his brother Robert presided over another at the 'Raven and Bell'.

Joseph could have surveyed his family with legitimate pride as the 1820s began. Panton was now a Member of Parliament, and made his maiden speech on 31 May, entirely appropriately calling for an inquiry into agricultural distress. He now lived with his family at Leighton Hall except when Parliament was in session. He had served as High Steward of Welshpool and had been nominated by Wilberforce as a member, and later a director, of the African Institution. 'If he resembles his father in intelligence, assiduity and order', Wilberforce had commented, 'he will be a valuable acquisition to us'. Uvedale was a successful barrister and, like his brother, a director of the African Institution, which must have rejoiced their father's heart. Uvedale had married Mary Lyon of a Norfolk family in 1817, and they moved to Tettenhall Wood with their two children three years later. Young Joseph, who since his ordination had taken over some of his father's clerical responsibilities, became incumbent at Holgate in 1819 in his father's place and then, with the enthusiastic support of the bishop, in 1822 became also vicar at Tugford where he enlarged the parsonage and made his home. Robert, for all his stalwart qualities, was still unsettled, having rejected farming and the Stock Exchange and been disappointed when a prospective post in Ceylon fell through. The youngest son, Waties, after Cambridge and his eighteen-month continental tour, was ordained in 1820 and began to take some services for his father. The next year he succeeded him in the living of Coreley but, when it became apparent that his father needed help in his local parishes and on the bench of magistrates, soon came back to serve as perpetual curate in Longnor and Leebotwood.

There is less recorded of Joseph's daughters, though they played a vital part in his life as they lived at home with him and took turns to accompany him when making visits or preaching elsewhere. None of them had yet married, and perhaps they had little opportunity to meet eligible men. They must have sorely missed a mother, for their maiden aunts could offer little guidance on finding partners for life. Although aged thirty-six in 1822 and a virtual invalid, Josepha managed to attend the school daily, visited poor neighbours and taught Emma French. Helen and Matilda, respectively twenty-seven and twenty-four in that year, were able to look after their younger sisters, especially Harriet who, though twenty, was so weak that she had to use crutches and slept downstairs in the library. When seventeen, she had spent six months lying on the couch, and it was fifteen months before she went out even in her wheelchair. Mildred at eighteen and Emma, twelve, were healthy but their lives were anything but exciting. Teachers of music, dancing and French regularly visited the Hall, and Katherine must have encouraged their artistic talents. Matilda, Harriet and Mildred all had violin lessons, but how many played the grand piano we do not know. They sometimes put on recitals at home. Outings to concerts and recitals at the 'Lion' or St. Mary's in Shrewsbury were not infrequent. For all the girls, times spent with Panton's and Uvedale's young families must have been special treats.

Joseph and his sisters were all in their sixties by 1822. Ann's health had never permitted more than the occasional minor excursion, and Katherine was much less active than she had been. Joseph himself was reaching the point when he was glad that his two clergy sons could relieve him of some of the responsibilities he had accumulated over the years. Yet as archdeacon, magistrate and school trustee he was still very busy, and wholeheartedly committed to the leadership of the Bible Society in Shrewsbury.

15   PRESIDENT OF THE SHROPSHIRE AUXILIARY BIBLE SOCIETY

The formation of the British and Foreign Bible Society in 1804 was one of the landmarks in what is often called 'the evangelical revival'. A modern historian warns, however, that 'that epithet is as slippery as it was ubiquitous',[1] because it sometimes refers to a spiritual awakening within the Church of England that had led, for instance, to the founding of the Church Missionary Society in 1799, but is also used to describe the wider movement (the Evangelical Revival, with capital letters) that included Methodism and other denominations. The striking feature of the Bible Society was its enthusiastic support by large numbers from the Church of England as well as Nonconformists, united by their concern to make the Scriptures more widely available both at home and abroad.

Its origins can be traced back to fifteen-year-old Mary Jones's famous twenty-eight mile walk from her home in Abergynolwyn to Bala in the summer of 1800 because she desperately wanted a Bible of her own. This led the Rev. Thomas Charles of Bala to campaign for a society that would supply Bibles for Wales and further afield. A Religious Tract Society had been formed in 1802 with the support of Wilberforce, and with the Rev. Rowland Hill, popular evangelist and brother of Sir Richard Hill of Hawkstone and M.P. for Shropshire, one of its founder members. But what was now sought was a Bible Society. It was born at a meeting in the London Tavern in Bishopgate Street, London, on 7 March 1804. A secular venue was deliberately chosen so that the proposed Society should not be associated with any particular church or denomination. Wilberforce was enthusiastic for such a body, though he could not be present at the meeting. It was chaired by the veteran anti-slave trade campaigner, Granville Sharp. Two contributions to the meeting stood out — the speech of the Rev. Karl Steinkopf, who spoke movingly of the scarcity of the Bible in Germany and throughout the continent, and that of the Rev. John

Owen, chaplain to the Bishop of London, who was mightily impressed by the presence of so many who had for long been kept apart by doctrinal and ritual differences. He subsequently wrote that, to him, 'it appeared to indicate the dawn of a new era in Christendom and to portend something like the return of those auspicious days when the multitude of them that believed were of one heart and soul and when as a consequence of that union, to a certain degree at least, "the Word of God mightily grew and prevailed"'.[2] The resolutions to establish the British and Foreign Bible Society to distribute Bibles, without notes or comment, throughout Britain, Europe and beyond, were carried unanimously. Henry Thornton of the 'Clapham Sect' was made Treasurer. Soon afterwards the Bishop of London, Beilby Porteus, who had backed the anti-slave trade campaign, and some other bishops announced their support, and Lord Teignmouth, former Governor-General of India, became President and served for its first thirty years.

When Joseph heard of the birth of the Society and recognised its great value, he thought at once of founding a local branch. He was encouraged to do so by some of the promoters of the parent body with whom he had worked closely in the previous decade to end the slave trade. Wilberforce had become a Vice-President of the Bible Society; Granville Sharp, Henry Thornton, Thomas Gisborne and others, all staunch supporters, had been his comrades in the earlier campaign. But when Joseph approached the clergy of Shrewsbury to elicit their support, 'they, to say the least', recorded a disappointed Katherine, 'did not appear to consider themselves called upon to step forward; on the contrary, there seemed somewhat of a feeling inimical to it among them'. They considered the Society for the Promotion of Christian Knowledge (S.P.C.K.), founded a century before, adequate to meet every call. Joseph had been one of the earliest subscribers in the neighbourhood to the S.P.C.K. and, opined his sister, 'a very excellent institution it is so far as it goes — but much is wanting, and the Bible Society appeared the most likely means of supplying all that may be wanted if it is properly supported'. The negative response from many of the clergy caused Joseph to drop the proposal, conscious as he was that Shrewsbury was not part of his archdeaconry. Had he been successful, Shropshire could have been the first place to have its own Auxiliary Bible Society, for it was not until March 1809 that the first such were established in Reading and Nottingham.

Shropshire was still not far behind, however, for a group of clerics, some Church of England and some Dissenters, many unknown to Joseph, went ahead in 1811 and formed an Auxiliary in the county town. Katherine rejoiced that they 'all unanimously have requested my brother to become their President'. It was not the easiest time for the archdeacon since there was much illness in the family and the scurrilous campaign over the Corbett inheritance threatened to end in the law courts. Yet 'he has accepted the office, for though his health and the cares of a large family have led him to decline all public business more than formerly, he would have considered it an injury to the true interest of Religion if he had declined this'.

Katherine went on to explain what lay behind the reluctance of many clergy to support the Bible Society. 'There is a party of the clergy (those who are denominated high church) who set their faces against the Bible Society; they object that it is much encouraged by dissenters, that it dispenses only the Scripture unaccompanied by any tracts in favour of the established Church, and that if the dissenters choose to promote such a Society they are welcome, but that it becomes the members of the establishment to give all their aid exclusively to the S.P.C.K. which not only dispenses Bibles and Testaments but the Common Prayer and various tracts in favour of the Church of England'. She believed, and no doubt had talked this through with her brother, that this argument was very ably and very fully answered by Anglican friends to the Bible Society who maintained that the Church of England could in no way be injured by joining an institution formed to dispense the Scriptures 'in the greatest purity, without note or comment'. Already in its first seven years the Society had circulated 'the unadulterated Word of God' in unprecedented quantities, because its subscribers were drawn from all the churches. Katherine was shocked at the opposition from some clergy and laity since the Anglican Church appealed to the Scriptures as the only foundation of the faith. Had such opponents lived at the time of the Reformation, she suggested, they would have shared the terrors that the most bigoted Roman Catholics then had at the thought of the Scriptures being read at all by the laity.

Joseph's experience at his first meeting as president of the Auxiliary was very positive. He was struck by the harmony between the different denominations, a harmony that transcended all those differences in forms and phrases that had too often embittered the minds of Christians and estranged them from each other. He told his audience how pleased he was with their committee meetings. Whereas in most public meetings the person in charge of the business had to defend this or that measure in opposition to some other measure, he had found an atmosphere of calm and quiet, reflecting the unity that diffused the whole Society. A little later he published a brief account of the Society's development together with a short address written by himself and signed by him as president of the Auxiliary. Copies were sent to the clergy throughout the county. He also established an organisational structure, with a number of vice-presidents to assist him, and a working committee that met quarterly under his chairmanship. Membership of the Society was open to those who subscribed one guinea (twenty-one shillings) a year; a subscription of ten guineas gave membership for life. If anyone was willing to subscribe five guineas a year, he/she became a Governor, with the right to attend and vote at meetings of the Central Committee in London.

Almost the whole family, including Josepha who had not been to Shrewsbury for two years, turned out to support Joseph at the Annual General Meeting in the Shire Hall on Wednesday, 7 July 1813, at twelve noon sharp. After the Annual Report had been read aloud, Joseph as president proposed its acceptance. Each year this was his opportunity to fire the enthusiasm of the subscribing members in the hall, to present a national, even international, picture of the parent Society's activities, and to defend the Society from the criticisms of some Anglicans. At this meeting he was able to tell them of the A.G.M. of the Bible Society in London at which he had been present. Once again he had been struck by the overwhelming sense of unity. He described the ovation given to Wilberforce, and the warm receptions accorded to two of the king's sons, as well as to lords, M.P.s and a bishop. He brought heartening news of new Auxiliaries that had been formed all over the country — and was able to announce two new branches in Shropshire at Madeley and Wellington. He went on to answer the sceptics who wanted to exaggerate divisions within the Church on account of the Society as well as those challenging the accuracy of the Biblical text. 'In this Society, Christians of different denominations are united in upholding the same identical Book. They are agreed on the transla- tion of it that they promulgate. They maintain it is the genuine Revelation from God to Man; and, that it may be removed as much as possible from all traces of human infirmity, they give it without note or comment'.[3]

Joseph was not an academic Biblical scholar, but as an active priest and a senior churchman he was very familiar with the Scriptures. In the last chapter it was noted that his religious reading had included the study of the six volumes of Orton's Bible Commentary in 1814 and later he noted how his daily Bible reading was accompanied by the use of other commentaries. So, though he repeated the Bible Society mantra 'without note or comment', he knew perfectly well that there were different interpretations of passages in the Bible and he therefore encouraged others to use learned commentaries. But the dissemination of the Bible as God's Word was even more important. To raise the necessary funds to distribute Bibles and New Testaments widely in Britain, and to support the work of translation into other languages and the subsequent distribution in other lands, it was essential, he believed, to support a Society where the different denominations could work together in unity. He shared the grand vision of the Society's original promoters that was nothing less than to make the Word of God available to all people throughout the world. Had not the prophets proclaimed that 'the earth shall be full of the knowledge of the Lord', and Jesus himself commanded that 'the Gospel must be preached to every nation'? As he had once been gripped by the great campaign to end the slave trade, it seems that he was now similarly fired by the aim of spreading the Word of God across the whole world.

The member who proposed the vote of thanks to their president praised Joseph for 'his unremitting attention to the interests of the Society'. Others, who took it in turns to propose and second votes of thanks to the vice-presidents, the committee, the treasurer and the secretaries, picked up Joseph's themes and added their own variations. In these early days the local press gave the annual meetings extraordinary coverage. In some years the almost verbatim accounts of the speeches took up a third of the four-page issue of the *Salopian Journal*. The meetings attracted audiences running into hundreds and lasted for up to four hours. But because the format remained basically the same and, of course, the fundamental message did not change, Joseph had to look each year for a new slant for his address. In 1814, he seized on the news of the recent death of Granville Sharp, the National Society's first chairman, to pay a fulsome tribute to his old friend's life, achievements and love of the Bible. He also welcomed the war hero, Lord Hill, as a vice-president of the Auxiliary, and heartened his listeners with the information that a Bible Society had been formed in St. Petersburg.[4] It was left to the hymn-writer Reginald Heber, soon to become Bishop of Calcutta, to raise the burning issue in the current peace negotiations of the right accorded to France to resume slave trading for five years — evidence that the Society was not just made up of narrow Bible enthusiasts, but included those who wanted to see Jesus's teaching on justice applied to the contemporary political situation.

The A.G.M. of 1815 was held days after the news of the Allied victory at Waterloo. Before the largest attendance yet, Joseph immediately picked up this theme, contrasting the background of peace talks at their meeting in July 1814 with the renewal of war in 1815. But, he maintained, 'we bear in our hands the sacred volume, the only sure guide in peace and plenty — the only source of certain consolation in danger and distress'. He then turned his attention to the Salop Infirmary, founded in 1745, because he saw its maintenance as another instance of co-operation across different denominations and across party political boundaries, too. He went out of his way to praise the S.P.C.K. for giving hospital patients a religious tract and, on leaving, if they could read, a copy of *The Christian Monitor.* The Bible Society, he pointed out, could follow that example and present patients with a Bible or Testament. In his own ministry, he told them, he gave away Bibles and Testaments supplied by the Bible Society and Prayer Books from the S.P.C.K. The Annual Report of the Shropshire Auxiliary had recorded receipts of £1,125 in the year 1814-15 and the distribution of 1,230 copies of Scripture. He was able to tell the meeting that the parent Society had distributed 1,250,000 copies of the Bible in its first ten years. In spite of Joseph's obvious attempt to preserve harmonious relations with the S.P.C.K., one of the vice-presidents, the Rev. Edward Bather, felt he had to defend the Bible Society against those who charged that it 'was conspiring to sap the foundations of the Church of England'.[5]

In 1817 Joseph paid tribute to the late treasurer, Robert Pemberton. The vacancy was filled by his son, Norgrave – who also invited the Corbett family to dinner as his father had always done on Bible Society Anniversary days. Joseph's main theme was the international growth of the Society. He was able to announce that Bible Societies had been set up in Norway, Sweden, Denmark, Russia (where, in the Crimea, seventy-six 'Mahometans' and five Jews were among the subscribing members), Poland, Prussia, Switzerland, Greece, Malta, India, Malaya, America and Asia. 'Let it not, however, be supposed', he went on, 'that we have already attained or are already perfect. If we look at a map of the world and see how small these islands are in comparison with the continents and islands of the globe, and then consider that notwithstanding our previous, as well as our present, distribution of the Scriptures, how much more remains to be done at home, we shall form some idea of the great exertions wanting to fill up the immense outline comprehended in this enterprise of grandeur and of glory'.[6]

Payment for the work of translating the Bible was another call on the funds of the parent Society. In 1812 they had received news of the tragic death from plague of Henry Martyn on his way home from Tabriz in Persia. Martyn, who had gone to India in 1806, had translated the New Testament into Hindustani and Persian for the Bible Society and had had plans for an Arabic translation.[7] In her journal Katherine had copied a letter published in the newspaper from the British envoy to the Shah of Persia, expressing the Shah's thanks for the translated New Testament and his intention to have it read to him from beginning to end. Martyn's death at the age of thirty-one was a grievous blow to the Society. All the more exciting, then, was the emergence of Samuel Lee, the son of the Longnor carpenter, who, only a month after his ordination, preached at St. Chad's in Shrewsbury on behalf of the Bible Society in April 1818. His sermon on the divine inspiration of the Bible lasted for about an hour, recorded Katherine, and was well argued with 'a powerful appeal on behalf of the grand object of the Society'. The collection of £67 was the largest ever known on this occasion. As he told the Annual Meeting later that year of Samuel's 'rare talents', Joseph went on to list his Biblical and liturgical translations in some of the seventeen languages he had mastered. 'Let us bless God, then', he continued, 'that such talents are so directed. Let us bless God that they are directed in an especial manner to the interests of the Bible Society; and, perhaps, after all, the grandeur and the simplicity, so apparent in the plans of the Bible Society, are the two adjuncts that best exemplify the mind thus devoted to its service'.[8]

It was difficult for Joseph and the committee to sustain the interest of subscribers who came only to the Annual Meeting. At the 1820 meeting he again expressed his delight 'at meeting so many Christians congregated together for the sake of bearing their undivided testimony to the Word of Truth'. Theirs, he believed, was the most efficient plan yet devised for the salvation of all mankind. Yet the needs of the Society seemed never to diminish. He could now report that since its foundation the parent Society had distributed 2,500,000 Bibles and New Testaments, but the £93,000 raised in the previous year had fallen £30,000 short of expenditure.[9]

Yet there was every reason to feel encouraged, Joseph told his audience on the twelfth anniversary of the Auxiliary in 1823. 'It is the natural effect of success to strengthen opinion, and when we observe the issue of Bibles augmented from hundreds to thousands and from thousands to millions, when we see county added to county at home, and province added to province abroad, each containing Bible Societies indefinitely multiplied and still continuing to multiply, when we see islands joined to continents, and continents so far united to each other that the whole world may be looked upon as cemented in this holy union — we must admire more and more the solidity of that foundation on which such a superstructure has been raised ... the foundation of the Apostles and Prophets, Jesus Christ being the chief cornerstone'. He went on to single out some heartening incidents from the previous twelve months. A letter from a former French ambassador told how he had been so impressed to see the way the Bible was prized in humble hands that he took back to France an example of the Scriptures distributed to the poor in England — and the Bible Society of Paris had resulted; the king of Prussia had sent the Society a gold medal struck on the anniversary of the Reformation and a portrait of Martin Luther; Armenian monks in Venice had sent some Bibles, at the English Society's expense, to their brethren in Asia. A tribute from Sweden read: 'The rest of Europe has caught the sacred flame from England,

and there is scarcely a country but has got its Bible Society. Our own is one of its glorious monuments'. But the president brought them down to earth again with his reminder that, 'Notwithstanding the large sums that have been given, and the many Bibles that have been distributed, this great work is yet in its infancy'.[10]

The Shrewsbury Auxiliary faced a number of problems as the years passed and its novelty wore off. One was their persistence with the same format for their annual meeting, with the reading of the Annual Report, followed by the president's address and a long series of votes of thanks, always seconded, and long replies, the whole lasting for up to four hours. The Rev. Edward Bather had raised the question gently in 1823 when he wondered aloud if they should continue to congratulate each other at such length and so obviously enjoy hearing themselves speak. But things did not basically change. A more serious problem was falling revenue as some of the original and most munificent subscribers died. Joseph tackled this issue in his address in 1826, saying that though they had raised over £1,000 in the past year he did not consider this large as compared with the extent and population of the county. A third problem is suggested by the comment of the *Salopian Journal* one year[11] that the Town Hall was 'crowded with elegantly dressed females', for the soul of the movement was endangered if attending Bible Society meetings became the fashionable thing to do.

One change was introduced into the proceedings in 1828 when Joseph announced that there would be a collection plate at the door for those who were not regular subscribers and for those who were but felt moved to give a little extra.

One change that did not happen was in the presidency. According to Katherine, her brother had proposed in 1824 that the Bishop of Lichfield should be invited to become the Patron of the Auxiliary — which he did the next year — and she hints that Joseph might have been prepared to stand down as president but had been pressed to continue. His diaries in the mid-1820s suggest that he was not completely satisfied with his own performance at the annual meetings: in 1827 he noted that he had got through his part 'without much mistake'. The truth is that there was no-one else — with the possible exception of the Rev. Edward Bather, who would become Archdeacon of Salop in the Lichfield diocese — of the same stature and as trusted by the other denominations to maintain the unity of the local Auxiliary, but there were signs that its initial impetus had been lost.

16   THE APPROACH OF OLD AGE

When Joseph had reached sixty-five years of age in 1824 his thoughts had not been on retirement. It is true that, as has been seen, he had gratefully handed over some of the responsibilities in the parishes where he was incumbent, and as a magistrate, to his sons Joseph and Waties. But he continued to serve as archdeacon, to take services in Longnor and Leebotwood and other churches, to sit on the bench at Petty Sessions (if less frequently), to attend some meetings of the Shrewsbury Corporation, and to be active on the boards of trustees of Shrewsbury School, Stretton School and the Salop Infirmary. He was about to enter his fourth decade as treasurer of the Clergy Widows' and Orphans' Charity, and had thirteen years of service behind him as president of the Shropshire Bible Society.

What encouraged him to maintain this level of commitment was the unexpected, but perceptible, improvement in his health. For years he had struggled in the winter months with heavy colds, coughs and sore throats, and lumbago, which had sometimes kept him indoors for weeks on end. He had seen many of his contemporaries reach the end of their lives, and was probably not expecting to survive much longer himself. On his sixty-sixth birthday he exclaimed in his diary: 'How few attain this age in comparison with those who fall short of it'. Perhaps to his surprise he began to find that he was well enough more often than not, even in cold weather, to conduct the services on Sundays and to preach in other churches when their clergy were ill or away. His increasing years were, of course, taking their toll, but he was able to express his gratitude that 'I suffer from decrepitude rather than pain'. He was even fit enough to walk 'through the fields to Leebotwood and back between dinner and tea — for the first time for thirty or forty years'.[1] On the eve of the new year of 1826 he gave thanks for the blessings of the past year — no serious illnesses or deaths in the family, and he had not suffered much pain or diminution of his faculties. Two years later he again thanked God that he had been able 'to take more exercise and to live more abstemiously than in some former years'. Not that thoughts of death were wholly out of his mind, for he asked for mercy and forgiveness so that he should 'be ready if suddenly called'.

No illness stopped him conducting his visitations each year (apart from when it was the bishop's turn); fortunately they were usually now held in May when the weather was warmer. The visitation at Ludlow was always a bigger affair than that in Stretton, with between fifty and sixty to dine with him. At Stretton the following day, amongst local clergy he probably knew better, there were about thirty-five parsons and some churchwardens — and he could have a cup of tea with Pemberton at the Rectory afterwards. His visitation charges continued to win praise: 'It was the sweetest charge I ever heard', his friend Norgrave Pemberton told Katherine one year. 'The instruction it gave the clergy, if followed, may save the Church, but no other kind of behaviour will — for our Church is much assailed'. Joseph's themes on that occasion were conciliation, mildness and attention to clerical duties. Unfortunately his words were not always heeded by some of his hearers. In 1823, for instance, he had to visit Clun to inquire into charges against the curate, 'a pious but indiscreet man'. He took evidence from twelve persons.

His other duties as archdeacon included visiting the parishes of his six deaneries, as when he visited Pontesbury and Minsterley on his way to Leighton Hall to return his grandsons who had been staying with him. While in that area — it was September 1828 — he preached at Buttington, to a very full congregation, and the next day went on to Worthen and Weobley churches to meet the clergy. On his way to Tettenhall with Matilda in 1833, he called on Mr. Reynolds at Coalbrookdale, met the vicar of Madeley, and inspected the progress on the new church being built at Ironbridge. Since Bishop Huntingford was at Winchester for much of the year, the archdeacon often had to institute new incumbents in their parishes on his behalf. Naturally, he particularly mentions his own sons — Joseph at Clee St. Margaret in 1823 and Waties at Acton Scott in 1833. His diary reference in 1828 to seeing Joseph Grainger 'about the Primitive Methodists who meet at his house', while typically giving insufficient detail for its significance to be understood, suggests the very wide range of issues that an archdeacon had to deal with.

Joseph was able to keep in touch with many of his local parishes by accepting invitations to preach or arranging to take the services in the absence or illness of the minister or during a vacancy. Over the years diary records refer to reading the service and/or preaching at Woolstaston, Stretton, Pitchford, Wistanstow, Acton Scott (many times), Stapleton, Smethcott, Pulverbatch (in the absence of Mr. Gilpin, a favourite of Katherine's, who

214

loved his large happy family), and Condover, where he spent a busy day in July 1828 conducting a wedding before the morning service, leading and preaching at both services with a 'churching' at each, and ending the day with a baptism! He also preached at or near Shrewsbury, although these churches were in the Lichfield diocese: at Uffington, Battlefield church, Meole (several times for his friend Edward Bather when his wife died), at Shrewsbury Abbey and St. Julian's on behalf of the National School Society (Panton had become chairman of the Shrewsbury branch), at St. Alkmund's, and at St. Chad's, giving the visitation sermon, preaching at the service for the Corporation, and when the vicar was ill and the curate's wife dying. It was after he had taken the service at St. Chad's in April 1823 that Katherine noted it was the first time that year that he had gone to a church without a stove. He also always took the annual service at Longnor for an organisation calling itself the Dorrington Club. Further afield, he was asked to give the sermon at Welshpool and Montgomery — Panton's area — and once in Birmingham at Mr. Hodson's Free Church on behalf of the National and Sunday Schools of the growing town. He retained his skills as a preacher right through to at least his mid-seventies. His son Robert, working in the capital, wrote to tell Katherine that his father's sermons were 'Very strict, yes. But very excellent – he preaches to the purpose, I can attend to him — I cannot attend to any of the preachers I hear in London'.[2] Later, Robert attested that he knew no-one who had his father's talent for explaining the Scriptures — and, according to Katherine, Mr. Hickman, the local butcher, said the same. Katherine attached an interesting comment of her own about his speeches — that he never wrote a line till he had delivered the speech, but could then recall and record it with great accuracy; this may not be so true of his sermons for he sometimes mentions how he had had to write his notes when under pressure from other commitments.

Although his son, Waties, had become perpetual curate of Longnor and Leebotwood in 1822 in place of his father, who had served there since 1784, Joseph continued to take many of the services, sometimes at Leebotwood now that there was a stove there, but more usually at Longnor, where, in a pulpit so close to the pews, he must have been a very familiar figure indeed. A reference in 1827 to 'choir money' suggests that Longnor had its choir by that time. He especially enjoyed preaching and administering Holy Communion at the great Church festivals of Christmas, Easter and Whitsuntide, and again at harvest time. Christmas was especially dear to him as the family re-assembled and, year after year, he distributed pieces of beef — a total of 700 lbs. in 1823 — or candles or clothing to the more needy parishioners. That year he also gave shoes to thirty-eight girls and twenty-six boys at the school. His diary prayer on Easter Sunday 1828 was of thanksgiving for Christ's resurrection and for our preparation for our own resurrection 'by seeking and co-operating with that good Spirit that puts into our minds good desires'. Four years later he prayed that he, his family and all mankind should know the power of Christ and his resurrection 'in faith, hope and obedience here, and in acceptance for His sake hereafter'.

Beyond his church duties, Joseph continued to attend Petty Sessions and fulfil his obligations as a magistrate, although on fewer occasions. He took Katherine and Emma to 'a special day at Dr. Butler's school' in June 1828, but his last recorded meeting with the Shrewsbury School Trustees was later that year. He kept his links with the other organisations he had been engaged with through the 1820s but, as we shall see — and not surprisingly as he reached his mid-seventies — he put in just token appearances, perhaps when an important election was to be held or an appointment made. Over and above all these, much time was consumed in acting as an executor for deceased friends like Mrs. Windsor of Preen, for whom he had to sort through twenty-one large boxes of papers, and Lord Muncaster, whom he had met through the anti-slave trade campaign. Years afterwards he was still meeting up in London with Muncaster's daughter and her husband, Lord Lindsey. What seems to have made friends writing their wills think of him as an executor was his reputation for integrity, administrative skill and scrupulous attention to detail.

It was the interests and activities of the members of his family that played a greater and greater part in his life as the years went by. Although Panton, now an M.P., had his own estate at Leighton with his wife, Lucy, and their three children, Favoretta, Richard and Edward, all born between 1815 and 1817, he kept in close touch with his father. When Parliament was in session they wrote to each other almost daily. Panton took his role seriously, sitting on a number of Commons committees and often so undecided which way to vote in important divisions that he wondered if he had been right to put up for Parliament. He therefore welcomed his father's views. Sometimes he voted with the government, sometimes against. When Joseph met Wilberforce in London the year after Panton's election, he heard his son's conscientious conduct praised. Joseph will have been interested to hear that Panton had voted in favour of the seats of the pocket borough of Grampound in Cornwall being transferred to Leeds in an industrial area, for it was an early sign of the battles to come over the reform of Parliament. On the other hand, he abstained in an important division on Catholic Emancipation in 1825, for although, on account of the state of Ireland, he favoured it, his constituents sent in a petition opposing (and his fellow M.P., Mr. Bennett, was still strongly pro-Emancipation). They were certainly interesting years to be a Member, with new ministers with liberal ideas, like George Canning who became Foreign Secretary after the suicide of Lord Castlereagh. In the general election of 1826 Panton came top of the poll in a three-cornered contest with 627 votes, nearly twice as many as R.A. Slaney who came second. Panton's appointments as President of the National School Society in Shrewsbury and of the Shropshire Agricultural Society will have brought further pleasure to his father.

Uvedale, meanwhile, was establishing a high reputation as a barrister. He now lived at Tettenhall Wood near Wolverhampton, with a family that increased in number almost annually. Sons Uvedale, William and Robert were followed by two other boys before the first of four daughters eventually arrived — and two more sons. His wife, Mary, clearly stood the strain of bearing children better than either of Joseph's wives. In 1825 Mary brought the children to stay at Longnor Hall for two months with their grandfather, who loved to play with them, as he did with Panton's children. Uvedale himself was working in London, and Joseph prayed that his son might have 'the protection of the Holy Spirit that he may think more of the happiness of heaven than prosperity in this world'. He also, at last, found a gift suitable for Uvedale to present to Pembroke College — a portrait of William Shenstone, another former Pembroke man.

The archdeacon's next son, Joseph, who remained single, lived in the vicarage at Tugford, but was also vicar of Holgate and, from 1823, of Clee St. Margaret on the slopes of the Clee Hills. This last was a surprise presentation by Mr. Pelham who, in the 1819 election, had vociferously opposed Panton's candidature. When he visited his brother's new parish, Uvedale said it reminded him of an Alpine village. Joseph's two younger sons were unmarried, too, but lived totally different lives. After years of looking for a settled job, and many failures, Robert at last was offered a position where he could use his business experience. Through the good offices of Mr. Williams Wynn, M.P., and with the approval of his father and the support of Panton, he rather reluctantly (he had been hoping for a post in Ceylon) accepted a clerkship in Mr. Williams Wynn's office in the India Board of Control. So the restless Robert, who would perhaps have been happier in the army had his father not talked him out of it, ended up as a civil servant. The career of Waties followed similar lines to his father's — indeed, he still lived with him at the Hall, shared his local ministry and sat with him (and slowly replaced him) on the bench of magistrates.

In the mid-1820s all his daughters, except Josepha, nearly forty years old, and Emma, still in her teens, were in their twenties. Josepha had fashioned a way of life for herself compatible with her poor health and unmarried status. She played a significant role in the local school where the master, who had a large family, was (in Katherine's eyes) indolent and only kept on by Joseph 'for motives of humanity'. She continued to make clothes for local families and to visit sick people in the village, but she spent considerable periods away in the warmer months at Plas Gwyn, Parkgate on the Dee, Chester, or with Panton's or Uvedale's young families. Helen's life took a very different course. In May 1825 she married the Rev. Edward Burton, an able young man 'highly regarded in a moral and religious light' (commented Katherine) of a Shrewsbury family well-known to Joseph. Already acquainted with each other, their lives seem to have come together when he was a curate at Tettenhall, highly esteemed by Uvedale. Joseph gave the bride away, while Waties conducted the wedding and Matilda and Emma acted as bridesmaids.[3] The servants at the Hall held a dance in celebration and Joseph gave them a wedding cake. The couple went to live in Oxford, where, Joseph noted on his visit the next February, they had a well-furnished house in The Broad. Helen's health continued to cause occasional alarms. When they visited Longnor her scholarly husband was always happy to take a service or preach. Of all Joseph's children, Matilda has the lowest profile in his diaries or his sister's journals, perhaps because she enjoyed generally good health. Matrimony, however, eluded her. The frequency of her visits to all her brothers who no longer lived in Longnor, or to Helen after her marriage, suggest that she was a popular sister and perhaps a favourite aunt.

Harriet, four years younger than Matilda, was the least healthy of the family. The problems, both chronic and acute, that had dogged her in earlier years, relented only slightly. On the eve of the new year of 1825 Joseph expressed his thanks to God that after seven years of decrepitude Harriet was now 'cheerful and capable of a little more exertion'. At first her father would take her short drives with him when he had visits to make; then she got as far as Tettenhall to spend a few days with Uvedale's family, and then to Tugford with Matilda for three weeks to be with their brother Joseph. She enjoyed learning Italian along with Emma from a visiting teacher. Harriet had always been close to Mildred, two years her junior, but in August 1826, perhaps spurred by Helen's wedding the previous year, Mildred was married to Colonel Hull. Since he had gone as an ensign to India in 1798, six years before Mildred was born, there must have been a considerable disparity in age. Katherine remarked that they had not known each other long. Joseph again gave the bride away and Waties took the service. The couple went off to tour Wales before spending the winter in Sidmouth; they settled in Wimbledon. Two years later Mildred gave birth to a stillborn baby. Joseph was in Oxford on a visit to Helen, with Josepha and Harriet, when he received the sad news. They all travelled at once to Wimbledon, where they found Katherine already comforting the grieving parents. After a fifteen-hour coach journey home from Oxford on the Friday, Joseph, aged sixty-nine, took the Sunday morning service at Longnor.

Emma, the 'baby' of the family, born six years after Mildred, grew up surrounded by older siblings. She seems to have had good health, enjoyed music and dancing lessons, and at fourteen began learning Italian with Harriet. She was confirmed by the bishop at Stretton in August 1825 — along with ninety-seven other females and thirty-six males — at the age of fifteen. Like her sisters she enjoyed going to stay with those who had married, especially where there were children.

It is clear from the above brief accounts of his children's lives in the 1820s that caring for the family, running a 'taxi service' when there were visits to be made, or just keeping in touch with them all was almost a full-time job for Joseph. Most of his periods away from Longnor were now spent with those of his offspring who no longer lived with him — or taking one or more of the others to visit them. Yet, of course, as he grew older they were also caring for him, and when he took one or two with him on a 'business' trip they will have seen it as not leaving their father to travel alone, as when Mildred and Emma accompanied him to Hereford in 1823, where he visited the cathedral and the graves of some of his departed friends. The road to Chester was a familiar one for he frequently conveyed Josepha or Matilda on one of their trips to see the Panton daughters now living there. Journeys to Tettenhall were even more regular as there was always a new baby in Uvedale's family that Joseph's daughters wished to see. Visits to Panton's family at Leighton tended to be longer affairs, and in 1825 included attendance at the Eistedfodd in Welshpool. Anglesey was a long journey, but in June 1826 he and Matilda did the ninety-eight miles by coach in fifteen hours at a cost of £8-7-5. He stayed long enough to go to Pentraeth church where he had married Jane

Josepha forty-three years before. On the way back they collected Josepha from Chester.

Oxford was a convenient stop on the way to London and from 1825 Helen and her husband lived there or nearby. In April the next year Joseph and two daughters paid her a second visit and then went on to London where they saw Robert and Panton and his family. Panton walked him along 'the new and significant street from Oxford Road to Charing Cross to the House of Commons', where he sat under the gallery to hear a debate. On the Sunday morning he worshipped at the Scottish church in Swallow Street and at St. Mary's, Bryanstone Square, in the evening. He found time to visit the Commons again, meeting various bishops, lords and other acquaintances. On the way home they stopped at Tettenhall where they left Emma.

Two years later, this time with Katherine and Emma, he was in Oxford again to spend two days with Helen before travelling on to Wimbledon for a brief stay with Mildred. A day in London enabled him to see Panton at the Commons, Uvedale at the Court of King's Bench, and their wives and families — and finally Robert. He left Katherine with Mildred and returned to Oxford, dining that day with the Warden of Wadham College. On the Sunday morning he was in All Saints' to hear his son-in-law, Edward Burton, preach, in the late afternoon at St. Mary's for the University Sermon, and after dinner at New College chapel for Evening Prayer.[4] He was home after a hectic week on 6 May. The sad news of Mildred's stillborn baby caused him to return to Wimbledon — and Oxford — only two months later, this time with Harriet. But the time was coming when such journeys would be rare, and it was for the children to visit him. Since friends of his own generation were even more reluctant to travel, he received fewer visitors; it was a special pleasure when Bishop Huntingford came to dinner after his visitation in 1828, and when three fellow magistrates dined with him that November.

All too often Joseph found himself recording another death. In 1825 it was Mrs. Peele, uncle John's married daughter, 'the only first cousin I ever had'. Deaths among former servants were common. Elizabeth Burgess, a housemaid at the Hall for forty-eight years before retiring, died at seventy-four; he took the funeral. When Henry Swannick, a labourer for many years and an honest, civil man, died aged sixty-seven, Joseph wrote, 'May he be rejoicing in his exchange'. The sufferings of 'poor Rogers', a servant for seventeen years (but aged only forty-seven), who had had his leg amputated, distressed Joseph and his family so much that as the end drew near they stopped dining at the Hall. Sarah Kyte, whose father and brother were gamekeepers on the estate, lived till she was eighty-eight. Joseph made a note, too, of deaths in the locality, often, no doubt, of people he had known for years — Samuel Smith, the mason, whose wife had given birth the day before he died of consumption; two labourers who collapsed and died in the field after drinking cold water on a blisteringly hot day in July; Mr. Holyoake, the respected owner of the paper mill, a good tenant and popular neighbour, deceased at thirty-eight; Mr. Harrison, the village blacksmith and a friend of the family, whom Joseph 'had known as long as I can remember', had reached seventy-two; Thomas Evans, a tenant at Cardington, aged seventy-six; and Mr. Maddocks, the rector of Abdon, and who also served as curate to Joseph Corbett jnr., who failed to recover after a fall from his horse.

The two deaths that caused Joseph the greatest distress both occurred in 1829, when within six weeks he lost his two sisters. They had been his companions as a child, the carers for his three little children when their mother, Jane Josepha, died in 1787, beloved and valued members of the family when they all lived at The Bank and since his move to Longnor Hall, his constant support and biggest admirers.

Ann remains a somewhat shadowy figure, plagued by illness, for much of her life a virtual invalid, and because of her immobility rarely featuring in journal or diary. Yet she was a loving and talented person. The little children loved her Bible stories, the growing children enjoyed performing for her on their various musical instruments — and perhaps shared their secrets with her — and the poor and sick of the neighbourhood blessed her for taking over her father's dispensary and providing medicines at little or no charge. Dr. du Gard said of her: 'If we were all equally good, the world would be a happy one'. It is surprising that one who had suffered so much should have survived so long. We know that she died on 22 July 1829, aged sixty-eight, but there are no other details as Katherine's journal had come to an end two years earlier, and Joseph's diary for 1829 to early 1832 is one that is missing. The family must have sorely grieved her loss.

Katherine was surely the one who suffered the greatest anguish at Ann's death, for they had lived together, in mutual love and support, for the whole of their lives. Katherine was the older sister and much the more active. Of her life and views we know a great deal as she had kept her journal from the day of Thomas Clarkson's first visit to Longnor in October 1791 down to June 1827. Since all her little notebooks have survived from those years, it seems unlikely that any written beyond the middle of 1827 have disappeared. As she had never made entries every day, there were sometimes long gaps that were only scantily covered when she took up her pen again. After weeks of lengthy entries at the time of the court case, she had written: 'I am unwilling to quite give up my old habit of preserving some recollections of the little incidents that occur'. Fortunately for us she maintained her journal for another fourteen years — fewer entries, shorter comments it is true, but still an illuminating account of her own and the family's life. This biography would not have been possible without Katherine's one hundred and fifty notebooks, packed with information, full of interesting observations and asides, and written in her own careful hand.

Writing was not her only talent. 'Drawing has from my earliest years been a favourite pursuit'. She had watched her father painting butterflies, insects and flowers, and had so absorbed his skills that today it is not possible to identify which of them painted the intricate and beautiful pictures preserved by the family. In 1813 she decided to try her hand at oil painting. At the age of eight she had begun having music lessons from Mr. Jones. Later she would play the piano as a comfort to Ann, and enjoyed accompanying young Joseph or Robert on the flute, or Uvedale who had a fine bass voice. She liked to go to recitals and concerts, but was irritated by 'the interruptions of those who love to hear themselves talk'.

That Katherine was deeply religious her journals make abundantly clear, for she was disciplined in her attendance at church, quoted regularly from the Scriptures, and gave her brother unstinting support. But she was no narrow-minded churchgoer: like Joseph, she was tolerant of others' different views and championed the inter-denominational Bible Society. Her liberal upbringing meant that from the first she supported the anti-slave trade campaign, favoured a measure of political reform, and wished to see the extension of educational opportunities. She taught Joseph's children in their early years and, when they were ready to start, French. She had a great appetite for reading and study.

Katherine kept 'commonplace' books and sometimes more extensive notes on what she had been reading, from which the remarkable range of her interest is evident. She was familiar with the term 'blue-stocking', but while she was learned and academic, there was nothing of the pedant about her. In another age one can imagine her as a university student and going on to thrive in academic life.

One of her less intellectual interests was revealed when she recorded an accident while she was making ginger wine, for she escaped severe burns when her clothes caught fire as she 'was reaching across the furnace to take the scum off'.

Katherine's strong constitution had enabled her to lead a very active life, but references to illnesses in 1821 and 1824 tell that as she advanced into her sixties her health deteriorated. It is touching to read in her brother's diary that he had taken her out 'for an airing'. Yet she could still enjoy a 'delightful walk' in Norgrave Pemberton's plantations at Stretton and along 'the pleasant paths that wind on the sides of the hills in his domain', no doubt what today is known as Rectory Wood. And she could record in a matter-of-fact sort of way that she had been burgled — ham and beef taken from her larder and clothes 'removed from the hedge', where they had presumably been left to dry. Reference in October 1826 to inflammation of her eye, which was lanced by du Gard, may explain why her entries ceased in June 1827. At the end of May she had made a dash to Oxford when Helen was reported to be danger-ously ill. As her niece improved, Katherine took advantage of the summer weather to walk in the gardens of some of the colleges — New College, St. John's, Trinity, Magdalen and Worcester, as well as Christ Church Meadow, are all mentioned. She recorded her return to Longnor on 19 June, but then the journal comes to an abrupt end.[5]

We learn from Joseph's diary that besides occasional 'airings' Katherine was well enough to travel to Wimbledon in June 1828 to be with Mildred after the loss of her baby, that she had a trip to Stretton with her brother in November, and that she got as far as Chester in December — but his next

The interior of Leebotwood church looking towards the east, with the Plymley memorials on the lower part of the south wall of the chancel

diary is missing. We simply know that, six weeks after Ann's death on 22 July 1829, Katherine herself died on 2 September at the age of seventy-one.

Joseph suddenly found himself the last survivor of his generation. With long experience of erecting stone plaques in Leebotwood church as memorials to close family members, he now provided the inscription for another, briefly paying tribute to the two sisters who had always been at the centre of his life:

In memory of Katherine and Ann, the daughters
of Joseph and Diana Plymley of Longnor.
Katherine departed this life September 2nd 1829 aged 71 years
Ann July 22nd 1829, aged 68 years.
They were women of superior mind which they had
Cultivated with great industry, and devoted to the service of
God and of their fellow creatures; no persons, perhaps,
Of equal means ever contributed more to the comforts of their
Nearer relatives, or the wants of an extended neighbourhood.

17   THE LAST YEARS

It is a great pity that we have no fuller account of his sisters' last days from Joseph's own pen; it is a matter of regret, too, that almost nothing is known of his activities between Christmas 1828 and Easter 1832, and nothing of how his seventieth birthday was marked on 17 May 1829. The special place of the family in his prayer of thanks for the resurrection of Christ on Easter Sunday 1832 is a reminder, if one were needed, of the importance to him of his children now that he no longer had his sisters.

During the three-year gap in Joseph's diaries Panton's ten-year career as an M.P. came to an end at the election of 1830, which in Shrewsbury was said to have demonstrated the 'omnipotency of gold'. Richard Jenkins, who had returned very wealthy after twenty years in high office in India, 'a proper nabob' in fact, headed the poll with 754 votes; R.A. Slaney, second in 1826, came second again with 563; and Panton came last with only 445, 'reputedly through failure to apply "gold spurs" to the electorate'.[1] Perhaps he was well out of it, for he had always spurned the idea of buying his way into the House. 'The electorate was now well over a thousand, and the constituency had regularly shown a disposition for venality and violence. Already local gentlemen were failing to come forward with their former alacrity'.[2] Because of the missing diary we have no account from Joseph of the poll or of his own involvement. Nor, of course, do we have Panton's thoughts on the historic debates before the passing of the Great Reform Act in 1832. Joseph does record in April 1833 that Panton had resisted the pressure to be a candidate for Montgomery Boroughs at the next election. He seems to have settled to the role of a landed gentleman — one hopes meeting the ideals that his father had set out thirty years before in his report on Shropshire Agriculture (see Chapter 10). We do know that he was soon travelling on the continent with his wife and daughter for over a year, with his sons placed at Eton. The younger son, Edward, would later emulate his father and serve as M.P. for South Shropshire in the heyday of Gladstone and Disraeli.

225

Joseph still had his concerns about public schools, for when Uvedale sent his oldest boy to Rugby, grandfather's prayer was, 'May he be saved from the trials of that trying situation'. Nor had Joseph's firm views on the army changed: he was unhappy when Uvedale's son, William, went to Sandhurst (and quietly rejoiced when his cousin, Richard, Panton's elder son, had to resign his commission in the Dragoons because of an injury). Uvedale himself was in the next decade to become a judge on the Shropshire circuit. About the son named after him, Joseph also had some anxiety, for his three country parishes were not without their temptations to a fit, young (forty in 1834) and single cleric. In that year his father prayed 'for a more aweful conception of his professional duties and less fondness for field diversions'. On the other hand, Robert had at last settled into a career and was ultimately to hold an important post in the India Office. Waties, the youngest, was perhaps the closest to his father — and not just because he lived in Longnor. He was dedicated in the performance of his duties in the home parishes, and only reluctantly accepted the offer of the rectorship of Acton Scott, made by Mr. Stackhouse, for he was opposed to pluralities. Waties demonstrated the same commitment as a Justice of the Peace. It was fitting that one day he should be made Chancellor of the Diocese of Hereford.

Because, apart from Waties, his sons all lived away from the village where they had grown up, Joseph was closer to his daughters in his last years. Josepha, who would reach fifty in 1836, enjoyed a fairly independent life, spending considerable periods away visiting her brothers and sisters and her close friends, the Pantons, in Chester. When she was at home she perhaps exercised a pastoral role in the parish, as Joseph specifically noted her visit to a poor girl, Margaret Newell, who lived near the Lawley. Helen had taken a different path in life, marrying the Rev. Edward Burton and moving to Oxford, where he was subsequently made chaplain to the bishop and moved to the parish of Ewelme. On a visit to see them in 1834 Joseph was invited to preach in what he described as 'the handsomest parish church I know'. Burton went on to become Regius Professor of Divinity at Oxford, but was to die young in 1836. Helen's own health continued to cause concern. Matilda and Emma were still unmarried when, in 1835, Joseph recorded that they were both now at The Bank, where their spinster aunts had once lived together — although it seems likely that Waties had moved there, too. Joseph must have been delighted with the news in September 1833 that Mildred, wife of Colonel Hull, had given birth to a son, William, the only grandchild by one of his daughters. He will have been cast down when the baby died at eleven months, bringing back memories of his own first child's death at that age fifty-six years before. It seems likely that Josepha and Harriet, who had suffered more illness than any of his children, were the only ones left living at Longnor Hall with him in his last years.

e

Visitors to the Hall were now more rare. Joseph was therefore delighted by the arrival in September 1833 of Bishop Grey, newly consecrated at Hereford. He came to dinner with Waties and Norgrave Pemberton on the Saturday, preached at Longnor the next morning, walked with Waties to Leebotwood for the Sunday evening service, and took the confirmation service at Stretton on the Monday. Joseph exchanged occasional letters with Samuel Lee, who no doubt called to see him if he came to Longnor. Dr. du Gard he sometimes saw in Shrewsbury, but more often, as he became frailer, at home. He was able to spend more time in the garden, doing some weeding and, once on an April morning, 'contemplating a bed of polyanthus and anemones with gratitude, admiration and pleasure'.

But whatever physical ailments troubled him, he had never forgotten the issue of slavery. The British slave trade had been abolished in 1807, but slavery itself had not disappeared. Joseph had attended a meeting in Shrewsbury called by the mayor in 1824 and proposed a petition to the Commons for the gradual but final abolition of slavery in the West Indies which a small audience had carried unanimously. Over the next years he had sent out various leaflets and pamphlets published by the Anti-Slavery Society. In 1828 he met several gentlemen at the 'Lion' and approved a petition for the amelioration and extinction of slavery in the British colonies — quite like old times! He carried on a correspondence with Clarkson as the campaign developed, finally noting in his diary that he had signed the petition in 1833 that preceded the Abolition of Slavery Act of that year, one of a series of major reforms passed after the Parliamentary Reform Act. He will have rejoiced that Wilberforce lived just long enough to see this second great victory.

Deaths of other friends and members of his household will have increased a sense of loneliness. He heard in 1833 of the passing of a very old friend, the Rev. Robert Taylor, who had given him his first curacy at Shelve on his ordination fifty years earlier. Taylor was eighty-two and, sadly, as the archdeacon must have been aware, in the King's Bench Prison, probably for debt. Mr. Stackhouse of Acton Scott died at the age of fifty-seven after years of suffering. And a succession of servants, both retired and serving, died in the early 1830s — Michael Dunn, gardener, at seventy-seven; William Heath, 'honest and much beloved', at seventy-one; Ann Hotchkiss at seventy-four; and, saddest of all, William Everall, aged twenty-one, 'a civil and well-disposed young man, but hurt his health by a fondness for Malt Liquor, the bane of thousands'.

On his sixty-ninth birthday, before he lost his sisters, Joseph had lamented, 'Of those who began life with me how few are left'. As he had grown older his greater awareness of his mortality had led to a search for deeper spiritual understanding. One Easter Sunday he included a prayer that 'I may this day arise to a more spiritual life than I have yet been enabled to lead'. He had recorded, when he was sixty-five, that he prayed daily for himself, his children, his in-laws, and his grandchildren that in small as well as great things they might act with reference to Christian principles. In the longer periods he then found himself spending at home, he began to pray at greater length and to study his Bible more assiduously. When any of his children were to make a long journey, he wrote a prayer in his diary for their safety. On noting the receipt of a letter from any one of them he added D. G. (*Dei gratia*). When, in 1835, he was suffering from a sore mouth, so painful that he could not pray aloud and could hardly speak, he wrote out a long prayer in his diary asking for forgiveness and that his scarlet sins should be 'as white as snow or wool'. Shortly afterwards, on his seventy-sixth birthday, he gave his thanks to God for His mercies and went on: 'May I be enabled to contemplate my approaching dissolution undistracted by pain or sorrow'.

Of course, his health figured ever more prominently in his diary jottings. Increasing sight problems, reflected in the larger handwriting in his diary, led to a minor operation; he got confused over the dates of his diary entries; he complained of various pains as a result of 'diseased nerves'. In the winter of 1832-33 he was confined to the house for four months; two years later he could not attend church for six months. He consulted Dr. du Gard with growing frequency.

But he still carried on with his chief responsibilities. It is evident from his archdeacon's records[3] that he was visiting parishes to inspect churches in the last year of his life and, as far as is known, he never missed his visitations. Other than in the winter months he regularly took the services at Longnor, but more rarely in other parishes. As a magistrate he seems to have limited himself to the meetings of Petty Sessions at Stretton, to which he was accompanied by Waties, though once, at age seventy-five, he went to Dorrington because his son would have been alone on the bench. From 1834 there is no reference to magisterial activities. He had already resigned from the Corporation in 1832. The Clergy Widows' and Orphans' Charity, however, still saw him present as Treasurer at their annual meetings to supervise the distribution of funds. His close ties with the school at Stretton caused him to continue to audit the accounts and to be present at the Annual Meeting at least as late as 1833. In that same year, too, is his last mention of a visit to the gaol. But he went on recommending patients for admission to the Infirmary, and was at a Board meeting as late as 1835 to appoint a new physician. The reason we cannot go beyond 1835 is that no diary remains after that year. The final diary entry is from Saturday, 22 August 1835:

> I rec'd letters from R.N. Pemberton and G.D. Pardoe Cls. I saw Mr. Watters. I wrote to the Bishop of Hereford. I took Mrs. P.C. [Panton's wife, and some others] to Penkridge Hall — and Harriet. I wrote to Archdeacon Bather. I rec'd letters from the Bp. of Hereford, Sir Rowland Hill, the Salop Bank.

With that entry, typically detailing correspondence and family movements, Joseph's final surviving diary ends.

Fortunately, reports in the press allow us to go beyond 1835 with his Bible Society presidency for, apart from his unfailing commitment to his roles as priest and archdeacon, it was this Society that held his loyalty longest. 'The Book we bring forward', he had told the Annual Meeting in 1829, 'like the Saviour it reveals, is the same, yesterday and for ever'.[4] It was perhaps because the Shropshire Auxiliary was itself unchanging that its membership and income slowly dwindled. In most years Joseph was able to announce that the parent Society's income had increased and more branches had been opened, but in Shropshire subscriptions fell on account of 'deaths, or discontinuance from other causes, of several contributors, without any material accession of new subscribers', according to the 1831 Annual Report.[5] The parent body was itself shaken by the secession of some members over the question of whether some Bibles printed should include the Apocrypha. As the local president, Joseph advised against any change to the rules 'under which the Bible Society was so happily established', but expressed his hope that those who had seceded had been 'diligent in dispensing other equally authentic copies of the Word'.

Although Joseph did his best to maintain morale in the Auxiliary, it was apparent that he was missing the strong backing of the original subscribers. Katherine was no longer there to praise his efforts, though at the 1833 meeting he quoted from one of her journals (without disclosing his source) to demonstrate how the Christian unity exemplified by the

Society was treasured. He was able to add that the parent Society had now issued eight million Scriptures — but the world population was estimated at eight hundred millions![6] The next year he had to announce the sad news of the deaths of the national President, Lord Teignmouth, and of William Wilberforce, whose friendship, he told them, he had been honoured with for nearly half a century. Joseph's trust in the Bible never wavered, though scholarship was raising new interpretations. 'It is', he told his audience, 'an inexhaustible store to learning and to contemplation, whilst former glosses are preserved, and new lights struck out by erudition acting upon erudition, it gives to the pious reader, however simple or uninformed, plain and sure rules of faith and practice'.[7] Nor did his confidence in the Bible Society waver: 'I cannot but look upon the Bible Society, not only as the greatest, but the happiest exertion that has been made since the cessation of miracles'.

The death of their Patron, Bishop Ryder of Lichfield in 1836 was a further blow to the Auxiliary. Joseph looked for crumbs of comfort in the Annual Report: 'If it is not a matter of congratulation it should be received with thanksgiving. If it does not exhibit the freshness of attachment some of our reports did, it is an improvement upon the languor of recent years'.[8] With the accession of Queen Victoria in 1837 he hoped that the fortunes of the Auxiliary had turned the corner. At least there was some novelty in the 1837 meeting for it was held in the new Shire Hall — which presented Joseph with the theme for his address. The hall would be the scene of controversies and legal trials in the future, he told his audience, but he rejoiced that this first visit had the 'sole object of the promulgation of the Divine Law which, if duly attended to, would supersede the necessity of appeals to human tribunals'. He recalled the old hall where he had assisted in the first steps towards the abolition of the slave trade. He had been delighted to read that 'a minister of colour' from Antigua had said that the first Bible distributed there had been hailed as 'the Emancipation Book'. He was pleased to announce that the national Society's income in the previous year broke all records and that though their own was much below their early years it had again risen a little. His closing words should be quoted in full:

> Whoever reads his Bible till he is convinced that the only real comfort attainable in this mixed scene must come from following its rules, and that they alone lead to the unmixed happiness of a future state, will be anxious to impart as widely as possible the same blessings to all his fellow creatures.[9]

That proved to be Joseph's final message because before the next Annual Meeting he himself had passed on to 'the unmixed happiness of the future state'. He had celebrated his seventy-ninth birthday the month before he died at Longnor Hall on 22 June 1838. His death was announced in the local press within days, but those issues were dominated by reports of the young queen's coronation. The reports on the Bible Society Annual Meeting on 10 July were also exceptionally short, though the coverage in recent years had been much curtailed compared with the early glory days. The *Shrewsbury Chronicle* reproduced the words of the resolution adopted by those assembled in the Shire Hall: 'The meeting feels called upon to record the most painful event that has ever yet occurred to the Society, *viz.* the decease of its truly venerable and greatly beloved President, the Rev. Archdeacon Corbett'.[10]

A local newspaper, in a fulsome obituary, wrote of the Archdeacon: 'Universally beloved, his death will be sincerely regretted by all classes. He possessed a highly cultivated mind and a generous disposition, and was not only admired for his talents and knowledge, but beloved for the amiable qualities of his heart.'[11] It fell to the family to compose the inscription on the plaque on the wall of Leebotwood church where he had been laid to rest. After giving details of his parentage, marriages and number of children it concluded: 'Having passed a long and useful life in the scrupulous discharge of the various duties incident to his station, He died at Longnor Hall June the 22nd 1838 aged 79 years'.

So, what sort of man was Joseph Plymley/Corbett? How did he develop over his nearly eighty years? And do the answers to those questions justify the publication of this biography?

Joseph had been fortunate to be born into a loving and cultured family, and to grow up in an intellectually stimulating environment. When he was born in 1759, his father at forty-three and his mother at thirty-four were old to be starting a family (Katherine was born only the previous year), but for that reason were perhaps determined to give their children the best possible start in life. It was in those vital early years at home that Joseph's character was shaped. The love and attention he received as he grew up instilled in him a love and respect for his parents and sisters, in time a deep love for his own children, and throughout his life a natural kindness and generosity, a warmth in his relationships with friends, and a tolerance of individual differences.

From his father he imbibed a lifelong interest in 'natural history' (a term that then embraced much of science) and a love for drawing and painting, from his mother a religious faith that would be central to his life, and from Sir Richard Corbett, who was more like a grandfather to him, an interest in politics, travel and invention. Serious conversation was encouraged in the home, where there was a predisposition, born of long allegiance to the Whigs, to champion the cause of freedom and political reform. At school in Chester his knowledge and understanding were extended, his religious faith nurtured, and lifelong friendships formed.

As a young man going up to Oxford in 1776 he was, then, well prepared to build on the intellectual and moral foundations already laid. But university life unsettled him. Perhaps the way many students comported themselves was too great a change from the ordered existence of home and school, perhaps other possible careers than the one for which he was intended became attractive to him. What seems to have happened was that his sense of vocation to the Church was lost and he decided to abandon his studies. Had he had his portrait painted at twenty years of age, with his mother seriously ill and his own future uncertain (for he had left Oxford without a degree and with little idea of the path ahead now that he had turned his back on the Church), it seems probable that it would have shown a handsome but insecure young man. The death of his mother, however, as has earlier been suggested, may have been the crucial factor in the recovery of his vocation and his subsequent ordination.

With the launch of his clerical career and his marriage there came a new stability in his life, a stability enhanced by the birth of three children in as many years. But then came the shock of Jane Josepha's sudden death. A profound nervous reaction followed. It was at this moment that a cause in which Joseph, his wife and sisters had become intensely interested, presented him with the opportunity to become directly and actively involved. It was, of course, the abolition of the slave trade. This not only assisted his recovery after the tragic loss of his wife, but opened up a whole new dimension in his life. Some may have seen this as a diversion from the career as a priest that he had only just begun. But this would have been a serious misunderstanding. His emergence as the leader of the anti-slave trade campaign in Shropshire and beyond enriched and transformed his ministry in the Church. Perhaps it presented him with the answer to the crisis of uncertainty that he had encountered at Oxford. Now he could see that his service to God and the Church could embrace a movement for human dignity and freedom that echoed the other major formative influence in his early life.

Through his leadership of the local anti-slave trade campaign Joseph discovered in himself the capacity for running an organisation, for influencing

232

others, and for working flat out for long hours. Meeting and then working with men of the calibre of Clarkson and Wilberforce widened his horizons and gave him a new confidence in his own abilities. Old Archdeacon Clive at once recognised his talent, as more gradually did his fellow clergy and the bishop. So when Clive died Joseph, aged only thirty-three and in clerical orders for a mere eleven years, was immediately appointed Archdeacon of Salop in the Hereford diocese.

How he had developed in those eleven years! He could hardly wait for his new wife, Matty, to give birth to their first son, before he was off round south Shropshire to compile an astonishingly detailed survey of the social, economic and ecclesiastical state of his archdeaconry. As his abilities became more widely perceived, everybody wanted him — as a preacher, as a magistrate, as a trustee, as a tax commissioner. At the time of his fortieth birthday in 1799 he was perhaps at the height of his powers and confident enough to agree to compile a comprehensive account of agriculture in Shropshire at the start of the new century. The uncertain undergraduate had matured into a confident leader in the Church and an energetic Justice of the Peace. He had become a formidable organiser and administrator, the man of integrity that local organisations wanted on their Boards and his friends wanted to name as an executor in their wills. He was also, it has to be remembered, father to a fast-growing family: when he reached forty he had six children by his second wife, in addition to the three from his first marriage now in their teens. This, then, was Joseph in the prime of his life. A portrait painted at this time would surely have shown a confident figure, brimming with energy. There would have been those who thought he would be made a bishop and perhaps be lost to the area.

But Joseph had driven himself too hard. His sister came to notice his irritability if disturbed by unwanted callers and occasional twitchings of arms and legs that had first been seen when Jane Josepha died. Katherine remembered how their friend Thomas Clarkson had burnt himself out. And the passing years brought additional burdens. Although inheriting the Corbett estates ended his financial worries for a while and provided in Longnor Hall a home appropriate to the size of his family, their management consumed precious time. His involvement in the Shrewsbury elections of 1806 and 1807 made him enemies, he suffered anguish over the death of his beloved daughter Jane, and the campaign to challenge his inheritance of the Corbett estates created further anxiety. Though that case was eventually won hands down in 1813, he had lost his second wife, Matty, in the intervening period, leaving him with ten children dependent on him, the youngest only two years old. He was a loving father, wanting nothing but the best for each of his offspring, but to give them 'quality time' when he had so many demands made on him was almost impossible. The strain was great and, though he was only fifty-three, his sister thought he looked venerable and had lost his old vitality.

As the children grew up, however, and the boys (apart from Robert) settled into careers, Joseph was better able to discharge all his many duties. He was at last prevailed upon to have his portrait painted just short of his sixtieth birthday. The picture that emerged shows a stocky, white-haired gentleman with a kindly face, a fatherly, even grandfatherly, figure, yet with an air of authority. As the years passed he was upheld by the love of his family and by the affection of his servants and neighbours most vividly demonstrated in the almost wild rejoicing that followed his triumph in the inheritance case. Through his sixties he continued to shoulder his manifold responsibilities, and to find a new challenge and new joy as president of the local Bible Society. This came to engage him more and more, led him to spend longer in reading the Bible and in prayer, and prompted the diary prayer on his seventy-fifth birthday asking forgiveness for not studying the Bible more when he was younger 'instead of following the customs and fashions of the world'. At seventy-nine years old — for he did not reach eighty — a portrait would have revealed a venerable old man with his mind less on the achievements of this life and more on how to make his peace with his Maker, whom he believed he would shortly face.

Joseph, then, was a good man, a loving and beloved husband and father, tolerant towards all, generous to those in need. He had a reputation for integrity in his public life and for scrupulous attention to the duties imposed on him by his office in the Church and the positions he had accepted in other areas. Yet because of these very virtues and his always serious approach to life, he was probably admired and respected rather than popular.

But what did he *achieve*?

As Archdeacon of Salop in the diocese of Hereford for forty-six years, he was a figure of authority in the Church in south Shropshire and also in Shrewsbury, even though the county town lay across the diocesan boundary. That air of authority is why he was always referred to as *Archdeacon* Plymley or Corbett — or just 'The Archdeacon'. That role gave him considerable influence on the Christian ministry exercised in the more than 150 churches in his six deaneries, for he had the supervision of the clergy as well as church buildings. His commitment to raising standards and to pastoral care will have been an influence for good, but he would not have over-rated the impact he made and nor should we. Yet the Anglican Church in the southern half of the county will have benefited from his leadership over nearly half a century, and the example he set of nurturing Christian unity will have improved relations with the other denominations. His low profile but valuable work as Treasurer of the Clergy Widows' and Orphans' Fund for forty years was another aspect of his commitment as a churchman. Nor must we forget the authoritative survey of the communities and churches of his archdeaconry that he compiled in his first years in the post, for that was an achievement from which all interested in local history still benefit.

Although he did not have the stature of Clarkson or Wilberforce in the Abolition movement, they paid tribute to his almost single-handed achievement in drumming up support for the petitions that added substance to Wilberforce's oratory by electing him as a corresponding member of the London Committee. He was largely responsible for turning a conservative rural area, remote from the slave trade, into one that national leaders could rely on for petitions and financial support. We can truthfully say that, as the leader of the local movement, he played a very significant part in the early years of the campaign that was ultimately victorious and that in its tactics provided a template for future political pressure groups.

The compilation of the *General View of Shropshire Agriculture* — his only significant publication — was a worthy achievement at a time when he was a young and busy archdeacon and an even newer magistrate. It took its place among the other county surveys that provide an illuminating picture of the state of agriculture at the opening of the century that would see the rapid advance of scientific farming. The report also highlights Joseph's deep concern for the welfare of the poor, his strong backing for new farming techniques, and his lifelong passion for improving roads.

His industry, commitment, good sense and compassion as a magistrate, and his generosity to local people — gifts of candles, clothing, beef at Christmas, and food in times of real hardship — contributed to the maintenance of social harmony when this was threatened by the self-interest of many landowners and the spirit of rebellion among some workers. All the work he did and the time he spent as a member of the Shrewsbury Corporation, as a Board member at the Infirmary, as a school or turnpike trustee cannot be classed as 'achievements', but should be seen as contributions to the welfare and advance of the local community by this public-spirited man.

What must certainly be credited to his list of achievements is his leadership of the Shropshire Bible Society for over a quarter of a century. He may fairly be regarded as the local personification of the movement to spread the

Word of God across the country and the world, for as he aged the Auxiliary lost its initial impetus.

There remains one further area of achievement that should not be overlooked — Joseph's place in what has been called 'the Shropshire Enlightenment'. As Barrie Trinder observed in his *History of Shropshire*: 'For a few years at the end of the 18th century a score or so of men of unusual ability were active in Shropshire'.[12] Most of those whom he names have appeared in the pages of this biography as they were Joseph's friends or acquaintances — the county surveyor Thomas Telford; Owen and Blakeway, the county's historians; Dr. Samuel Butler at Shrewsbury School; the Reynolds family at Coalbrookdale; Thomas Eyton; Rowland Hunt; the philosopher Archibald Alison; and Dr. Robert Darwin. In addition there were Thomas Beddoes of Shifnal (though he went to Bristol), Dr. Robert Townson the geologist, Dr. Thomas du Gard, Richard Wilding and Professor Samuel Lee. They were all men who wished to extend human knowledge, who practised innovation, and who favoured reform in a variety of areas. They were not a close-knit group for, in a rural area, regular meetings like those held by the Lunar Club in Birmingham were not practicable, but if there was one person who constituted some sort of link between them it was the Archdeacon. His energetic support of the anti-slave trade movement, riding out to all parts of the region to recruit subscribers, his programme of visits to all his churches as a new archdeacon, and over the years his participation in so many local organisations meant that he got to know all these people, and most of them came to dine with him at The Bank or Longnor Hall and to join in the intellectual discussions that followed the meal. In this way Joseph introduced men from different disciplines to one another, causing new ideas to be diffused more widely and encouraging the adoption of progressive attitudes.

Whether Joseph was a sufficiently significant figure for this Life to be published is for others to determine. He was not a man of national stature like Wilberforce or Clarkson, he was not an original thinker like Thomas Beddoes, nor a practical genius like Telford or William Reynolds, nor was he a prolific author. But as a humane man of great breadth of mind and interests, an outstanding organiser, and an exceptionally active proponent of reform he rightly stands tall among the key figures of the Shropshire Enlightenment of that day.

It happens that the 200th anniversary of the birth of Charles Darwin falls in the same year as the 250th anniversary of Joseph's birth. As the archdeacon was a long-standing friend of Charles's father, Dr. Robert Darwin, he and the young Charles knew each other well. Indeed, Charles sometimes joined shooting parties on the Longnor estate with Joseph's sons and other young men.[13] On one occasion in September 1825, when Charles had recently left Shrewsbury School and was preparing to go to Edinburgh University, Katherine recorded that he and others — probably members of a shooting party — dined at Longnor Hall with Joseph and his family. Charles Darwin would go on to win international and enduring renown for his work on the origin of species. He is properly regarded as Shrewsbury's greatest son. Yet his field work on the theory of evolution began on the other side of the world, and after the voyage of the *Beagle* he returned to Shrewsbury only briefly before moving to London and then Kent. Joseph, however, was every inch a Shropshire man. Born at Longnor and living there the whole of his life, he dedicated himself to the service of the Church and of his fellow Salopians and to the development of the county community. In his lifetime he was not without honour in his own county; in retrospect, we may justly hail him as a true 'Son and Servant of Shropshire'.

Joseph Plymley's memorial in Leebotwood Church

Sources and Bibliography

Primary Sources

Shropshire Archives (S.A.)
    Katherine Plymley's Journals: S.A. 1066/1-141
    Archdeacon Plymley's Visitation Records: S.A. 6001/6860-5
    Archdeacon (Plymley) Corbett's Diaries: S.A. 567/5/4/1/1-6
    Plymley family papers: S.A. 567/2F/1-38
    Corbett family papers: S.A. 567/2F/39-46 and 567/3/1-57
    Katherine Plymley's Journal of Visit to Anglesey: S.A. 567/5/5/1/1-3
    Rev. Joseph Plymley's Sermon 1792: S.A. CO 1 1650
    Shrewsbury Chronicle
    Salopian Journal
    Shrewsbury News and Cambrian Reporter
    Salopian Shreds and Patches
    Transactions of the Shropshire Archeological Society (T.S.A.S.)
    Salop Quarter Sessions Orders, 1783-1839
    Rev. W.D.G.Fletcher: *Collections for Shropshire:* Microfilm 40
    Morris J.: *Shropshire Genealogy* vol 5: Microfilm 151
    Country Life, 1964
    Registers of Leebotwood and Longnor churches

Herefordshire Record Office
    Diocesan Ordination Papers: HD 6/15
    Diocesan 'Subscriptions': HD 6/57/2-3
    Little Hereford parish register

Anglesey County Record Office
    Pentraeth parish registers

Bodleian Library, Oxford
Gentleman's Magazine

Cheshire Record Office
The Cheshire Sheaf

Pembroke College, Oxford, Archives

Bibliography

Bellamy, V.   *The Making of Shrewsbury* (2004)
Black, J.   *Pitt the Elder* (1999)
Blakeway, J.B.   *The Sheriffs of Shropshire*
Boswell, J.   *The Life of Samuel Johnson* (1791)
Briggs, A.   *The Age of Improvement, 1783-1867*
Clarkson, T.   *The History of the Abolition of the Slave Trade* (1968 ed.)
Darwin, C.   *Autobiography* (ed. N.Barlow, 1958)
Desmond, A.
  and Moore, J.   *Darwin's Sacred Cause* (2009)
D.N.B.   *Dictionary of National Biography*
Evans, E.J.   *The Forging of the Modern State, 1783-1870* (2001 ed.)
Foster   *Alumni Oxonienses*
Gash, N.   *Mr. Secretary Peel* (1961)
Grounds, A.D.   *The History of the Church of St. Laurence, Church Stretton*
                     (2002)
Hague, W.   *William Pitt the Younger* (2004)
Hague, W.   *William Wilberforce* (2007)
Hibbert, C.   *George III* (1999)
Hilton, B.   *A Mad, Bad and Dangerous People? – England 1783-*
                     1846 (2006)
Hochschild, A.   *Bury the Chains* (2005)
Hulbert,C.   *The History and Antiquities of Shropshire* (1837)
Langford, P.   *A Polite and Commercial People – England 1727-83*
                     (1998 ed.)
Leach, F. (ed.)   *The County Seats of Shropshire* (1891)
Leonard, J.   *Churches of Shropshire and Their Treasures* (2004)
Macleane, D.   *A History of Pembroke College, Oxford* (1897)
McLynn, F.   *1759 – The Year Britain became Master of the World*
                     (2005)

Midgley, G.   *University Life in Eighteenth Century Oxford* (1996)
Mitchell, L.   *The Whig World, 1760-1837* (2005)
O'Gorman, F.   *The Long Eighteenth Century, 1688-1832* (1997)
Oldfield, J.R.   *Popular Politics and British Anti-Slavery* (1998)
Owen and
   Blakeway   *A History of Shrewsbury* (1837)
Pattison, A.   *The Darwins of Shrewsbury* (2009)
Plymley, Rev. J.   *A General View of the Agriculture of Shropshire* (1803)
Porter, R.   *Enlightenment – Britain and the Creation of the Modern
                      World* (2000)
Reddie, R.S.   *Abolition! – The Struggle to Abolish Slavery in the British
                      Colonies* (2007)
Schama, S.   *Rough Crossings: Britain, the Slaves and the American
                      Revolution* (2005)
Smith, P.   *Houses of the Welsh Countryside*
Steer, R.   *Good News for the World: The Story of the Bible Society*
                      (2004)
Taylor, T.   *A Biographical Sketch of Thomas Clarkson* (1839, 2nd ed.
                      1846)
Thomas, H.   *The Slave Trade* (1997)
Trinder, B.   *A History of Shropshire* (2nd ed. 1998)
Trinder, B.   *The Industrial Revolution in Shropshire* (1981)
Uglow, J.   *The Lunar Men* (2002)
Venn   *Alumni Cantabrigienses*
V.C.H.   *Victoria County History of Shropshire*
Walpole, H.   *The Castle of Otranto* (1764)
Walvin, J.   *Slavery and the Slave Trade* (1983)
Weyman, H.   *Members of Parliament for Shropshire*
Wilberforce, R.
   and S.   *The Life of William Wilberforce* (1838)

References

For abbreviations and titles of works referred to by authors' names see the previous list entitled Sources and Bibliography.

CHAPTER 1
1. McLynn F., p.252
2. Black J., p.161
3. Mclynn F., p.388

CHAPTER 2
1. S.A. 567/2F/4-5
2. S.A. 567/2F/38
3. S.A. 1066/139
4. Owen and Blakeway, I, p.584
5. V.C.H., VIII, p.110
6. T.S.A.S., Series 4, vol 4, pp.66-7
7. *Ibid.*
8. S.A. 1066/63
9. S.A. 1066/80
10. *Ibid*

CHAPTER 3
1. V.C.H., VIII, p.108
2. Black J., p.3
3. The Cheshire Sheaf Ser.3, vol XIII (March 1916)
4. S.A. 1066/140
5. Foster
6. Midgley G., p.x
7. Macleane D., p.373
8. Midgley G., p.66-7
9. Macleane D., p.394, quoting Chalmers
10. S.A. 1066/141

CHAPTER 4
1. 1066/141
2. H.R.O., HD6/15
3. H.R.O., HD6/57/2
4. Anglesey Record Office: P.Smith, 'Houses of the Welsh Countryside' – Plas Gwyn
5. S.A. 567/3/55
6. Anglesey Record Office: Pentraeth Parish Register
7. H.R.O., HD6/15
8. Leonard J., p.206
9. *Ibid.*, p.207
10. Macleane D., p.363

CHAPTER 5
1. Taylor T., p.12
2. Clarkson T., I, p.210
3. *Ibid.*, I, p.230
4. Hochschild A., p.95
5. Clarkson T., I, p.465
6. Oldfield J.R., p.49
7. Hague W., (2007) p.195
8. Hochschild A., p.190
9. *Ibid.*, p.190

CHAPTER 6
1. Oldfield J.R., p.76
2. Schama S., p.511
3. Hochschild A., p.90
4. Thomas H., p.421
5. S.A. 1066/5

CHAPTER 7
1. Hague W., (2007) p.232
2. Oldfield J.R., p.61
3. Thomas H., p.528
4. Hague W., (2007) p.235
5. Thomas H., p.529
6. S.A., 1066/14
7. Wilberforce R.& S., II, p.228
8. Hilton B., p.187

CHAPTER 8
1. S.A. CO/1 1650
2. Venn
3. There was another 'Archdeacon of Salop' in the diocese of Lichfield and Coventry who covered North Shropshire
4. In 1877 the title Archdeacon of Salop in the Hereford diocese was changed to Archdeacon of Ludlow. Today the holder of this position has been made a bishop.
5. S.A. 1066/16
6. S.A. 6001/6860-5
7. S.A. 6001/6862

CHAPTER 9
1. Katherine's reference is to the 'Gothic Story', entitled *The Castle of Otranto* by Horace Walpole (1717-97) first published in 1764
2. Darwin C., p.10
3. S.A. 1066/15
4. S.A. 1066/31
5. S.A. 1066/33
6. S.A. 1066/39
7. S.A. 1066/49

CHAPTER 10
1. V.C.H. IV, p.220
2. V.C.H. IV, p.177
3. Plymley, Rev. J., Chapter 5
4. Trinder B. (1981), p.67
5. *Ibid.*, p.85
6. Plymley, Rev. J., p.307
7. *Ibid.,* pp.354-5

CHAPTER 11
1. V.C.H., VIII, p.110
2. S.A. 1066/69
3. V.C.H. III, p.204
4. 'The Mountain' was the name given to those who sat on the banked seats at the extreme left in the French Convention (National Assembly). They were regarded as extreme revolutionaries. In England the name was given to ultra radicals.
5. *Shrewsbury Chronicle*, 19 Nov. 1806
6. S.A. 1066/70; Thomas H., p.555
7. V.C.H. III, p.273
8. 'Plumper' – vote for one candidate only

9. A plaque, bearing the Archdeacon's coat of arms and the year 1808, may still be seen in a corridor at the Royal Shrewsbury Hospital in a long line of such plaques commemorating those who served as Treasurer to the Salop Infirmary.

CHAPTER 12
1. S.A. 1066/79
2. S.A. 1066/80
3. *Gentleman's Magazine* vol LXXIX, 1809, pt.2, p.599
4. *Salopian Journal,* 4 April 1810
5. D.N.B.
6. *Salopian Journal,* 24 March 1813
7. S.A. 1066/97

CHAPTER 13
1. Salop Quarter Sessions Orders 1783-1839 vol 3, p.xviii
2. V.C.H. III, p.122
3. T.S.A.S. Ser.2, vol IV (1892), pp.82-3
4. V.C.H. III, pp.125-6
5. *Ibid.,* p.123
6. T.S.A.S. Ser.2 vol III (1891), p.229
7. V.C.H. III, p.127
8. Gash N., p.308
9. Plymley, Rev. J., pp.349-50

CHAPTER 14
1. S.A. 1066/103
2. Hilton B., p.251
3. Evans E.J., p.228
4. Diary in private hands, 19 April 1818
5. V.C.H. III, p.375

CHAPTER 15
1. Hilton B., p.175
2. Steer R., p.66
3. *Salopian Journal,* 14 July 1813
4. *Ibid.,* 13 July 1814
5. *Ibid.,* 12 July 1815
6. *Ibid.,* 9 July 1817
7. D.N.B.
8. *Salopian Journal,* 2, Sept. 1818
9. *Ibid.,* 12 July 1820
10. *Ibid.,* 9 July 1823
11. *Ibid.,* 12 July 1826

CHAPTER 16
1. S.A. 567/5/4/1/4 Diary 19 April 1826
2. S.A. 1066/116
3. S.A. 567/5/4/1/4 Diary 12 May 1825
   S.A. 1066/134
4. S.A. 567/5/4/1/5 Diary 4 May 1828
5. S.A. 1066/137-8

CHAPTER 17
1. V.C.H. III, p.275
2. *Ibid.*
3. S.A.6001/6860-5
4. *Salopian Journal,* 3 July 1829
5. *Ibid.,* 13 July 1831
6. *Ibid.,* 10 July 1833
7. *Ibid.,* 9 July 1834
8. *Ibid.,* 20 July 1836
9. *Ibid.,* 19 July 1837
10. *Shrewsbury Chronicle,* 13 July 1838
11. *Shrewsbury News and Cambrian Reporter*, 23 June 1838
12. Trinder B. (1998), p.79
13. Desmond A. and Moore J., p.14

Index